Louis Horst

Louis Horst

Musician in a Dancer's World

Janet Mansfield Soares

DUKE UNIVERSITY PRESS *Durham and London 1992*

© 1992 Duke University Press

All rights reserved

Printed in the United States of America

on acid-free paper ∞

Library of Congress Cataloging-in-Publication Data

Soares, Janet Mansfield.

Louis Horst, musician in a dancer's world / Janet Mansfield
Soares.

Includes bibliographical references and index.

ISBN 0-8223-1226-3 (acid-free paper)

1. Horst, Louis.   2. Composers—United States—Biography.

3. Modern dance—United States—History.   I. Title.

ML410.H86S5   1992

784.18′82′092—dc20

[B]   91-32933 CIP   MN

*For Martha Hill,
Maxine Greene, and
Virginia Mansfield —
three exceptional
women*

Contents

Preface

As an auditioning hopeful for admission to the Juilliard School, I was introduced to America's dance luminaries—Doris Humphrey, José Limón, Antony Tudor, and Louis Horst—by the director of the Dance Division, Martha
Hill. During the ensuing years in Louis Horst's choreography courses, I
listened to his monosyllables between puffs on a cigarette that had the
longest dangling ash imaginable, and waited for those words and those ashes
to drop.

Making sense of Horst's concepts about dance-making began to absorb
my professional life. I was an easy addition to his entourage of admirers. He
was fun to be with. The years spent in his company were a nurturing time for
me as a developing dancer-choreographer and teacher. Throughout, Louis
was there to remind me that my work was valued. He placed me in his
charmed circle of dance artists.

There have been few in my experience who could equal Louis's ability to
discuss the beauty of an Emil Nolde painting and, at the same time, pull the
tip of his tie from his bowl of minestrone and wring it out—all without
missing a beat. I am still fascinated.

This book is essentially a chronology of eighty years lived by Louis
Horst. It aims to present a fair assessment of his achievements by drawing on
resources that are, in most cases, first-hand accounts. At times these sources
offer too simple, too subjective, too harsh, or too loving a portrait, but they
give a history as seen by its participants. What people say, and do not say
about their own lives is intriguing. If there is a certain beauty in this telling, it
is because these lived experiences have a common thread. Almost everything

discussed is about art-making. I have resisted analysis and conjecture in an attempt to reveal only the special circumstances that made it possible for Horst to project his aesthetic beliefs on an entire art form. Readers who manage to plow through the thousands of references, names, and tangled events are asked to compose their own conclusions, balancing content with form, the real with the abstract. Louis would have liked it that way.

Janet Mansfield Soares

Acknowledgments

Special appreciation goes to the following people who gave generously of their time in interviews, conversations, and correspondence quoted in the text: Bonnie Bird, Sam Bryan, Ann Crosset, Agnes de Mille, Anne Douglas (Doucet), David Diamond, Kathy Ellis, Nina Fonaroff, Virginia Freeman, Martha Graham, Harriette Ann Gray, Baird Hastings, Martha Hill, Hanya Holm, George Jackson, Hazel Johnson, Gertrude Lippincott, Ruth Lloyd, Evelyn Lohoefer (Debueck), Otto Luening, George McGeary, Helen Mc-Gehee, Jane McLean, Barbara Morgan, Alwin Nikolais, Beth Osgood, Shirley Ririe, Doris Rudko, Geordie Graham Sargeant, Marian Seldes, Jane Sherman, Gertrude Shurr, Anna Sokolow, Ralph Taylor, Umanya, Marian Van Tuyl, and Yuriko. Particular thanks to Jeanette Schlottman Roosevelt, who allowed me to read the transcripts of her 1960–1961 taped interviews with Louis Horst.

Three institutions made the writing of this book possible: Barnard College of Columbia University, the Dance Collection of The New York Public Library for the Performing Arts, and the Juilliard School. I also want to express my deepest regard for the many talented students whom I have taught, and from whom I have learned, at Barnard College and at the Juilliard School over the years. Likewise for Barbara Palfy, a brilliant editor, and for my editors at Duke University Press, Joanne Ferguson and Pam Morrison.

Thanks to those who contributed to these pages in other important ways: John Abrahams, Nancy Brancart, Dan Buttress (Western History Museum), Stephanie Cimino, Barbara R. Geisler (San Francisco Performing

Arts Library and Museum), Jan Gill (Bethlehem Public Library), Diane Gray, Louis L. Humber, Daniel Jahn, Luanne James (Missouri Valley Room, Historical Archives, Kansas City), Pearl Lang, Judith Willis Lesch, Lloyd Morgan, Genevieve Oswald, Daphne Powell, Rhonda Rubinson, Lois Rudnick, Henry Van Kuiken, Gerald Weinstein, and most especially Arthur, Sabrina, and Tristan Soares.

Louis Horst

Introduction

"To Abstract a work is to

sublimate it . . . to give it

an aesthetic pattern."

— Louis Horst

Louis Horst found himself in a dancer's world by chance. His childhood of serious musical study brought a new standard of excellence to America's illustrious Denishawn Dance Company when he joined it as musical director in 1915. But when asked about his earlier life, he remarked offhandedly, "That's a closed book." He might eventually have moved on from Denishawn to another freelance job if Martha Graham had not appeared there in 1916. Although he deeply respected Ruth St. Denis, it was Graham who stirred him to become an instigator for change in dance. In 1924 Louis inscribed on a music score, "for Martha"—a dedication that might serve to explain every major decision he made in his life after that point.

Information about the early years of this taciturn man gives little indication of the role he would eventually play in shaping American modern dance. Once Louis resolved that Martha Graham would be a major dance figure in America, he did everything in his power to make that happen. He badgered colleagues into action to stimulate a fledgling concert scene where she could star. He acted as Martha's iron-willed disciplinarian and protector of her ideas. Always her mentor, he was in the studio when she choreographed, accompanied every concert she gave, and composed scores for her dances when nothing else worked. He was also her lover for almost two decades.

For the first half of his eighty years, Louis was a performer on the go. Before his encounter with dancers he made a living as a violinist in music halls and vaudeville orchestra pits, and occasionally found himself at the keyboard accompanying singers in concert halls. A skilled professional who placed his trust in schedules printed on tour cards, his experiences as a "hack" musician served as a prelude to his influence on the emerging art form of modern dance. "Things started late with me. I joined Miss Ruth when I was thirty-one, went to Vienna to study music composition when I was forty-one, played Martha's first concert when I was forty-two, and only began to teach when I was forty-four."[1]*

Ted Shawn sanguinely observed, "Horst went from Nietzsche and Schopenhauer to high art."[2] But Louis's notion of high art developed through his association with some of the finest dance artists of this century in a period when there was "no such thing as choreography."[3] He staunchly opposed the tyranny of Europe's art heritage that governed ballet's method of arranging codified steps — "Dance isn't made up of steps. It is made up of movement."[4] — and insisted on contemporary and relevant subject matter. His particular vision of modernism evolved into choreographic theories as stringent as ballet's compositional devices. He worked with Martha and generations of other dancer-choreographers who desperately needed his special brand of strictness and caring. His regard for dance as a unique aesthetic experience remained unshakable.

By the mid-thirties Louis had become a leader in the dance "establishment" as pianist and composer for dance, teacher of dance composition, and editor and critic, declaring dance an independent art form on every front. A half century later he reflected, "At the time things happened I felt, this is it! This is it! My enthusiasm for the work has been endless, and I still have it. I still must instigate young dancers to do this and do that. Working creatively you get very close to people. And the young all need guidance — especially the talented ones. They do it themselves, really, but they need a tail to their kite. And they get a feeling that without me they wouldn't have done what they have. It would have happened, but it might have been different. These children, as I think of them, are my satisfaction."[5]

Louis — pronounced Louie: "You wouldn't write Louie the fourteenth, would you?"[6] — was an ardent collector of fact and detail. The biographical materials in the following chapters are drawn from Louis's own words, his personal chronology, and from interviews with an array of people who knew him well. From 1901, just before his seventeenth birthday, until 1962, two years before his death, Louis wrote one-line entries in a "life" itinerary, giving explicit data — with scant subjectivity. This journal reveals little in the way of unusual behavior or signs of impetuousness from year to year; it does reveal his steadiness of purpose and almost obsessive need for organization. By his

*All otherwise unattributed quotations throughout the text are by Louis Horst.

eightieth year he had compiled twenty-seven scrapbooks full of newspaper clippings, contracts, and memorabilia. As an editor, author, and critic, Louis wrote exclusively about dance. Personal recollections by others shed light on the man as they saw him. These interviews, graciously offered, along with Louis's own recounting in audiotaped sessions, are a biographer's dream, as are the thirty years of his *Dance Observer* magazine. An archivist and authority of the first order, Louis wrote the definitions of dance for the *Encyclopedia Britannica* for years. He was a stickler for "getting it right" — whether it was the word in print or the choreography on stage.

Louis's activities as a freelance musician, in contact with literally hundreds of people each week, makes this tracing an elaborate one. But as a subject for historical study, his life objectives were clear. Throughout his career he determined that the "condition of simplicity," in the words of T. S. Eliot, costs "not less than everything."[7] His own world was consumed by one passion: "To see a great dancer or a great dance and be moved by it without knowing exactly why is the highest kind of communication, for that is kinesthetic communication. . . . To abstract a work is to sublimate it . . . to give it importance and to give it an aesthetic pattern — that is what we are concerned with in art."[8]

Martha Graham wrote in 1984, "I feel so deeply that without him I could not have achieved anything I have done."[9] Yet to someone interested in writing about him, she warned, "Louis was too private a man to write a biography on."[10] Graham's word "private" prepares us for a biographical journey into the complex maze of activities led by a man whom an extraordinary number of dancers worshiped, yet few really knew.

An epitaph for Louis Horst (1884–1964) might read "music director, composer, and first teacher of formal composition for dancers." He has been labeled innovator and general force for progress, strict taskmaster, and opinionated ogre by those who knew him best. Doris Humphrey was the one who affectionately called him "a bundle of contradictions."[11] He fit all of those descriptions.

chapter one

1884–1915

"I always drank beer as all

children do in Germany."

— *Louis Horst*

Louis Horst was the son of immigrants: "They were farmers, more or less — just peasants. It was a soldier and servant girl kind of affair. I don't think they were ever married. I know they weren't."[1] The soldier was his father, Conrad Horst, who grew up in the farming village of Gilsa in Hesse-Kassel, Germany. For nine years Conrad had played the cornet in a regimental band for the Prussian army. Louis remembered "being on the Rhine in a boat" when at age six he accompanied his mother to her hometown of Wiesbaden, outside of Frankfurt in the province of Hesse-Darmstadt, where Conrad had first met and romanced the young Caroline "Lena" Nickell.

In 1882 the increasing oppression that followed the Franco-Prussian War threatened a second conscription in the army for Conrad, giving him good reason to head for the United States. He convinced his brothers to sell the family property and then the men booked passage on a steamer to America, along with Fräulein Lena, by then six months pregnant with Conrad's child. The small entourage joined other "lateiners" who, encouraged by pamphlets circulated throughout the Rhineland, traveled up the Mississippi.

Conrad found work in Belleville, Illinois, a town that supported the second-oldest philharmonic orchestra in the country and where popular "sägerbunds" gave concerts in the new Liederkranz Hall. The others left to farm the rich lands of the area. "My father lost track of his brothers. I probably have cousins all across the United States I don't know about!"[2] This left Louis the lone source for his genealogy. A daughter, May, was born in Belleville, and after two years Conrad moved his family farther west, where prospering land speculators supported a wide variety of musical entertainment in Kansas City.

Louis Horst was born there on 12 January 1884, in the same year as the American journalist Damon Runyon and the German composer Anton Webern. He was a sensitive child, prone to illness. "The doctor told my mother that she'd never raise me."[3] In contrast "kid sister" May, the rebellious one, could be counted on to show her brother what to do: "She was a tomboy and I was rather a quiet one,"[4] tracing early childhood patterns. Fussed over by a mother whose poor English forced her to bond even more to her children, Lena encouraged Louis's aesthetic nature. Certainly his relationship with these two women — one as comforter, one as leader — found parallels throughout his adult life.

Although Louis was raised along the Missouri River instead of the Rhine, he spoke German before he learned English and attended a German kindergarten in a town that was virtually bilingual. "I always drank beer as all children do in Germany. We'd have a little beer with each meal. My father was playing in a theater in Kansas City. I was sitting in the first row in the balcony and when my father came out in the orchestra pit I yelled, 'Papa Bier, Papa Bier!'"[5] When the area became depressed in 1890 "Papa Bier" again moved his family — this time to Bethlehem, Pennsylvania, where he took a job instructing the local bands for the steel mills of Catasauqua. For the next three years they lived in a tenement overlooking the Lehigh River into the ironworks. Louis remembered the dramatic night sky as "being red and in flames," and his sense of loneliness. "My father was away a lot. I used to sit in the window and copy the signs on the stores across the street."[6]

During "the real depression of '93, my father decided to try California."[7] Once in San Francisco the family moved with fair regularity from one working-class neighborhood to another — all within walking distance of San Francisco's Civic Center, close to Van Ness Street and the theater district. A number of excellent musicians had already established themselves in the sizable German community of San Francisco, alongside immigrants from China, Japan, and Russia in neighborhoods replicating their own homelands. The city was rich in cultural diversity, with choral societies and brass and marching bands to enhance the lives of the generations following California's fortuitous 1846 Gold Rush; enlightenment and vice had evolved hand-in-hand. By the 1880s a forty-piece orchestra was founded under the baton of Louis Homeier.

San Francisco's new "symphony" orchestra, under the direction of Fritz Scheel, put Conrad's solid musical training to use in the brass section as a trumpeter in 1893, giving him a salary of twelve dollars a week. He also joined the stock company of the Tivoli Opera House when they needed him and supplemented his income with additional fees earned as a music "professor" at the local conservatory. Sporting a handlebar mustache and a fresh flower in his lapel, the robust musician cut a dashing figure. In contrast a studio photograph of Louis at this time shows a round-faced boy dressed in high-top shoes, velvet knickers, and shirt complete with lace collar, looking slightly dismayed. The qualities that made Conrad a popular rabble-rouser among his colleagues often overwhelmed his son, who was frightened by the household tirades of his bellowing, red-cheeked father.

Lena kept her children on their best behavior in an orderly, frugal household, while the professor caroused with his friends. It was her idea to share their living space with outsiders. She was an excellent cook, "a hausfrau who took in roomers to pay for my music lessons,"[8] who enjoyed weekly "kaffeeklatsches" and attended whenever she could Conrad's performances under Scheel's baton as a member of the "Imperial Vienna Prater Band" and the Philharmonic Orchestra. Suffering from chronic asthma, which had worsened in the polluted air along the Lehigh, she reveled in Sunday strolls after church in Golden Gate Park, built to rival Paris's Bois de Boulogne by the engineer William Hammond Hall. Lena delighted in the arboretum filled with rhododendrons and the Japanese cherry orchards, complete with a Japanese Tea Garden among the lakes and fishponds, as she picnicked with her children. May and Louis loved to scamper in the midst of the annual Civil War veterans' meetings and political rallies held during the summer months. But they sat quietly when Conrad conducted his small pickup band in arrangements of crowd-pleasing ballads and German marches for the throngs surrounding the park's gazebo.

Controlled by strict doctrines of propriety, Louis usually obeyed his father, who considered any emotional display unmanly. "When I was growing up you were either a good boy or a bad boy."[9] As a young child Louis was a "good boy." He was delicate, with small agile fingers, good rhythm, and an acute ear. With no questions asked, priority was placed on a strict schedule of musical training. Conrad believed that his son had the makings of a fine string player and set him to study violin, a popular melodic staple for all musical events at the turn of the century. He was sure that its mastery was a solid choice for his son. "At nine, [papa] wanted me to be a violinist. He told me, 'If you want to be a musician you have to practice all day.' "[10] A regime of two practice sessions a day, "two in the morning, both violin and piano . . . same in the afternoon," was set up. "After four or five years, I was sort of his prodigy. By the time I was thirteen, fourteen, and fifteen, I was playing piano all over. Everyone said, 'Oh, you ought to go to Germany to study!' "[11]

Louis graduated from the Adams Cosmopolitan Public School at fifteen and never returned to formal schooling. His career, like his father's, would be in music. His daily schedule increased to four hours of violin practice and four hours of piano lessons designed to teach harmony and counterpoint. "When I was a boy studying piano, I would never have thought of going to my teacher without preparing the assignment. It was a foregone conclusion that I would be ready."[12] But he also practiced the latest popular rags on the piano whenever he had a chance, preferring to emulate his father's image as a band leader rather than as a prestigious orchestra member.

Louis always mistrusted education's power to sanction talent. In later years he told anyone who asked about his schooling, "I never went to college. I only teach there."[13] Awarded an honorary doctorate from Wayne State University at the end of his long career, he congratulated himself: "Not bad for an eighth-grade education."[14] Self-educated, he confessed that as a child his reading was limited to Horatio Alger's dime novels and Tip Top Weeklies featuring stories about a clean-cut Yale man portrayed as gentlemanly, adventurous, brave, handsome, brilliant, athletic, and wealthy. "We had no books at home. I thought *Ivanhoe* was an abstruse book. Then I got hold of some old Nick Carter things: *Ragged Dick, Frank Merriwell at Yale, Civil War* by Castleman. At that time I said, 'You was,' and 'I seen.' A flute player said, 'You're such a good pianist, why don't you improve your speech and grammar?' So I started to read Scott and Dickens — classics that we all know."[15]

Louis began a journal on the first day of 1900.* Perhaps the dawn of a new century evoked the teenager's interest in record-keeping. He placed his address in San Francisco — 439 4th Street — and the names of his music teachers on the opening page. He studied violin with John Marquardt, a musician from Cologne who played at San Francisco's Tivoli Opera House with his father, and piano with F. Dellepiane, "an Italian Jew who played in the Catholic Church."[16] Destined for the concert stage, he frequently rehearsed in ensembles with other young musicians under his father's supervision until a series of events changed the course of his career.

Louis's sister May was generally described as precociously brilliant and beautiful, her charm attracting many suitors throughout her long life. At eighteen, she married Ernest Forbes, a handsome and ambitious diplomat

---

*Hereafter, all excerpts from Louis Horst's journal are in quotes without endnote citation.

who served the United States government in South America. He advised the Horsts to invest their savings in a gold mine outside of Acapulco. Rekindled by the discovery of Canada's Klondike, gold fever returned to Californian opportunists, and must have lured Conrad as well. The same impulsive wunderlust that had resulted in booking passage to the United States caught his imagination when another opportunity arose. Conrad combined the journey to Mexico to witness his daughter's wedding with a business scheme: he took Ernest's advice.

The family moved out of their apartment and arranged for Louis to reside in a tenement on Turk Street with Karl Goerlich, a German tuba player from the symphony, and his wife. During the three months that his parents watched over the mining operation in a search of precious metal that depleted their funds, the sixteen-year-old was expected to continue his musical studies. Free to venture out on his own he quickly adopted independent ways. Immediately after their departure he played "a dance in Colma," some twenty-five miles south of San Francisco, with a friend. Each of them received five dollars.

A month later the two companions traveled to Randsburg, in the Mojave Desert near Los Angeles, where they played a three-week job in a "theatre-dance hall." Unperturbed by the moral teachings of his German Lutheran background, Louis discovered the less-than-reputable side of San Francisco life. He haunted popular cafes, where musicians played the syncopated jazz tunes he practiced in secret, and visited gambling clubs and whore houses. This desire to be part of visceral experiences continually presented a paradox in his personal life. He admired the freer attitudes of others, if usually at a distance, and attempted to adopt the bohemian way of life — at least in his mind.

By the time his parents returned penniless to San Francisco to reside in a flat on Hayes Street, Louis was confident that he could make a living as a popular entertainer. He passed the musician's union entrance exam and found work as a musician at various cafes, first in San Francisco and then farther afield. Happy in the raucous atmosphere of wild women and heavy drinkers, he took every entertainment job that he was offered, plainly enjoying his position as a musical conduit for pleasure-seekers of the day. Usually he played in surroundings where gambling, drinking, and whoring were the major attractions.

I played in dance halls in the Mojave Desert at the mines. [There were] two big gold mines then, with a town nearby called Johannesburg. When we asked where the nicest place to live was, they said, "Oh, go down to Belle's." I stayed with four girls. . . . We'd have breakfast around twelve. It was awful nice. Just like home.

At the pike, miners had three shifts and changed shifts at two in the morning. They'd come in for beer, drinks, and to dance with the girls. I'd play from eight to two or three in the morning. We played a lot of sweet waltzes — "After the Ball Is Over" and "Under the Old Apple Tree" and some Strauss. . . . [But] the rough miners and girls weren't dull people. Men used to come in and shoot out the lights sometimes.[17]

Louis liked to tell about his adventures and playing for the "patrons of ladies of ill-repute" in gambling houses. One friend said, "He had a kind of perverse pride and a sort of thrill about shocking people. I think it was part of an antiromantic, anti-German, reaction to middle-class respectability. A nice boy of good parents, of good upbringing, of Lutheran background. I think he delighted in that like so many teenagers through history. He loved to think that he was living the life of a bohemian."[18]

"When musicians were out of work in San Francisco, they would go to Nevada."[19] In 1903 Louis traveled with two friends to play for six weeks at the Elk Saloon, a gambling casino in Elko. "It was just a cow town then — a railroad town and little huts and Chinese restaurants run by Chinamen that didn't serve Chinese food."[20] With the help of a little gambling on the side, he saved $800 that year. Worried about his son's decadent ways, Conrad wrote that there were jobs waiting for him in San Francisco. After a reluctant return to the Bay Area, Louis was soon working in more respectable places — "fancy" restaurants, playing "sentimental" songs on the piano at the Bay State Grill and then violin duos with John Marquardt, his former teacher, at Cafe Zinfand and the Techaw Tavern.

He went from one freelance job to another, returning intermittently to lessons with the first violinist of the Symphony Society, John Josephs, oboe studies with two different teachers, and occasional lessons at the keyboard. His new piano teacher was Sam Fleischman, "quite a virtuoso technician with a beautiful tone,"[21] produced by dropping the wrist when striking the note. He also studied the organ for a brief period. In the middle of this decade of contrasts, the population was more excited by Franz Lehar's latest operetta, *The Merry Widow,* than by Albert Einstein's Theory of Relativity. Louis was no exception. Although rising early on Sundays to play the organ for church services might provide a steady income, he chose the more lucrative and faster paced night work, where the newest dance rage, the cakewalk, was just coming into vogue.

Increasingly dissatisfied with his violin studies, Louis resisted his father's constant pressure to excel. Considered the most complex of all instruments the violin demanded unrelenting, near schizophrenic duplicity between bow and fret, while maintaining an eternally awkward stance of crooked neck and tension-filled shoulders, to Louis's complete discomfort. Furthermore, although the violin received prominence in the orchestra, its extensive repertoire from the Classic and Romantic periods bored him. He sensed that he would never be a strong enough player to fill the first chair in an orchestra. "I never was really an excellent violin player. I just got by!"[22] But he had learned to balance the disciplines of a musical career with popular diversions of the day — a pattern that continued throughout his life.

Twenty-one years old in 1905 and with $1,557.20 in his savings account, Louis moved into a rooming house on Bush Street to begin a fully independent life for a period. He gave piano lessons, "some in, some out," during that first year, and he underwent minor surgery. A Dr. Black first removed a tumor from his nose and later "a bone from a nostril," possibly accounting for an unusual aquiline nose that distinguished his profile and contributing to the odd snorting sound for which he was famous years later.

San Francisco was a thriving city until the devastating natural disaster of the new century — the earthquake of 1906 — changed the lives of its inhabitants. Louis's journal recorded April 18 at 5:11 A.M. as the exact time he felt the first sharp tremor. "I was [working] in the Columbia Theater. I was usually in bed by four and slept till noon. I was just in bed an hour." The impact sent his piano sliding across the room. "We had gas in our house and there was a light fixture right above my head. It shook above my bed in my room, so sharp that glass things all fell on me. I heard the sideboard open. All my mother's dishes fell out. Yet, we still had phones."

Fortunately, the row house at the end of Bush Street where Louis was staying temporarily with his parents was far enough away from the center of town to avoid the fire that broke out and spread quickly along the damaged gas mains for the next four days. "Other little fires started because all the flues were broken. We didn't move. We were house-bound four days and nights with just the food my mother had in the house. We could see little fires miles down the street. We'd get bricks and everyone cooked meals on the sidewalk in front. There had to be marshal law to stop the ransacking."[23] The city was in chaos for months after the catastrophic quake, and the fire that followed destroyed a good portion of the city. Of its 450,000 residents, 100,000 fled.

Louis, with a friend, left San Francisco a month after the quake for work in Eureka, two hundred miles north on the California coast. They signed on as pit musicians from August to December 1906 at the Margarita Theatre, which was "known as a combination house, where all the traveling shows come . . . the good, old road, you know! . . . That was nice, but it wasn't a successful venture."[24]

Theaters had cropped up all along the coast, most of them owned by circuit organizations such as Orpheum or Pantages that booked popular variety shows, vaudeville, light opera, silent movies, and "legitimate" stage plays. With millions of Americans becoming weekly theatergoers, these organizations grew into big businesses, operated by theatrical agents and managers who paid excellent wages to their artists. Musicians practically lived at the theater and, with their knowledge of current music, adaptability, and skill, had to handle each of the acts, many of which were excruciating agony for these sufferers in the pit. Generally the size of the orchestra varied with the size of the theater, making a violinist who could "double" at the keyboard a valuable commodity. Louis played the violin with the orchestra for the two main-show house bills and often stayed on as pianist, "playing out the audience" at the end of each show or accompanying the "undivided middle" (fillers between main shows) with other artists who did "three turns" a day.

Returning home for his birthday in January 1907, he took a job at the Novelty Theatre, hastily built "just like a mining camp . . . like a little tin shed."[25] At age twenty-three, Louis moved into a San Francisco boarding house and bought a new Chickering piano with the intention of building his private teaching clientele. But versatile musicians were in demand and his schedule allowed little free time for giving lessons. Even between the two shows at the Novelty he often played at the Aquarium Grill and the Cafe San Francisco. A highlight at the Van Ness Theatre, where he also played in 1907, was Ethel Barrymore, who performed in *Captain Jinks*. She earned $3,000 a week from the Orpheum circuit as a star in *The Twelve Pound Look*. Louis played for several runs of the show. He was also in the pit for Cyril Scott's performances in *The Prince Chap*. Louis took little notice of dance in those days. "Vaudeville had hoofers, [performing] soft shoe, buck and wing, and what was called fancy dancing—with scarves and little elves. I never paid any attention to it. I was more interested in accompanying singers."[26]

Occasionally Louis did rehearse and perform with a chamber ensemble, but "serious" recital work was usually scheduled around better-paying jobs. He tended to work for the duration of a theater's season and then travel for pleasure—often for months at a time. Quick to adjust to new situations he worked tirelessly for long stretches, cramming his schedule with every job that was offered to him until physical exhaustion eventually led to illness. Louis's chronology is peppered with visits to doctors, usually followed by sudden vacations. One such entry lists a Mount Zion Hospital visit in May for a circumcision by a Dr. Hoffman. Taking an unusually long eight-month break after the surgery, Louis went on a cruise along the Mexican coast with his sister and brother-in-law and began to put his musical ideas on paper. He signed his first attempt at an arrangement — scoring a piece by M. Magalanes for violin and piano — on 14 February 1908. He called the piece *Passion: Danza* — words full of portent for a man who would leave a legacy to dance.

During the summer months of 1908, Louis worked as a resort musician at the Casino in Santa Cruz. While there, he was hired to conduct the orchestra for a show, *Don't Tell My Wife,* marking his first official position as a musical conductor. He became an adept gambler during this period of playing in casinos; his account sheet shows a steady increase of personal savings from $1,451.75 in 1907 to $2,101.95 in 1909. In the fall, again contracted as a pit musician at the Van Ness Theatre, Louis played for prestigious shows such as *Peer Gynt* and *The Lion and the Mouse.* Once settled into a schedule at the Van Ness for another five-month stretch he also managed to play the 6:00 P.M. set at the Hotel Argonaut with a friend. Seeking diversion from the continual demands of his work as a theater musician he began to socialize, in the Germanic tradition, at clubs where he could enjoy the comradeship of men. At this time he was elected to the board of directors of the local musicians' union.

During this period ideas about healthy living were being introduced by Christian Scientists and influencing California Arts and Crafts Movement architecture. Louis was an interested participant. Earlier, inspired by Teddy Roosevelt's Rough Riders and his historic decision to create nationally owned parks and preserves throughout the West, Louis had joined the ranks of young men who adventured in the "great outdoors." It was a splendid antidote to long hours of work. Filling his free time with healthful activities, such as mountain climbs and walking tours, Louis returned to the relaxed atmosphere of Santa Cruz whenever he had a chance. With a natural ability for sports that demanded eye and hand accuracy, he took up the game of tennis, sometimes bringing his mother along to watch his matches.

But Louis had another reason for these return trips. He had fallen in love with a young high-school student, Bessie Cunningham, a telephone operator at the Casino. "Betty," as she was called, lived in Santa Cruz with her family. Louis's carefree life took a formidable turn as he began at age twenty-five what appears to have been his first relationship with a woman. He was an ardent suitor. Seven years younger than Louis, Betty was a voluptuous redhead, feisty and fun-loving, with a lively Irish temperament. After a rapid succession of trysts during the spring and summer, Louis left for a series of short vacations over the next few months, including a visit to Tacoma for the Alaska-Yukon Exposition.

He paid four more visits to Betty in Santa Cruz that fall—each a month apart—among a flurry of other activities. Once romantically involved the couple dispensed with any idea of a long courtship. "I knew I wasn't meant for marriage. I just thought everyone got married. It was a date, then you got married."[27] He took a two-week break from his Van Ness Theatre performing schedule and they traveled to Oakland, where they were married on 29 November 1909. They then boarded a train for Salt Lake City. After introducing his new wife to his sister and brother-in-law, then living in Ogden, he and Betty returned to San Francisco and an apartment on Post Street to begin their married life.

A photograph taken that year shows a dapper-looking Louis sitting on the stoop in front of their San Francisco row house with a mongrel pup in his arms. For the next few years, he snapped photos of his good-natured Betty leaning indolently against giant redwoods, on tops of mountains after strenuous climbs, and looking crisply dressed on hotel verandahs. With pleasant, "Rubensesque" appeal, Betty's joviality seemed to complement the romantic Louis's full figure in these candid shots. And it is apparent that Betty doted on her more mature and sophisticated husband.

In January 1910, Horst left his playing jobs at the Van Ness Theatre and the Monroe Hotel to become a pit musician at the Columbia Theatre in San Francisco, playing the violin for musical productions and piano for dramatic shows such as the Shakespearean dramas produced by the theater. His schedule also included playing for the touring companies booked around the busy "in-house" schedule, as in April 1911, when he accompanied Ruth St. Denis's *Oriental Dances* at the theater. Occasionally he played other engagements with some of the resident musicians; they called themselves "The Columbia Boys Band."

After almost two years of continuous work at the Columbia Theatre, Louis and Betty decided to travel east. "My wife and I wanted to see New York. I took a winter off."[28] Vacationing in a carefree manner they enjoyed a tour of Niagara Falls in September 1911 before arriving in New York City. After a day with friends in Sea Cliff on Long Island Louis noted in his log: "First View of the Atlantic." With lodgings secured on West 96th Street his two immediate concerns were to get tickets for the World Series and to find work.

In November Louis was hired to accompany the actress Annette Kellerman in rehearsals for the Fox movie *Daughter of the Gods,* in which she starred. (Four years later, he again worked with Kellerman for the movie *Neptune's Daughter.*) He then joined Lucius Hosmer's Orchestra, commuting to Westchester for nightly performances at the Briarcliff Lodge or the

Hotel Gramalan in Bronxville. The couple's move to New York was brief. Restless, Louis eagerly accepted interim work at the chic Princess Hotel in Bermuda from December through the following April. Betty went happily along. "In Bermuda's Princess Hotel, she worked at the telephone. I was in the orchestra. We played tennis on grass courts, and I learned how to swim, but I hate swimming. I hate the water. We were there in April 1912 when the Titanic sank."[29]

The Horsts returned to Manhattan, where they found temporary living arrangements with a Mrs. English in her boarding house on West 124th Street. He rejoined the orchestra at the Briarcliff Lodge for a brief stint until he had made contacts for other resort jobs for the summer. Betty traveled with him to New Jersey, where he worked for two weeks at the Laurel House in Lakewood. Then they toured New York and New England, sightseeing on their way to a three-month summer position at the Maplewood Hotel in New Hampshire. Always observant of luminaries around him and in the audience, Louis noted President Taft's presence. It was a particularly pleasant stint. "I played with all Boston Symphony men — seven musicians at the hotel. We played lunch, dinner, and dancing on Thursday nights. Every Sunday we had nothing to do except for the concert that night. We'd climb different mountains."[30]

In fact, Betty's and Louis's chief recreation that fall seemed to be mountain climbing. They traveled at a leisurely pace from Montreal to Quebec and then cross-country before returning to San Francisco in November. Back in their familiar neighborhood they moved into the Vernon apartments on Hyde Park after a few weeks' stay with their folks. Throughout their first trip to the eastern seaboard Betty had missed her relatives in California. Louis felt at this point that New York City was the only place for an artist to live, but he could not convince his wife that they should move there permanently. He began to face the sober realization that, no matter where he settled, married life was not for him.

Having spent a good portion of their savings — the remaining $846.19 was the lowest amount ever recorded in his journal — they stayed in San Francisco and Louis went back to work as a pit musician at the Columbia Theatre. For the next two years he played every show there, including one of the most popular hits of the period, *Peter Pan*, starring Maude Adams. The heavy schedule of continual performing once again affected his health. In February 1914 he contracted lobar pneumonia and the following year he was hospitalized for a tonsillectomy. After this the couple went to El Pajaro Springs for a vacation.

Louis's journal documents more mountains climbed, a Christian Science treatment, and his father's naturalization as an American citizen. After nearly fifteen years as an entertainment musician, Louis returned to occasional concert work as a member of an ensemble trio that played classical repertory, accompanying Metropolitan Opera singer Bernice de Pasquali at the official opening of San Francisco's Municipal Auditorium, playing with Nathaniel Firestone in a concert for the Pacific Music Club, and accompanying several other singers at the Civic Auditorium. However, it was his work in the commercial theater that paid his bills.

Silent movies were becoming a popular form of amusement. Louis began to play the piano for "silents" four times a day, accompanying films such as *The Chorus Lady* and *Paid in Full*. He played from "mood" music collections and worked with "cue" sheets, which were usually handed to pianists just before the theater went dark. The player often had to improvise on the spur of the moment, using these "pasticcios" of small pieces of musical themes that already existed while synchronizing sound to the image on the screen. The music also had the practical function of drowning out the noisy projector. Arthur Lass, a "silents" pianist with a background similar to Horst's, wrote:

> My piano teacher . . . had given me an excellent grounding in the traditional classics and piano techniques. My musical memory was pretty good; I had a fairly broad and varied popular and classical repertoire; and I played easily, naturally, and quite accurately by ear. I could, in addition, improvise and compose, on the instant, the music I thought would fit the shifting moods and scenes. So I improvised and composed my way through fires; terrestrial upheavals of all kinds — volcanic eruptions, rain and snowstorms, typhoons, hurricanes; confrontations between the forces of good and evil; love scenes; pursuits; rescues, et cetera.[31]

Adept at using the popular cut-and-paste technique of the day, Louis well understood the procedure of "raping" the works of Bach, Beethoven, Mendelssohn, Grieg, Tchaikovsky, and Wagner for "adagio lamentosos, sinister misteriosos, weird moderatos, and majestic pomposos," as Lass explained. This new technique of accompanying would prove a valuable asset for Horst's future role with dance.

While studying the organ, this time with Wallace Sabin, Louis returned to work as a pit musician for the *Ziegfeld Follies of 1914*, followed by other movie stints at the Alcazar and the Cort Theatres, accompanying D. W. Griffith's *The Clansman*. This juggling of a variety of jobs continued throughout Louis's long life as a freelance musician. Jockeying between seriousness of purpose and lighthearted pleasures suited his temperament. It also gave him the opportunity to withdraw from personal conflict and avoid confrontation.

Married life had become a series of episodic vacations between constant moves from one boarding house to another for the couple, and Louis began to question the value of domesticity. Still bound by the traditional mores of his Lutheran upbringing and his strong sense of duty and propriety, he did not consider legal separation. But he began to demonstrate in subtle ways that his only honest commitment was to music-making. Showing little emotion, he noted his father's death at 1:25 A.M. on 14 June 1915, with the same clinical accuracy as the other factual information he jotted during this period. After a brief bereavement Louis took another movie job before returning to work at the Columbia.

chapter two

1915–1925

"The powers of art are

the wings of the soul."

— *François Delsarte*

ouis was thirty-one when he encountered the Denishawn Dance Company, billed as the first "institutional" dance theater in the nation. Its star, Ruth St. Denis, had a particularly furious row with her accompanist while performing in San Francisco and appealed to the theater manager for a new music director. The manager asked around. Louis found out about the job through a violist playing at the Alcazar. His varied experiences as a professional musician made him a likely candidate for the position. He had often conducted from the keyboard, but he warned St. Denis that he had no experience in playing for dancers. "I had a knack for holding a tempo, which a lot of musicians lack, so I agreed to take the job for two weeks."[1] Hired on the spot, Louis went home to pack, placed his violin under a friend's bed for safekeeping, and said a temporary goodbye to his wife.[2]

The musical director for Denishawn had to be quick-witted, willing to put up with less than ideal conditions, and able to recognize vast numbers of sight cues for the smooth running of the dance numbers. Before Louis joined the company St. Denis and Shawn had selected music from the classical repertory to suit their dramatic ideas with the same reverence as producers of the period "commissioned" piano scores matched in mood and tempo to their "two dollars a seat" movies. Louis's own dance experience ranged from "a little grizzly bear to a one step and hop. I never actually studied dance. Oh, Gosh, no! Not a step! But, I have a photographic eye. Once I saw a dance, I felt the movement."[3]

After making it through the first performances he went to Miss Ruth:

"If I don't get a rehearsal I'm going home." "But it's going all right," she said. "But I don't know it," I said. And then Ted would come and say, "Now tonight Miss Ruth is doing *Radha*." And then, without an orchestra rehearsal, there was *Radha*. Big, long things with difficult music [from the divertissement of Leo Delibes's *Lakme*]. And then Miss Ruth said, "Well, Mr. Horst," — she didn't call me Louis — "when we get to Seattle we'll give you a rehearsal because we'll be there two days. But it will have to be the second day because we won't have time the first day. We'll be too busy getting the show up."[4]

Pleased that he kept the orchestra going and the dance tempi steady, St. Denis asked him to stay on for the remainder of the tour. Louis was in the pit at the piano when she approached him. "Kind of crooning in her Irish way, she stepped down on the top of the piano. And she said, 'Do you have to be back in San Francisco at the end of two weeks?' 'No,' I said. 'We just wondered whether you wouldn't stay on?' 'I'd be delighted,' I said."[5] This temporary two-week job continued for the next ten years, placing Louis at the center of ceaseless dance activity, performing, finding new scores and arranging old ones, accompanying classes, and teaching. From then on Louis referred to his life after 1915 as "A.D.": "I've had two lives — B.D. and A.D. — Before Denishawn and After Denishawn."[6]

His one stipulation was that Betty must travel with him. Within a few months Shawn had choreographed Louis's wife into the show, and the willing Mrs. Horst became one of Denishawn's dancing women. If fairly innocent of formal dance training, Betty's charm and spirited demeanor evidently sufficed, as it did in varying degrees for others when they first joined the company. Evidently satisfied with her work Shawn choreographed a solo, *Serenata Morisca,* that she performed regularly. Louis, too, adapted easily to his new role as he began to appreciate the uniqueness of dance as a performing art.

> There were character dances, will o'wisps, sunrises, dragonflies, bubbles, showers, rainbow, sunset, torch dances, crescent moons and bats and then Miss Ruth did her *Spirit of the Sea*. There was the lion ballet. Then a facing west from California. She did her Japanese flower arrangement, *Egypta,* an ancient Egyptian ballet [that] was very popular, and *The Legend of the Peacock*. It was all pictorial. . . . It was just enough romantic theater — nothing abstruse, although some of Miss Ruth's religious studies got a little metaphysical. Sometimes when I was conducting I'd hear a woman in the front row say, "Oh, that's nothing! I could dance like that," but generally they liked it.[7]

This lucrative touring (for the directors, at least) was difficult on the company members, who spent a good portion of their lives backstage in vaudeville house dressing rooms, and Louis's job was not much easier. At each theater after spacing and brush-up rehearsals, while the dancers tended to their elaborate costumes he briefed the pickup orchestra members, rearranging scores depending on the instruments available. "They had musicians ready for us. I used whoever came and those who could play the music. In the big towns I had eight, nine, or ten. I always conducted from the piano, because we didn't get time to rehearse all the show. I played with my left hand and conducted with the right. A lot of things I performed absolutely alone when I knew they couldn't play the music."[8]

The zealous Shawn and charismatic St. Denis were showmen who filled their audiences with wondrous respect for dance along with well-paced entertainments. Their arduous transcontinental jaunts were vividly described in Shawn's memoirs: "We performed twice a day, matinee and evening, for a total of twelve times a week for forty weary weeks. An advantage of the full week engagement over the one night stand was that of being settled in one place for six days. No matter what our accommodations, they seemed luxurious when we slept in the same bed six nights in a row."[9] According to Louis, "Generally we went to theatrical hotels that gave rates, and always ate out. In Texas you could get a dinner for twenty-five cents."[10] Recalling the differences among the vaudeville circuits that booked Denishawn, he explained that "Pantages was a lesser theater [that gave] three shows a day. With the Orpheum it was always two—matinee and night. This was top vaudeville—'top time.' If you saw Orpheum or Keith's that meant it was first run."[11] Before long Louis had a good sampling of all of them, and by the end of January 1916 he took on other operational responsibilities when the Keith managers "liked the show so much they told us to get a thirty-minute act together."[12]

Louis's next run as musical director featured Ruth St. Denis "assisted by Ted Shawn and eleven dancers" for the 1916 Orpheum circuit, which was routed from Minneapolis to Winnipeg, Calgary to Vancouver, Seattle and Portland to San Francisco, Los Angeles to Denver, then Omaha to Chicago over twenty-eight weeks. Vaudeville "concert" audiences applauded the aesthetic barefoot dancing on their local stages. Press coverage usually amounted to photos in the tabloid section of St. Denis and her dancing girls, with captions such as "More Than An Eyefull [sic]."[13]

Occasionally notice of their arrival in town was more dramatic: "Go See Ruth, Ted and the Girls and Tear the Daylights Out of the Spud Patch in the Backyard When You Get Home."[14] The San Francisco *Chronicle* promised that "Ruth St. Denis. Orpheum Star — Dancing Act — Costume Scant" would entertain with exotic, "lavish ceremonies of the senses."[15] But an article in *Musical America* saw "nothing radical about the works of Debussy, Schoenberg and Ornstein." Deploring the "delicatessen idea" of art, the reviewer pleaded for a "greater Correlation of the Arts. . . . Pavlowa [sic] creates — Ruth St. Denis imitates! . . . Miss St. Denis gives a series of pretty pictures, and her work is pleasing, but it lacks the vital elements of art which Pavlowa expresses."[16] These reviews went into Louis's music satchel to be pasted into a scrapbook at the end of each tour, along with an unusual one containing the headline, "Ruth St. Denis Foils Bandit By Means of 'Stocking Bank' and Manages to Save her Money: Dancers and Several Members of Company Are on Train During Hold-up Near Hanna, Wyo."[17]

Ruth St. Denis (a name given to Ruthie Dennis by the great theater director, David Belasco, to describe her virginal ways) had learned how to deliver enlightened entertainment early in her career. "I will be Egypt," she had declared in 1904, taking her cue from a cigarette ad glorifying the Goddess Isis on a soda-shop poster. At the time she was playing in Belasco's *Madame DuBarry* as Mlle LeGrand, a dancer from the Grand Opera. Her reputation as an actress-dancer and vaudeville artist as well as her unswerving sense of mission were well developed before she met Ted Shawn.

Ruth combined her own brand of Eastern mysticism with the words of the French movement theorist, François Delsarte. For her, the word "Art" must always be capitalized. "Art is divine in its principles, its essence, its action and its end. The essential principles of Art are the Good, the True and the Beautiful. . . . The powers of Art are the wings of the soul," she told her followers, quoting Delsarte.[18] St. Denis was also practical. "Any technique is sufficient which adequately expresses the intention of the artist," she told student Jane Sherman. "One should *think* of dance as an art, although one may have to *do* it as a business."[19] Sherman found out later as a company member that *talking* ideals and *working* ideals were two different things.

Ted Shawn attended the University of Denver as a pretheology student, where he enjoyed performing ballroom exhibitions, much to the chagrin of his fraternity brothers who told him flatly that "men don't dance." When a sudden illness caused temporary paralysis he turned to America's Transcendentalists and Christian Scientists for spiritual guidance and to ballet lessons for physical therapy. Then, moving to Los Angeles where "everybody . . . was pioneering in business or the arts," he began his professional career in dance with a partner, Norma Gould.[20]

Together they demonstrated the latest dance crazes at Tango Teas, formed a small company to make a movie, *Dance of the Ages,* for the

Thomas A. Edison Company, and entertained vacationing employees along the Santa Fe Railroad line. Inspired by St. Denis in performance, Shawn auditioned for her. She hired him immediately to perform the now essential ballroom dances, as popularized by Irene and Vernon Castle, on her programs. After creating a mazurka coined the "Denishawn Rose" in a dance-naming contest in Portland that received much attention in the press, the endearing Ted convinced Ruth that they should join forces and call their company "Denishawn." In August 1914, they married.

"Papa" Shawn, twelve years younger than St. Denis, became the financial protector and principal administrator of the company; St. Denis continued to have the last word on the artistic aspects of their work. From then on their private lives and public images presented an odd dichotomy of philosophical messages to those around them. Sensitive to the popular idea of the European ballet dancer as an entertainer of questionable moral standards, they wanted to be taken seriously in puritanical America, making every effort to represent themselves as a passionate, yet stable, happily married couple.

Los Angeles was one of the first places to welcome the theatrical couple and their free-spirited ideas. St. Denis and Shawn saw themselves as pioneers in pedagogy as well as dance performance. They were also opportunists, leasing glamorous surroundings for short durations between tours for their educational enterprise. At the Ruth St. Denis School of Dancing and its Related Arts, students were trained in Denishawn techniques designed to "inspire the soul and free the body." Discipline and devotion were demanded, as well as a dollar into the cigar box by the door, at the 6th Street building, complete with a "practice-performing platform" on its terrace.

In 1916 they moved to the recently vacated buildings of the Westlake School for Girls, which offered space for out-of-town boarders and a tennis court "floored with fine sanded wood, and shaded with a canvas tent top."[21] Ted's anniversary surprise to Ruth, a lone peacock, strolled beside the swimming pool and among the eucalyptus trees. The following year they purchased a bungalow they dubbed "Tedruth" and Shawn oversaw the building of a 400-seat theater in the suburbs of Eagle Rock, where the company could present recitals. As Ted had anticipated the Denishawn school attracted a growing number of students.

In turn the school became an important resource for talented dancers entering their company. Remarkably, the dancers who came to study with St. Denis and Shawn over the next years were to become the future leaders of the new modern dance movement in America. Doris Humphrey, Martha Graham and her sister Geordie, Pauline Lawrence, and Charles Weidman learned enough about theatrical dancing from Denishawn to eventually effect a profound change in America's art.

When twenty-two-year-old Martha Graham appeared on the scene for the summer session of 1916, few would have predicted that she would change dance history and stir Louis's unending passion. "The first time I ever saw Martha she was running across the tennis courts at Denishawn. I watched her from my window, her black hair flying. She had a special quality — like a wild animal."[22] Unlike Humphrey, Graham had had no dance experience when she went to her first lesson in the open-air studio. She confessed it to Miss Ruth, who is said to have signaled her pianist: "Louis, play a waltz."[23] Martha returned to the school to study in 1917 and, according to Shawn, "applied herself in class without distinction but with a diligence that was just short of dedication [becoming] . . . so well trained in Denishawn techniques that she taught classes of business girls at night."[24] Shawn took advantage of her skill as a teacher when he opened the new Ted Shawn Studio on South Grand Avenue in 1920.

The renamed Denishawn School attracted twenty-two-year-old Doris Humphrey. Humphrey, like Shawn, had performed for the Santa Fe Railway Men's Clubs. In her one private lesson Miss Ruth asked, "What do you do?" To the answer "I teach," St. Denis replied, "You shouldn't be teaching, you should be dancing."[25] Still, a perfunctory period of teaching was necessary before Humphrey was hired as a performer. She joined the Denishawn entourage as it zigzagged the United States for the better part of 1917, observing the pianist in his fully appreciated role as music director. She was also one of the women (who only occasionally included his wife) whom he escorted to the best restaurants in town. A few years later an affable young man from Lincoln, Nebraska, joined the company after a typically brief introduction to the art of dancing. "Charles Weidman showed up in 1919. He was nineteen years old — as old as the century. We liked him right away, and he fit right in."[26]

Newspaper clippings began to cram the Denishawn scrapbooks. One announced "Plans to Establish a Dancing Studio in Hollywood for the Moving Picture Girls,"[27] showing photos of the company residence where Ruth Chatterton, Myrna Loy, and Dorothy Gish were among the starlets sent to learn emotional expression for their roles on the silent screen. The school quickly became a center for potential talents. Its reputation caught the attention of prominent Californians, among them the movie maker D. W. Griffith, who believed in the "spiritual" values of dance. The movie mogul often attended Denishawn recitals and was particularly impressed by fourteen-year-old Carol Dempster. Shawn agreed that she was so beautiful off-stage that theater makeup tended to reduce rather than heighten her beauty. After touring briefly with Denishawn she became Griffith's lover and leading ingenue.

Griffith wrestled with the problem of silence and its deadly effect on celluloid rushes. In one of his attempts at matching accompaniment to his moving images he asked Louis, along with other Denishawners, to participate in his latest venture, *Intolerance*. He cast the dancers as the god Ishtar's priestesses, along with hundreds of extras and six elephants. St. Denis staged the dancing at Belshazzar's feast on the massive Babylonian set, while Louis played a score concocted by a popular composer of the day, Joseph Carl Breil. Adept at sight-reading and already familiar with Breil's score for *The Clansman* (with its 214 cues drawn from Schubert, Dvořák, Schumann, Mozart, Tchaikovsky, Grieg, Mahler, Wagner's "The Ride of the Valkyries," and a handful of Civil War and Stephen Foster tunes), Louis gallantly plodded through the elaborate score for rehearsals and shoots. Afterward he understood why Griffith once said after a quarrel with his arranger, "If I ever kill anyone, it won't be an actor, but a musician."[28]

Another of Denishawn's more illustrious summer activities helped the company's — and Louis's — reputation. Their momentous *Dance Pageant of Egypt, Greece, and India* production in 1916 had filled William Randolph Hearst's Greek amphitheater in Berkeley with a large cast that included numbers of children. The event must have impressed Conrad Horst and his colleagues at the San Francisco Symphony Orchestra when his son stepped before the "forty men" to conduct. The pageant also marked Martha Graham's debut as a dancer.

When Martha attended the better-organized and more expensive twelve-week Denishawn summer school as a student in 1917 she paid $500 for classes in technique (consisting of barre work and "free" movement), guided reading, arts and crafts, a private lesson with Miss Ruth, and room and board. Louis recalled that "We gave concerts there. They had a studio house, a craft house . . . and a faculty dormitory, where I stayed. Doris was teaching. Pauline Lawrence was a pianist. I lectured on the symphony. . . . It was expensive but we had pupils."[29] Betty taught children's classes. As the school's music head, Louis gave piano lessons and accompanied Miss Ruth's classes, which taught "plastique" dancing and movement phrases based on Delsarte's principles of the body as an expressive instrument. (St. Denis admitted to being more inspired by ideas than music and to being more of an "eye" dancer than an "ear" dancer.)

From 1915 to 1920 Shawn studied with a Delsarte teacher, Mrs. Richard Hovey, from whom he learned the nine rules of attitude, force, motion, sequence, direction, form, velocity, reaction and recall, and extension, based on the premise that all human movement has meaning. Shawn was more excited about these pedagogical notions and understood them more thoroughly than St. Denis, who later confessed, "I was never a good teacher. . . . I confused rather than clarified, and someone's help was frequently needed to finish what I started."[30]

When he resumed his place at the piano during the summer, Louis began to suggest experiments that were later labeled "musical visualizations." In the classroom as well as the theater, waiting for the sight cue that signaled his upbeat, he saw a need for greater discipline, craft, and attention to detail among the dancers. Simple musical concepts, second nature to a practicing musician, were rarely considered by Denishawn except in occasional "eurhythmics" classes, in which rhythms were translated into movement patterns in an analytical system devised by the Swiss musician, Emile Jaques-Dalcroze.

Other dance artists influenced the Denishawn work. Isadora Duncan performed at the Mason Opera House each time she came to Los Angeles and Louis went to her performances.

> I didn't particularly like her because we were more theatrical, although we had done the musical visualizations, which was my idea. I had read about Isadora Duncan and Mary Wigman doing dances without music and also doing things to good composition, instead of just using character music. It started with Ted and [me] talking about rhythmic things, doing things so they'd know music, so we taught the Bach *Inventions* to the class. We had two groups — one did one voice, and the other did the other — and they danced each one, note for note.[31]

As helpful as Louis might have been at the time, no one could have predicted his eventual importance in this world of dance into which he had so casually drifted. But as he worked each day with dancers struggling for their own mode of expression, he became aware (as Jaques-Dalcroze had earlier) of the strong link between music and dance, sensing that the kinetics of dance movement were drawn from the same rhythmic impulses that musicians understood. As he became increasingly interested in the potential of movement and its theatrical powers his own ideas about dance began to take shape. St. Denis relied on him in the studio, accepting his encouragement and support as she began to experiment with musical form. He tried to be helpful as she struggled to find new material. "Miss Ruth wasn't really a choreographer. She just could put a show together."[32] In his usual gentle manner he suggested to her that she might experiment with these ideas in the same way he had earlier tried to interest Shawn in Bach.

In an interview at the time St. Denis mentioned her latest choreographic attempts and the importance of her pianist:

> I muse upon . . . [the movement's] silences, its infinitude, its impressions it has made upon me emotionally and mentally . . . I see the dance forming. . . . Next I research for music to fit the mood. I tell Louis . . . to hunt up several pieces and when I have heard them I move through them, trying for music to fit my conception. . . . We now need musicians to formalize what we dance. And I intend to work out this plea next. I expect to cajole or threaten some musician into writing such music — even to train him myself. This is logically the next step in dance development artistically.[33]

She mentioned this ruefully, perhaps hoping that her pianist might take the hint.

In the 1918 catalog these concepts, such as "visualization of pure music themes," appeared in course descriptions. "I said, 'Why don't we take some pieces by Schubert or Grieg or Schumann and do them?' And she said that would be fine. . . . Then Doris got to do them, and we started Schubert impromptus where we didn't do the rhythm. Doris oversaw it, while Ted would sometimes have suggestions."[34] Anne Douglas, then at the Denishawn School, recalled that "Louis would play the part that each instrument had separately, and Miss Ruth would start dancing while we sat and listened. Martha was given the bassoon passages because she was dark."[35] Doris, more experienced at choreography, "took to it like a lark," according to Horst, and received credit as co-choreographer with St. Denis for the musical visualization works developed with his guidance.

Louis was a sophisticated figure of experience to the dancers. "We all looked up to him. He offered avenues of understanding about things in the imagination that we never knew, and his word was the law," one acolyte said. "He did preach Nietzsche. That was his main pressure on the girls, on everybody — it was Nietzsche."[36] His gentlemanly manner was a strong asset for the trailblazing Denishawners, particularly since its leading artists were often not on speaking terms. As self-elected guide he escorted his favorites to exhibitions at local museums, where their discussions of the most recent happenings in the arts seldom mixed with headlines warning that the European war threatened the country's neutrality.

By the end of the first years of touring during his ten-year tenure, the artist-directors considered Louis an invaluable associate. He had learned to use his quiet wit to cajole the performers, ward off rising tempers, and cope with next-to-impossible schedules. The confidence they gave him allowed for acts of favoritism, sometimes painfully apparent. "Louis was in charge on the road and Betty had solos," Anne Douglas confirmed.[37]

Louis noted the April 6 declaration of war in his journal, along with his list of eighty-two shows over two months on the Orpheum circuit during the spring of 1917. His interest in politics, the economy, and world issues widened, as it did for every citizen preparing for total war and its consequences during this first world threat to peace. World War I and its influence on future activities preoccupied the Denishawn artists as they traveled from one theater to another. Various assignments with the company included a two-week run in September of Shawn's choreography for the Zodiac Ballet Company. After receiving his draft notice Shawn enlisted in the Army Ambulance Corps and was placed in officer's training at Camp Kearney in nearby San Diego. For the duration, he managed to return to Denishawn on weekends to keep the school functioning.

Louis had registered for the draft, although at thirty-four he was over the age limit. There was little chance that he would be called into service. Concerned with the growing sentiment of radicals who distrusted German-Americans and demanded loyalty oaths, he learned to be more cautious about his family's German ties. "When we went to Canada, I had to have a birth certificate because my parents were German."[38] He was jubilant when Conrad wrote to say that he had become an American citizen.

Faced with a company of women and needing income, St. Denis relied on her pianist to help reorganize the company's touring program without Shawn. Back on the Pantages circuit, Louis explained that "it was Ruth St. Denis, Margaret Loomis, and myself. We did what was known as the 'Interstate Time' for the Interstate Amusement company. Miss Ruth was a headliner."[39] More rigorous than the Orpheum tour, but paying three times as much, the group gave thirty-one performances in rapid succession and then 216 more in twenty-two Pantages theaters as the company crossed the country twice. "Sometimes there were cancellations — once or twice a theater burnt down."[40]

Louis survived the tour without incident until the final week, when he contracted German measles and was quarantined in his hotel room. The Los Angeles *Record* published Denishawn's "New Rules" in an article that said, "Ruth St. Denis, esthetic dancer, is doing her bit to teach the world that patriotism is first with the American girls. 'I want you to include a course in useful patriotism; and get it started quickly,' she told the manager of her dance school. 'From now on I shall teach these girls useful patriotism and this course will include hygiene, first aid, economy and probably simple cooking.'" She stated that the dancers "must attend war lectures two times a week, and they will be taught the democratic principles that forced the U.S. into the War."[41]

However, Miss Ruth's commitment to the war effort did not keep her away from vaudeville's stages. The months of combined Pantages and Liberty Bond touring from November 1918 through September 1919 featured *Dance of the Royal Ballet of Siam* on the same bill with *The Spirit of Democracy, or Triumph of the Allies.* On breathers between runs, the company returned to the compound at Eagle Rock, supporting the war effort by entertaining the enlisted men at Camp Kearney, playing for U.S. Bond concerts, and working at the polls during elections.

On the road, Horst continued to conduct his pickup orchestra with his eye on the dancers' entrances and exits. "Places" called, his portly tuxedoed appearance was the cue for the house manager to dim the lights, transforming the dark outside world of forboding realities into the magic of theater's fantasies and musical delights. The curtain opened to reveal the extravagantly costumed dancers of the St. Denis company. Humphrey now performed a solo, *Dance of the Sunrise,* but it was St. Denis's performance of the ever-popular *Nautch,* with *Greek Veil Plastique,* or *Kuan Yin* to Satie's Gymnopédie No. 3, that filled the stage with wonder for audiences, most of whom had never seen dance under lights before.

As score-maker, Louis had learned to use bits and pieces of oriental-sounding themes to give an Eastern flavor to the dance materials, filling in transitions with his own music. He explained that he assembled scores for a new Denishawn work by taking pieces they had selected from phonograph records, "a bit of this and a bit of that. . . . The idea back of it was that dance was considered the handmaiden of music. The dancer caught the mood of the music and made a dance to it. If the score was too long — as it frequently was — I was asked to cut it. Often the cuts amounted to chasms. The method was invalid, both musically and choreographically, but this is what my first experiences of dance music were like."[42] Once in a while he was sent off on a buying spree, returning with $100 worth of music, occasionally slipping in some modern works. Later, when he played through the new acquisitions, St. Denis would stop him and inquire about these rhythmically and harmonically unusual pieces, and this sometimes gave her ideas for new choreography. After the piece was completed, Louis made sure that the dancers had copies of the musical score to which they danced.[43]

The world's greatest period of bloodshed and destruction to date came to an end on 11 November 1918, when armistice was declared by German delegates, followed soon after by President Wilson's signing of the Treaty of Versailles. The aftermath of the "Great War" brought unexpected changes to the lives of many Americans. Easy money was made from a soaring stock market during President Harding's corrupt "period of normalcy," when Prohibition was in effect and no saloon operated legally. Racketeering ushered in the "roaring twenties," with speakeasies that featured bathtub gin and hot jazz.

Discharged from the army at the war's end, Shawn was ready to go back on the circuit, but by then St. Denis was committed to her company of five women, which included Doris and Betty. For the next three years the two artist-directors conducted separate projects under the Denishawn Company name.

Although devoted to one another as partners in dance the Shawns' intimate partnership had ceased when both began to take male lovers. Gossip often centered on the couple's latest conquests. At one point there was actually a company "kidnapping," as Louis called it, when an ex-lover stole Shawn's boyfriend away during the night. Despite their own promiscuity, St. Denis and Shawn insisted that those in the company keep some semblance of respectability or get married. Uninterested in love relationships with men, Louis's sexuality was very different from Shawn's. Louis often fell in love — although without expressing his adoration — with the young women who surrounded him. These relationships later became more complex, as did that of St. Denis and Shawn when they both fell in love with the same man.

The contented appearance of the Shawns' marriage was duplicated by the only other married couple within the company, Louis and Betty Horst. Being on tour helped to smooth any emotional difficulties the pair might have been experiencing. Perhaps the only advantage for Louis was that he was relieved of the burden of maintaining an apartment for a wife at home. Before long the Horst marriage had deteriorated to a point at which everyone (except his mother) understood that their relationship was a free-wheeling arrangement. It was rumored that Betty was always popular with the stagehands. Completely involved in their careers with Denishawn, time spent together was marginal. They were comfortable with separate sets of friends, although his sense of propriety held fast.

In this, St. Denis and her music director shared similar attitudes. In an unpublished essay she wrote, "Marriage [is] an invented law designed to keep two people together whether they want to stay together or not."[44] In later years Louis would state that artists should not marry. Live together, but don't get married, he advised, lamenting his own unfortunate mistake: "The domestic pattern will ruin the artist."[45] Although his opinion on the subject strengthened to near heretic proportions, Louis himself never forgot his marriage vow "for better or for worse," and he made sure that Betty was included in all of Denishawn's plans.

All who knew him agreed, "Louis always had a weakness for young women."[46] One of his favorites was Anne Douglas.

> I was one of Louis's girls. Not bad or sexy — that was Denishawn gossip. [He was] very insecure. Betty was going out with some fellow in one of the acts and I was with Louis. He was educating me. We went to museums in one city, and then the next city where there was a museum I was supposed to guess the artist without looking it up. I was reading Neitche [sic] and Schopenhaur [sic] and arguing with him about it. One argument I kept [having] was that the family group was the greatest influence of all and he kept saying you had to live to be a great artist. I was eighteen and he was thirty-six then [in 1920]. . . . Although Louis spoke of free love, his own habits were more puritanical than others were led to believe. But, he always sponsored some girl. Even with Betty in the show, I went with Louis. Thank heavens sex wasn't involved, or I wouldn't have known what to do. One time Miss Ruth made a remark to someone that even if he was with different girls, they all learned something. Oh, I did. I did! I was called stubborn because I wouldn't change some of my ideas.[47]

Still, Louis's journal seldom mentioned any women, noting instead peculiarities in the weather and keeping track of the theaters and towns in which they played. There were those who speculated about his sexual prowess and questioned the nature of his relationships with women. During his young adulthood Louis sought various forms of "treatments," giving substance to the notion that he suffered from some form of sexual dysfunction. Whatever the case, he managed to become one of the most beloved figures in modern dance, and he took an ardent stand in support of female dancer-choreographers, beginning with Ruth St. Denis.

When the company returned to Los Angeles in 1919 for a summer of teaching, they prepared for the newest enterprise commissioned by Alexander Pantages for his vaudeville houses. Shawn created *Julnar of the Sea* as an Arabian Nights spectacle for seventeen dancers, featuring Lillian Powell as narrator. Louis was placed in charge of the entire operation while Shawn stayed behind. This eight-month circuit run of the Ruth St. Denis Concert Dancers also featured an assortment of musical visualizations. Less than a week after *Julnar* opened, a fire destroyed the bungalow at Tedruth. Ruth wrote in her diary, "Little Tedruth is in ashes. And now my soul is naked and I can see it and can tell how spotted and soiled it is."[48] The Shawns lost everything but a trunkful of photographs and an East Indian rug. Undaunted, the tour continued and Shawn began a new project.

Louis said proudly, "We gave 1,205 performances of *Julnar*. I was entirely in charge for two years. I kept the books. Ted said they were marvelous. *Julnar* made $1,600 a week. I used to send Ted $500 a week after I paid all the salaries, my own and all expenses. I had to manage the hotel and railroad people — get the tickets and pay the transfers. We carried two stage hands, myself and the company. There were always disputes to be settled and jealousies."[49] When he mentioned jealousies, Louis was most likely thinking of his own difficulties.

During the long *Julnar* tour Spanish influenza had become an epidemic, taking the lives of a half-million Americans, five times as many as had died in the war. The Denishawners did not escape the dreaded virus. "The audience sat in the theater with their mouths and noses covered. People were dying like flies. I was conducting an orchestra of thirteen or fourteen men. I'd come to a matinee and I'd say, 'Well, where's the trumpet player today?' 'Oh, he died last night.' " When another fellow musician died Louis went to the undertaker to identify the body and arrange the burial. "I conducted with a 102-degree temperature. I just went on and the dancers did too. They were dizzy and couldn't see straight with cold or fever, but they'd dance. And they didn't die, either."

But Betty almost did: "The influenza backfired into tuberculosis. Even though she got through with it, the next year she had to give up dancing. We didn't have antibiotics. We had to wrap her in blankets, and carry her to the railroad station. She didn't dance, she just went from the railroad station to the hotel. We got a doctor. She began to dance a bit in Buffalo."[50] But when Betty's health became worse and a second doctor confirmed the diagnosis, she was forced to leave the tour. According to Douglas (who had resumed her relationship with Louis), Betty went on an ocean voyage with a relative who was a doctor and could take care of her. She then tried unsuccessfully to keep up with the rigors of the Denishawn schedule, and finally went to Guatemala to stay with May and Ernest for seven months.

Julnar of the Sea had its last performance in Butte, Montana, on 20 March 1921 — the end of the lengthy run. When the company returned to Los Angeles, Shawn worked out plans to merge St. Denis's troupe with his and sent Douglas to the group performing in Minneapolis to separate her from Louis. Douglas knew that "Mr. Shawn had a talk with Louis before I left, and Louis swore it was all gossip. It was. I must have been so dumb.

Why didn't I hear it? The Shawns had a lot of managing to do to keep everything O.K."[51] When Betty came back from South America Louis joined her for the summer months in San Francisco, where he polished his piano technique in preparation for the next tour. He bought a Buick roadster for his wife with money saved on the *Julnar* tour. It was to be a farewell gesture: he signed his next Denishawn contract alone.

While most of the Denishawn dancers were touring with St. Denis and Horst in *Julnar,* Shawn had begun to work with the intensely dramatic Martha Graham. He choreographed the first version of *Xochitl* to suit her unusual qualities. *Xochitl* was a Toltec drama to commissioned music by Homer Grunn. Using movement ideas drawn from Aztec reliefs, twelve dancers moved completely on half toe, framing the fiery episodes between Shawn and Graham. "Martha was perfect in the role that made the most of her exotic features and allowed her body freedom of movements that ranged from tigerish and primitive to passionate and regal," Shawn wrote in his reminiscences.[52] Thrilled finally to be a part of the Denishawn troupe, twenty-seven-year-old Martha told her hometown newspaper, "I love this dance-drama and have every faith in it; it has brought the joy of life to me."[53] After *Julnar* completed its run Shawn designed an abbreviated version of *Xochitl* for a tour of the Pantages theaters, which continued to feature Graham in the role of the Indian girl. In addition to the lead Martha was assigned the job of paymaster. The rest of the program consisted of solos danced by Shawn himself, with Louis at the piano playing interludes by Scarlatti and Satie.

The posters for this second tour of *Xochitl* read, "Ted Shawn — America's First Man Dancer — Assisted by Louis Horst, Concert Pianist," and Louis began to receive favorable reviews. The Omaha *Bee* noted, "As a soloist, Horst displays a clean and facile technique, a beauty of tone and a musical and authoritative interpretation which makes his playing a delightful addition to the program."[54] The *New York Mail* reviewer wrote, "Louis Horst was the whole orchestra!"[55]

On the Ted Shawn and Dancers tour Louis would disparage Martha's little sister Geordie (who joined the company at this time) as difficult, but he did continue to enjoy her roommate, Anne Douglas. Geordie's account reinforced Anne's: "We were a threesome and went around together, Louis, Anne and I. We'd go to dinner and he would get so mad with me, because I was always dieting. Sometimes I'd only order a baked apple and he didn't like that. He loved women, but he was not promiscuous. We went out quite a lot but he was not sexual at all. He was wonderful. He gave us a great education and opened up a whole new world for everyone that he touched."[56]

At first Louis resisted the charms of Geordie's sister, Martha, whose eloquent abstract statements at museums took him by surprise. After seeing a red-slash-against-blue Kandinsky painting in a gallery in 1920 she was quoted as saying, "I will dance like that."[57] Soundly challenged by her intense nature and brilliant mind, Louis had never encountered a woman as provocative as Graham. He began to spend more time with her. Anne explained, "I stepped out of the picture and Martha Graham stepped in."[58] Louis described their first romantic encounter in October 1921:

> We were in Omaha for two or three days with no concert. Martha and I were staying at the same hotel, and she was evidently bored. This was when all the things started with Martha and [me]. Martha said, "Can I come in?" I said, "Yes." So she came in and sat down. I was arranging music. Pretty soon she stretched out her arms to me, wanting me to come over and kiss her. That started the seventeen years of living together.[59]

Ten years older than Martha, Louis began his relationship with her much like the other attachments he had had with other young women in the company. More often innocent than not, friends confirmed, "Louis always was interested in the flirtation more than the ultimate conquest."[60] But Martha's flirtatious overture blossomed into a passionate love affair, as unusual as the Shawns'. Ted was well aware that a relationship was brewing. He wrote to Ruth that he had finally won Horst's respect through the cool handling of financial crises on the tour, and he also mentioned Louis's "very sweet friendship." He later observed the love affair between Martha and Louis from another perspective: "Apparently during that tour there was a sort of constant argument going on — Martha wanting Louis to divorce Betty, and Louis for reasons of his own, just saying 'no.'"[61]

Louis confirmed Shawn's observation: "All through this tour Martha and I were always together."[62] Martha admitted many years later, "I was out of Santa Barbara. Nothing erupted there except a nice day. He saw me as something strange and different. He schooled me in certain behavior, discipline and a deep respect for music. He introduced me to Nietzsche, Schiller, Wagner. He became my lover, yes, but it was like loving a child, because I was a child."[63]

During this period Louis entered diverse notes in his log that indicated his attempts at finding relaxation away from the theater — taking a vacation alone, more swimming lessons, undergoing "special treatments" with a Dr. Hart. Ever a sports enthusiast and fascinated with action of all kinds, he faithfully read the sports pages and had even managed to endure an ice hockey game at Calgary in $-30°$ temperature.

The concept of dance as an expressive independent art intrigued Louis as he continued to brood over the German philosophers Arthur Schopenhauer and Friedrich Nietzsche. He translated his German editions of Nietzsche's epigrams and musings, and quoted them in earnest simplicity: "It is terrible to die of thirst in the ocean" or "The more abstract the truth is that you would teach, the more you have to seduce the senses to it,"[64] delivered as easily as he told old vaudeville jokes when things got dull. Graham's words reflected this influence when she told a reporter in her first printed interview, "I owe all that I am to the study of Nietzsche and Schopenhauer."[65]

Louis persisted in matching the ideas of German and French contemporaries in the other arts as he searched for possible new directions for dance. He followed the establishment of the Bauhaus in Weimar by Walter Gropius as well as the work of European artists such as Arp, Duchamp, Giacometti, and Grosz who, in this "golden era of Expressionism," were concerned with function and form. Louis had introduced the music of Aleksandr Scriabin as well as Erik Satie and Ernst Toch into the Denishawn programs, and he paid close attention to the twelve-tone and serial composing of Schoenberg's Vienna Circle and the bitonal and atonal methods used by the French group called Les Six. (When he was later asked what he considered the major influence on his work, he replied, "Music, foremost, and painting."[66])

Gradually Louis influenced the dancers by constantly making analogies among dance, music, and visual art — a means of thinking that would become his forte. Having read German newspapers and periodicals about Rudolf von Laban's studies in movement analysis and its connection with Mary Wigman's studio work in Berlin, he translated this information for his colleagues and encouraged them to match the experiments of their European counterparts.[67] "We began to hear about what Mary Wigman was doing in Germany. She, we were told, thought of dance as an independent art, one that could come into being and exist without music. For her, the motivation was not the work of another person — the composer — but her own feelings. The dance was created from within."[68]

The Ted Shawn and Dancers company counted their blessings at St. Marks in the Bowery Church in New York City at the final performance just before Christmas 1922 in a choreographed service by Shawn. Fortunately an Apollo Theatre matinee had drawn enthusiastic crowds, recouping some of the financial losses incurred on the tour. An agent, Daniel Mayer — who booked concert artists of the calibre of Pavlova and Paderewski, and wore white tie, tails, and top hat to his client's concerts — saw the show and was enthusiastic. He asked for the creation of a production that would be the most extravagant ever created from Denishawn. The two artists must perform, and Horst's musical talents should be augmented by three permanent musicians, Mayer insisted. A contract was signed in February 1922 by a reluctant St. Denis, who had hoped to retire from vaudeville, and an elated Shawn. Again they had to face the months before the tour with no income and again the troupe dispersed temporarily.

In an effort to consolidate the company's money-making ventures Shawn invented the name "Greater Denishawn." He then began to work out plans to open a New York school and affiliate branches throughout the country. Strapped for cash, he suggested that Martha might teach classes for "department store girls" as she had in his 6th Street studio in Los Angeles. In his biography on Graham, Don McDonagh related her reaction to the plan, proposed during a luncheon date. Furious, she stood up and in one stroke ripped the tablecloth off the table, sending its contents flying. She grabbed Louis's arm and the two made a quick exit. "Shawn settled with the owner for $20 and stormed after Graham and Horst, who were entering a cab. Grabbing its door, Shawn shouted that Graham would never dance with Denishawn again; slamming the door, he smashed the window and left Horst to deal with the driver."[69] No mention of this is in Louis's log. Instead, he recorded amiably: "Christmas dinner and tea at Ted's Beaux Arts." Accustomed to temperamental outbursts among Denishawn's dance artists, and now particularly Martha's, Louis somehow managed to keep a steady, focused eye on day-to-day operations at the Chadwick on West 72nd Street, where Shawn had created a temporary studio complex for rehearsals and living arrangements.

St. Denis, who had little interest in how Shawn worked out the finances, remained uninvolved in his "Greater Denishawn" schemes. She had agreed to join him, five dancers, and Louis in a brief United States promotional tour as part of the Mayer contract, to be performed before scheduled dates in England. Under Mayer's management the "concert" program, featuring Louis's Instrumental Quartet for piano, violin, cello, and flute, received praise wherever it appeared. The *New York Dance Review* lauded Louis's "fine technical mastery and sterling quality of musicianship"[70] in a concert that contained works such as *The Album Leaf and Prelude,* to music by Scriabin, that Jane Sherman said was "shocking for those expecting to see Denishawn dancers tripping the light fantastic with scarves and garlands."[71]

Graham, who had grown increasingly unhappy with her position, was enraged to learn that Louis had insisted on Betty's return to the company for the English engagements. To complicate matters, the Shawns could not agree on a cast: St. Denis wanted only "our three little stars" (Dorothea Bowen, Marjorie Peterson, and Betty Horst) and Louis to go; Shawn wanted to hire

Graham. When Betty arrived in New York heavier than before, the couple was still in a quandary. Her temporary return as a dancer finally made sense to both directors when Louis offered to contribute a portion of his salary in order to pay Betty's expenses.

The situation was resolved by hiring both Betty and Martha for the Denishawn tour to England. Betty had two weeks of rehearsals before the company sailed for England on the *Samaria*. Charles Weidman loved to tell of the intrigue on board ship, with Martha and Louis's trysts in secret places, and everyone getting a little too drunk and trying to keep their balance on the rolling sea each morning during Shawn's required warm-ups. Louis was in love with Martha but guilt-ridden over his lack of attention to his wife; his allegiance to the two women and their demands made his life impossible. Cautious about changes of any kind, he later confided that staying married saved him from making the same mistake twice.

After the performances as part of the London vaudeville circuit, the company managed to do a little sight-seeing and to attend a performance of Diaghilev's Ballets Russes. Some also went with Shawn to visit his most ardently admired author, Havelock Ellis, who encouraged free love as a means of increasing artistic enrichment. But in his memoirs Shawn wrote of spending an inordinate amount of time with Martha in shared misery, while St. Denis herself was in the throes of a new love affair: "Louis had insisted on having Betty Horst and was sharing a bedroom with her as man and wife. Martha was in agony. We would wander the streets . . . hand in hand."[72] Horst lists "Trip up the Thames to Hampton Court and 26 performances at the Hippodrome, London" in his chronology, but later recalled the tour from a different perspective: "Martha was on tour and my wife — she came along, just for the trip to England. They thought Betty ought to have it. . . . So she joined us. She was in the Egyptian dance and one of the others. We were all together, and of course, it was a triangle feeling with my wife and Martha there. It was just one big unhappy family."[73]

The second half of the tour, to Manchester and Bristol, required only the principal dancers. When Betty went off to Paris for a week Martha and Louis spent time together. "We did go places — saw everything. In Manchester there was nothing to see. The Manchester museum had an awfully nice collection of Tanagra figurines that Martha and I went to, but otherwise it was just like a dirty Pittsburgh."[74]

In keeping with Denishawn's shift of activities to the East Coast, when the English tour ended Shawn organized a summer residency at Mariarden in Peterborough, New Hampshire. In return for room and board for himself and Betty, Louis arranged Spanish music for Shawn's new work, *Cuadro*

Flamenco, while rehearsing St. Denis's *Ishtar of the Seven Gates* for the upcoming Mayer tour.[75] The Mariarden School for Dancing and Dramatic Arts had been established in 1919 on forty forested acres, adjacent to the well-known Theater-in-the-woods and two miles from the MacDowell Artist's Colony. Marie and Guy Currier directed the school, in which students received occasional classes with St. Denis or Shawn and performed their dances on an outdoor stage. When reminded of Mariarden, Louis referred to the idyllic countryside, rather than the activities happening there: "I lived in town and walked up to camp. . . . I used to walk through the MacDowell Colony, past MacDowell's grave every day."[76]

Mayer encouraged Horst to compose for the musicians contracted for the tour.[77] While at Peterborough he tried his hand for the first time at an original composition unrelated to dance. *A Sahara Romance* was dedicated "To Betty," an indication that his sense of duty continued to interfere with his passion for the dark-haired dancer with whom he had fallen deeply in love.

The company of seventeen dancers, which included fifteen-year-old Louise Brooks, again crossed the continental United States from October 1922 to April 1923. With scores arranged for the quartet of musicians, Louis's job as musical director became less hectic. Instead, it was St. Denis's three-ton set for *Ishtar,* with seven fully hinged gates, that created havoc at each new theater.

Again finishing on the East Coast, most of Denishawn's dancers continued to survive between tours by teaching when they could. Geordie went back to Santa Barbara for a brief, if intense, teaching stint and made enough to pay her tuition at Mariarden. (Evidently "Papa" Shawn found it necessary to charge tuition to company members.) "We had a whole summer there, and I loved it. I had never really studied with them, except for that,"[78] Geordie explained, grateful for the opportunity. Louise Brooks, too, studied at Mariarden before joining the 1922–1923 tour. Betty returned to teach at Shawn's studio in Los Angeles — a well-known landmark because of its all-black interior and Egyptian motifs — and "taught very successfully," according to Shawn. Graham and Weidman stayed in Manhattan to teach at the Denishawn School.

Once Betty was in California, the relationship between Louis and Martha resumed. To Shawn's dismay, Martha pronounced to her classes that she was "living in sin" and believed in "free love."

Martha began getting on her soapbox and shooting off in front of our students. Here was Martha saying she was living in sin, and she believed in free love. Finally when this had gone a little too far, I called her in and said, "Martha darling, your private life is your private life and I'm not going to tell you what to do or what not to do, but you are a teacher on my staff, and paid a salary to teach representing Denishawn. This does not represent Denishawn, it's not what we stand for." This made her very angry at me.[79]

For the next year-and-a-half Louis conducted an average of twenty-seven performances a month. Mayer's tightly booked tour played in six cities and gave at least eight performances a week. Again Louis documented the names and addresses of each theater, noting occasional mishaps such as missing baggage along the way. Shawn commented succinctly, "There was no way to know in advance whether we would be feted or swindled, ridiculed or lionized, eulogized or ostracized."[80] Things ran smoothly under the impresario's management, although St. Denis admitted to not knowing whether she was in Utica or Ithaca at one point, or whether speaking to an audience in Detroit or Duluth—"Oh! They both start with a D, anyway," she excused herself. Once, Shawn and St. Denis found themselves at a street corner in a town that neither could identify.

After Denishawn's final concerts in New York City, Martha accepted an offer to work as a soloist. "When we closed in Town Hall, John Murray Anderson came to the show and he liked Martha, so he got her for the *Greenwich Village Follies of 1923.*"[81] Shawn counseled Graham's departure: "Martha came to me and said, 'Ted, I feel I should take this. I cannot go on being in such close association with Louis when Louis will not separate himself from Betty. It's tearing me to pieces, and I've got to get away from this thing.' So I choreographed two solo dances during that summer of 1923 and early fall for Martha to do in the Greenwich Village Follies."[82] Some company members returned to Mariarden, while others trained to become "certified" teachers by taking Shawn's Greater Denishawn "Normal Course," now housed in a brownstone on West 28th Street. Although living at the Mariarden colony, Louis traveled into Manhattan to accompany dance classes taught by guest teachers such as Ronny Johansson from Sweden and Margarethe Wallmann, the first Wigman teacher to come to the United States— and to spend time with Martha whenever he could.

The second Mayer tour, booked from October 1923 to April 1924, was danced by Doris, Charles, Pauline, Geordie, St. Denis, and Shawn. Louis, the only available outside observer to correct spacing, lines, entrances, and timing, continued to serve as the company drill sergeant. Whenever possible he took odd moments to compose, completing a score for St. Denis's *Pompeiian Murals* (the section called *Dancer with Tambourine* later became *Byzantine Dance*) for a January 1924 opening. The dedication on that manuscript reads, "For Martha Graham" — finally admitting openly that he cared for a woman other than his wife. On January 12, Louis turned forty. Little disturbed by his age, although his hair had by now turned prematurely white, he joked that finally he was a man of means. An annuity set up by his mother had come due. Evidently his mother did not think him a "responsible enough person" to have received the money any earlier.

After this tour the performers went for their usual "cures," in which they swam, took sun baths, received daily massages, slept, and ate properly for several weeks, while Shawn dealt with a debt that rose from $30,000 to $60,000 by the end of the summer. For Louis, however, rest simply meant returning to Manhattan — the place he found most invigorating. For a few weeks on his own he could visit galleries, museums, and bookshops and go to concerts. Then he made his annual visit to California to see his relatives. Once there, he treated his return as he would any other musical assignment, accompanying classes at Shawn's school during his brief visit with Betty and his mother. He also stayed with May and Ernest in Monterey, where he wrote two short dance scores for Betty. She choreographed them for a concert at Carmel's School of Theatre of Golden Bough, where she now taught. During their time together the couple reached an agreement about their relationship: Louis would send money to her on a regular basis and visit her annually in California — an arrangement that implied they would never divorce. He returned to New York City to accompany classes at the Denishawn school on West 28th Street as well as for newly formed ones at "Studio 61" in Carnegie Hall.

In a situation that repeated itself among these professionals during their lives, Martha was invited to Mariarden that summer, rather than St. Denis and Shawn. Years before it was Humphrey who had first been hired to teach dance at the Outdoor Players Camp in Peterborough, and thus seeded the area for Denishawn's connection. Now it was "Papa" Shawn's turn to be overshadowed.

> Mrs. Currier went direct to Martha and said, "I don't need Ted Shawn anymore." And Martha accepted. I said even in the shoe business, this would be considered very bad ethics. It was Denishawn material. This also made Martha very mad, and I think affected the whole history of Modern Dance, because she flared up, that famous cobra-like hiss, and

reared back and said, "I will never again teach anything I ever got from
Denishawn! I will create all of my own material from now on."[83]

Throughout the scuffle Louis tried to remain a neutral bystander, although he
did manage to visit Martha at the end of her residency at Mariarden and
spend a few days with her at Lake Placid before the third and last Mayer tour
began.

Again on the road, over the next six months Denishawn traveled to 293
cities and performed for over one million viewers. The company's continual
adding onto and editing of the repertory on this tour kept him frantically
busy, and was best described by Louis as "rocky." One performance in
particular was given with armed policemen on stage to protect the women,
costumed in what Denishawn called "fleshings" (leotard-like body suits,
sometimes veiled with pieces of chiffon). To St. Denis this body covering was
not only practical, but also "aesthetically" correct, with the body's lines
uncluttered. "In Shreveport, Louisiana, they wanted to stop the show. Un-
dressed women couldn't appear on stage — the Bible Belt down there, you
know. The moralists threatened to bomb the place, and there were big stories
in the papers. The girls had to go out and buy long winter underwear and
dance in that. Luckily, the mayor had a little eye for art. I think he saw a
rehearsal and he said it was a good show. 'They'll give that show. I'll see that
they do.' "[84]

This final Mayer tour made a profit of $200,000, giving Shawn enough
capital to start negotiations for the purchase of the Steinway building in New
York City and for a two-year stint throughout the Orient. St. Denis was so
exhausted from the long tour that she went for a "water cure" in upstate
New York. She wrote to her mother, "I am a vegetable that is being well
washed."[85]

Without Martha this difficult tour had taken its toll on Louis as well. But
he had built a reputation of sorts for pianistic virtuosity. Other accompanists
praised him for playing "out of the keyboard, not into it" with an extraordinarily light touch. Although Louis continued to suggest new musical directions for St. Denis, he suspected that her interest in more exotic and theatrical
ideas for dance was not likely to change. The lack of integrity of Denishawn's
scores convinced him that he needed to improve his own compositional
skills. When time permitted he worked on counterpoint exercises, using
Percy Goetschius's popular texts *The Material Used in Musical Composition*
and *Models of the Principal Musical Forms* and the musical theories of
A. Eaglefield Hull as guides.

It seemed to Louis that the creation of new art styles called expressionism, dada, futurism, and constructivism could be paralleled in dance and, of all his colleagues, it was Martha who was most likely to find the means to do it. Something in her uncompromising personality and her inside-out way of working intrigued him.[86] Louis was convinced that he could help her find her way and at the tour's end, when they met in Boston for a few weeks, their conversations centered on plans for their own artistic ventures together.

chapter three

1925–1926

"Whatever is done from

love always occurs beyond

good and evil."

—*Friedrich Nietzsche*

Louis needed time alone to sort out his musical as well as emotional state and to rethink his relation to the dance world and its dancers. After months of indecision he found the courage to tell Shawn that he planned to resign at the end of Denishawn's third Mayer tour. The ten-year association with colleagues who had become his intimate coterie made this parting a difficult one. He intended to go to Austria, he told Shawn. Whatever reasons he gave, it was clear to Shawn that this unhappy frame of mind was caused by Martha. Shawn wrote in his diary: "Louis states not going to Orient. Talk until 3:30 A.M. about this and other matters pertaining to whole question of 'free' love."[1]

Remembering their talk the April night they closed in Boston, Louis admitted:

> Arrangements had been made for the Orient and I didn't want to go. They didn't ask Martha. I went into Ted's room and I said, "Ted, I'm not going to the Orient. I can't because I feel I want to study composition." And he said, "Why? Is there anything in this company that you don't like? If there is, we'll change it. Is there anyone going you think shouldn't go? Is there any one not in the company that should be? We can arrange it. But you must come with us." I said, "No, Ted, you know I wouldn't do any hold up like that. There's nothing at all. I'm perfectly satisfied. I'd love to go. But I can't leave for so long. I haven't studied composition except for a long time ago. I'm planning to go to Vienna

and study for a year or two." . . . I could hear Miss Ruth boo-hooing in the room next to us because she got to rely on me so.[2]

He conceded later that Martha did have more to do with his leaving than anything else: "They all thought that it was because Martha wasn't along. [Ted] would have gotten Martha, but she was in the *Greenwich Village Follies* of '24 and '25. See, Martha and I had a little tiff in those days too, and I wanted to get away from under her too much."[3] Having continually disparaged the concept of marriage, Louis remained stolidly opposed to it "in principle," but his refusal to take any action toward a divorce had deeply troubled Martha. His association with her must be spared this meaningless contract; her own art form deserved freedom from domestic attachments, Louis told her. He considered the nineteenth-century bourgeois way of loving obsolete. Following Nietzsche, who saw marriage as merely "society's permission granted to two persons for sexual gratification," he asked Martha, as he had earlier asked Anne Douglas, to agree that marriage was not a question of love, but rather a crass, middle-class affair. Their relationship must be beyond society's moral questions, Louis felt, again taking his cue from Nietzsche: "Whatever is done from love always occurs beyond good and evil."[4]

At forty-one — mid-life — Louis felt Vienna would be an excellent place to reflect on his past, consider ways to handle his present situation, and weigh prospects for the future. Adept as the patient arbitrator between Shawn and St. Denis, he had been content to be a catalyst and not interfere with the aesthetic choices of these artists. But his conversations with Martha had spurred exciting possibilities for the two of them, away from Denishawn. "I wasn't in sync any more with those oriental spectacles they were putting on"; he wanted to devote his full energy to "new things happening."[5]

"I didn't mind going to Vienna on my own, but to be way over in the Orient [was different]. So suddenly, on a day's notice I sent a letter to [music pedagogue] Dr. Stöhr and some friends of mine in Vienna I met through St. Denis and other people."[6] Having earned from $150 to $250 a week while with Denishawn, Louis had saved $3,652.21 by the end of the third Mayer tour, according to his account book — enough to live comfortably as a student in Europe for two years by his estimate. (A distressing letter, asking him to report to the United States income tax bureau, gave an additional reason for a quick departure date.)

Before his last performance as Denishawn's musical director, Louis told St. Denis, "These have been the ten happiest years, but I feel I just have to make a change."[7] The star did not take his decision well. "I waited in the pit for the flashlight cue to begin the show. It didn't come and didn't come. People got restless. The manager went backstage. [Ruth] had cried so much her makeup came off. She had to put on more makeup, and it would come off again. She was so upset that night after the show, I got out. I didn't want any emotional scene."[8]

St. Denis wrote in her biography that his leaving was an omen:

> There was never another Louis: gruff, hard working, enormously gifted. . . . We learned that Louis Horst was not going with us, but to Germany instead. Our consternation was shattering, but Louis had made up his mind. . . . In a sense, when he left the camp . . . the signal was given for the dissolution of Denishawn. Of course we did not realize this at the time, but it turned out in retrospect that Louis, as one of the chief pillars of the church, let the roof sag at the place where he had been, and it was never really mended again.[9]

On the other hand, experimentation was seething in Europe. Arnold Schoenberg, in a 1923 lecture in Prague, had asked fellow avant-gardists to abstract traditional harmonies. He himself had recently adopted the twelve-tone row as a means of musical organization, and his students Alban Berg and Anton Webern were revolutionizing concepts of sound with their methods of atonality. Louis may not have been ready to put an end to the homophonic compositional system as they did, but he agreed that there was a crucial need for forms "in which the laws of earlier art can be applied to the new."[10] Intrigued with this radical call for a break from an "epoch that has run its course," Louis "had reached the point where he never wanted again to hear the tinkle of a temple bell."[11] But it was not Schoenberg's teaching of concepts to rid the "pathos of subjective feeling" that Louis sought. He gravitated instead to the Viennese theorist, Richard Stöhr.

A respected teacher of harmony, whose popular manual *Praktischer Leitfaden der Harmonielehre* had been published in 1909, Stöhr had initially trained in medicine. Inspired by young men dancing at a midsummer's eve festival in Scandinavia, he theorized about the intrinsic relationship of dance and music. This popular professor at Vienna's Akademie, who believed that dance had created much of musical form, was recommended to Louis. Although Austria and Germany held a long-standing reputation as the place to find the best musical training, younger Americans such as Aaron Copland and Virgil Thomson were more apt to take up residence in France to study with Nadia Boulanger. For Louis, however, "Dr. Stöhr was the only one who could show the relationship between dance and music."[12]

Louis wanted to see Europe's dance exponents for himself. He knew about the Wiesenthal sisters and Rosalia Chladek in Vienna as well as Mary Wigman's Ausdruckstanz (dance of expression) in Berlin. Wigman's solos — *Lament, Spell,* and *Chant* (1920–1923) and *Ceremonial Figure* (1925) — exemplified Germany's new dance art for him. The Dalcroze method was taught at Wigman's Central Institute in Dresden, where the prominent dancers Yvonne Georgi, Margarethe Wallmann, and Harald Kreutzberg were in residence. Rudolf von Laban's followers throughout Germany and Kurt Jooss's "New Dance Stage" in Münster stirred Horst's interest as well. Comfortable with the idea of returning to the culture of his upbringing, Louis expected to enter an exciting climate in which to learn about music while watching dance.

There was also new art. Paul Klee, who taught at the Bauhaus, fascinated Louis, as did other prominent painters such as Emil Nolde and Gustave Klimt, a forerunner of expressionism and a founder of the Vienna Secession Movement in 1897. Louis admired the originality of Klimt's brooding figures, so dramatically different from Klee's childlike sketches, and the dark expressionism of Nolde. These artists' works suggested to him that choreographers must also consider the importance of variety in line, shape, and texture. He soon discovered that these innovators grew strong in spite of a resistant artistic climate.

Conflicts of love and anguish, creation and destruction, health and neurosis were significant qualities in the artistic milieu Louis planned to enter in 1925.[13] Sigmund Freud's work in psychoanalysis was adding to the intellectual richness of Vienna, and Louis intended to find out more about him, if only to stroll past Berggasse 19 as an observer rather than a participant.

Before leaving New York, Louis wrote an article, "The Musician Comments," for the *Denishawn Magazine,* to be published that summer while he was away. As a philosophical analogy, this first piece of published writing sheds light on his feelings at the time. As a dance musician he saw himself as *music,* the supporting masculine figure to Graham's feminine role as *dance.* A farewell note to Denishawn and the conventions of married life, these passages aptly describe his emotional state and present an idealistic statement of intention toward Martha.

Any preconceived notion a musician may have as to dance requiring only an expert rhythmic technician will soon be dispelled when he seeks to wed his art to that of the dance. And this wedding of music and dance has been for years the greatest interest of my art life. But, as with the human relationship, it is not always successful. Both arts must sacrifice too much at times. In the purer branch of "music visualizations" dance yields to music; and in the field of the usual characteristic pictorial dances music is sacrificed; it is rushed, dragged, changed dynamically and "cut" without mercy; and permissibly so, if it helps to serve towards the creation of a striking colorful dance.

Thus, in the union of two arts, music can generally be classed as the masculine element (man, being the more subjective, or egocentric) and dance as the feminine element (woman, being the more objective, or allocentric). When dance becomes as highly subjective as music, it will gain its independence and will no longer need music; it will then express that indefinable something that nothing but a movement, a gesture could express; just as the great music creations contain movements of that inexpressible quality that no objective visualization could adequately convey to the eye. Here is where the two arts must and will separate. And as husbands of the past have objected to feminine independence, so the "old school" musicians can not conceive of the independence of dance. But both are happening. Dancers rightly complain that no great music has been written for the dance. It is true that even great composers, when essaying that branch of their art, have "written down" to what they hold dance to be. And they will continue to do so until dance establishes itself upon a firm scientific basis and proves to music that union with a partner as independent and scientific as itself will be a greater honor than even its present glorious batchelorhood [sic]. Then, indeed, their very separateness will make them more at one than they are now; and composers will study the science of dance, and dancers study the science of music.

The last sentence perhaps indicates more clearly than any other Louis's most private reason for going away. He then summarized, "Years of dedicating one's abilities in one art to the service of another should obviously have gained a mine of impressions as to the relations of one to the other, their interdependence, and, most important, their independence."[14]

At the end of May 1925, for the first time in seventeen years of marriage, Louis did not spend vacation time with Betty. Instead, he boarded the *Bremen* for Europe. After debarking in Bremen and traveling by train to Vienna he moved into temporary quarters at the Meissl und Schadn Hotel. Louis began his studies with Dr. Stöhr at the Vienna Akademie on June 4, as planned. The next day he attended his first dance recital in Europe.

After settling into Pension Honer at 61 Lange Gasse he wrote to St. Denis:

I have been in Vienna three weeks now—the sudden transition was too much. I was not trying to follow your advice to forget you all—after ten years of such play and labor as ours, one can't forget. I have had about 10 lessons already with a Dr. Richard Stöhr, the head of the theory department at the Akademie here. So far it has been dry, pedagogical, but like sowing seeds—I only hope there will be some harvest. Won't attempt a tabloid version of my impressions of Vienna, except that so far it is the most charming city I have ever been in. I have been painfully lonesome, but am gradually making a few acquaintances. Have been to the opera a few times, but have only seen one dance-program so far—one given by a Lucy Kieselhausen; very popular here evidently—but, Lucy danced like her name—a little heavy. But she did one thing to a sacred song by Haydn in a Madonna costume that opened like your Quan Yin, and progressed through many religious poses—quite beautiful. Otherwise, nothing—old music—(including the Blue Danube) and the pianist—well, you've had a better one. I am quite comfortably located in a Pension—and quite reasonable. I do hope Clifford [Vaughan, Denishawn's new music director] will be completely satisfactory although I would like to have you miss me a little bit. [He promised to write again] after I get my chaotic impressions sorted and labeled. . . . Your words of faith and affection helped a lot—and you must know how grateful I felt for them. And someday I hope to bring you your tithe of the harvest.[15]

St. Denis replied on July 7, writing on the back side of stationery embossed "Pacific Coast Musician, Los Angeles, Calif.," "the old trige [tush] is full of vaccination marks and typhoid germs, which is the great preparation for the celebrated trip to the Orient, so you see, you escaped that much anyway." She mentioned his replacement: "Our new man is a good man and he has a hard job to follow in your footsteps. He is not a 'Louis' and we didn't expect him to be, but he is doing very well. So rest your mind about us for the present but I have a feeling that some day when we are ripe for it that there will be big doings again for you and me."[16]

Louis's daily log while in Vienna looks more like that of a tourist than of a dedicated music student. At first he relished the city's rich cultural heritage. He enjoyed "outings" to the horse races at the Freudenau area of the Prater, the sulfur spas in nearby Baden (with a Maria Zell and "S. B." for companions), and a weekend trip to Salzburg with new acquaintances.

Stöhr, his amiable guide and sympathetic teacher, became a regular eating companion. Together they enjoyed leisurely evening meals of Wiener-schnitzel, dumplings, and Sacher torte, fast contributing to the pianist's already portly stature. On his own Louis rummaged through bookshops for editions on art and dance, and bought recent collections of new music to bring back to the States.

In August, American friends Frances Steloff and her business manager David Moss (to whom she was briefly married) were on a buying excursion for their Gotham Book Mart on West 47th Street in Manhattan. They had received Louis's address from Martha, who had asked them to deliver the cloth cap he left behind. When they arrived he had already located sellers that carried books that might interest them. Their kaffeehaus conversations convinced Steloff that Louis's mission abroad now centered on the gathering of ideas for Graham and a new modern dance. She knew his letters urged Martha to strike out on her own. Steloff agreed to help make things possible for Martha when she returned. (She had advanced money to the writer, Anaïs Nin, for her first novel, repaid with the first one hundred copies printed on her own press, and would soon loan Graham $1,000 for her first endeavor.)

An ardent museumgoer, Louis lived close to the Kunsthistorisches Museum, Vienna's national gallery of art, and its concert halls. He viewed the museum's vast resources of paintings by Brueghel, Dürer, Rubens, Rembrandt, and Vermeer whenever he had a chance, and among the collections of folk and archaeological artifacts found American Indian relics on display. They were unexpected reminders of home. Shawn's interest in the Southwest and that of the composer Henry Cowell, who even used Indian thundersticks in a composition, had earlier piqued his interest. Martha's recent letters about a possible visit to Taos, New Mexico, added to his growing fascination with the rhythms and images of Indian ceremony. A renewed awareness that it was his cultural rather than ancestral roots that were most important to him sharpened his longing for America.

He also began to question the value of study with musicians who, in his opinion, had limited vision when it came to contemporary ideas. His piano teacher would carry on about Brahms by the hour and barely tolerate any discussion of Debussy or Ravel. This attitude upset Louis. "I was reading a paper one morning in the coffee house where I had breakfast—the Paris edition of the *New York Herald Tribune*. It said Erik Satie died. I went to my teacher that day for a lesson and I said, 'What do you think? Erik Satie died.' 'Satie? Who? Never heard of Satie.' And I thought, Well this is the end! They weren't interested in anything that wasn't Bach, Bruckner, Brahms, and Beethoven. It was kind of an old folk's home."[17] What contemporary musician wouldn't be upset by this news, he wondered.

After this incident, Louis concluded that he had made a poor choice for study. His restlessness increased in this "old world" environment he had envisioned so romantically months earlier. His complaint that the conservatory's faculty had little interest in any composer past Chopin mirrored his earlier dissatisfaction with the tastes of his musician colleagues from the San Francisco orchestra. Europe could not supply for him the answers he needed to create new avenues for a modern dance in America.

Horst was not particularly productive as a composer while in Vienna. Even before, his output had been meager. On the last leg of his final tour with Denishawn, he did complete several short pieces: *Tango* for piano (signed "March 1925, South Bend, Indiana"); two songs, *Ivory Petals* to a poem by C. Wentworth and *Autumnal* to words by Henri Faust; and a few compositions for dance or voice, showing his penchant for breath and emotional content.

By comparison a German counterpart, Kurt Weill, was well on the way to developing "song plays" that dynamically infused jazzy dance rhythms, while Louis's sensibility lingered stubbornly with St. Denis's romantic mysticism. If his Denishawn experience was dramatically different from that of other conservatory-trained composers making their mark on American contemporary music, and more akin to Weill's work in cabarets, it had not yet released any innovative ideas in his composing.

In Vienna he composed *Scene Javanaise* for piano (a score Martha used for a solo within the year). He continued to explore vocal writing with a song, *Toys,* to a poem by Arthur Symons. By August Louis finished *Harvest Dirge,* to a poem by Alfred Kreymborg, and *Mule Pack,* to words by William Haskell Simpson. During his remaining month in Vienna he also sketched out a partial score for a ballet, *A Viennese Nocturne,* a kind of romantic homage to the great city.

Although he relived Vienna's rich musical history with visits to the homes of Beethoven, Haydn, and Schubert and enjoyed evenings in the Volksgarten, where open-air concerts featured work by Mahler, one of Louis's most revered composers, he felt out of place. "After awhile I got tired of Vienna. It was beautiful — a marvelous musical city to be in but there was no real dance. It was so old fashioned. I couldn't work there, because if I wasn't an Austrian citizen, I couldn't even play a dance class in a studio. I realized I didn't want to study all day, so I decided suddenly, this is not the place. I can go back and study better in New York and be busy."[18] His change of heart was complete when in mid-summer Martha wrote to say that she had made a decision of her own.

While Martha had worked at developing social skills for charming an inner circle of benefactors, she had also spent time alone, ruminating on her future. She frequently visited the zoo to watch the lions move, observing, "No animal ever has an ugly body until it is domesticated."[19] She tried to envision ways that the human body might recapture its sense of "physical adventure," divorced from popular notions prevalent in the theater and those of flappers, speakeasies, and dance marathons. Deciding to give up the good salary and high living as soloist with the *Follies,* she accepted Rouben Mamoulian's offer to become associated with a music conservatory for its 1925–1926 season.

As instructor for dance and body movement in the new School of Dance and Dramatic Action at the Eastman School of Music in Rochester, New York, she would also be responsible for choreographing the season's operas. Excited at the prospect of working on a purer form of concert dance, away from the commercial theater, she now had an opportunity to develop her own choreographic ideas. Mamoulian agreed to let her divide her schedule between Rochester and New York, so that she could remain on the faculty of the John Murray Anderson–Robert Milton School of Dramatic Arts.

Her new position changed everything in Louis's eyes. "I didn't want to be separated from Martha, because it was too close a thing to me at that time." He decided to leave Vienna on a day's notice. "I sent a letter to Dr. Stöhr and some friends of mine I met through him, and I took a very slow boat home."[20] Leaving Vienna on 16 September 1925 Louis toured Venice, Florence, Rome, and Naples before boarding the *Martha Washington* in Trieste on October 3. Bound for New York, the steamer stopped at the ports of Patras, Palermo, and Lisbon, beginning its voyage across the Atlantic nine days later.

> I should have been in New York in ten or twelve days, but we were late because there was a terrible hurricane. The boat was slowed down. We'd get wires that little boats near us had sunk. Martha wanted to meet me at the boat, and every day she'd get a wire from the boat company. "Arrival is delayed another day on account of the storm." She was always on the verge of coming down from Rochester to see me. Finally they said, "Boat will arrive tomorrow, surely. Storm is over."[21]

Louis's European journey amounted to a summer of study mixed with a good share of sightseeing and relaxation. Distanced from his ten years with Denishawn he returned to New York anxious to begin work. Margaret Lloyd, the dance critic for Boston's *Christian Science Monitor,* wrote about his brief study, "He found no 'arty' atmosphere in Vienna, no hands over hearts bursting with inspiration, but straightforward, orderly, scientific procedure. This composing was a job, a craft to be learned, and no nonsense. Seven months of it, without emotional trappings, equipped him for his subsequent plunge into the new dance movement."[22] In fact, Louis had been away for only five months from the time he set sail until the day he returned to New York, but his colleagues understood that he came home with two sure strengths: a sense of what the modern artists were doing in Europe and a fierce commitment to the future of dance as an art form.

"Martha met me at the dock,"[23] Louis said about his arrival in New York on 21 October 1925. As Martha fussed over him, Gertrude Shurr (who had taken over teaching responsibilities while the company was in the Orient) hailed a cab, after arranging for his trunk to be delivered to a "dormitory" room on the top floor of the Denishawn School on West 28th Street. Louis then "went to Rochester with [Martha] for a week. I picked up my life, playing for Martha Graham. This was the beginning of [my work with] Graham and the first concert."[24] An historic collaboration was about to begin.

Still Denishawn-like in style, their work together would be significant not because of any dramatic change in content, but because it represented their first explorations as a team.

> She began working out new exercises, coming down every week [from Rochester to New York City] and we'd talk and rehearse. She began to develop some of her own dance materials. She'd get the idea for the dance, and I'd look for music, or I'd bring music and she'd get an idea, or she thought she wanted to do something in the class in an interpretative manner and she did the Brahms rhythms. Mostly I became very interested in modern music and played a lot to her. I'd buy Hindemith — Bartok for her. Then we began to go and look at all the modern art paintings and we bought books. There was a little bit about Wigman in German books, but when we were looking for new ideas we always had to turn to painting. We could see the way things were going. Our music was becoming more dissonant [with] different rhythms and uses of music. I said, "You've got to give a concert."[25]

That summer of 1925 Martha had investigated the latest happenings in the arts, such as director-actor Constantin Stanislavsky's innovative methods, and listened to the bold statements of artists in Greenwich Village. One, the composer Dane Rudhyar, had been offered "a tepee under the fruit trees" as Mabel Dodge Luhan's guest in Taos.[26] Enthusiastic about Graham he wrote to Luhan on her behalf, hoping that she, too, might enjoy an invitation to Taos — a suggestion that received no reply. Like other "new" women such as Georgia O'Keeffe and Frieda Lawrence, Martha was a perfect candidate for Luhan's salon gatherings, but it would take several years before Luhan would accept the modern dancer into that world.

When Louis resumed his compositional studies, this time with arranger Max Persin, he began a song, "Change," based on a poem full of Native American imagery by Witter Bynner. He completed it in early December 1925. Louis's modest output for the next five years centered on composing for the piano and voice, ending with *Spring Song* and *Civil War Songs* for Agnes de Mille. Typically, the scores emerged in A-B-A format with a good beginning, middle, and end — a shape that naturally enhanced choreographic materials, unifying the most disparate components. His use of songs also gave dramatic logic and uncomplicated ease for presenting the dynamics and range of breath — an efficient match for dance accompaniment. If his music occasionally explored strange harmonies and leaned toward dissonance, more often it was akin to Ravel's lyric style.

Otto Luening, composer, vocal coach, and at the time director of the opera department at the Eastman School of Music, befriended Martha that fall, finding her company "warm, friendly and stimulating . . . [and her] integration of music and movement superior. . . . She made suggestions about the visual aspect and movement in various works and although she was just beginning to launch her own solo career, she was extremely coopera-tive and helpful."[27] His assessment of Martha's way of working helps to explain the nature of her dependence on Louis:

> Martha and I didn't discuss technical details of music or dance. It was the expressive content of the works that was at the core of our conversa-tions. When she spoke, she gestured; she tried to speak from the depths of her personality, for her subconscious and her unconscious. . . . Music for her was related to movement and her subconscious groping and often unclear initial yearnings led her to create art works with music and movement from her inner experiences.[28]

Luening understood that Louis was determined to see Martha's talent mature. As her mentor, Louis must provide a protective environment in which she could create. Now "living" with Martha, as he put it, thus con-firming their intimate liaison, the nature of their intimacy soon became a guarded topic among colleagues. Some saw the attraction as a paternal one. (Her relationship with her father — once an "alienist" at the Dixmont Asy-lum in Pittsburgh, a hospital for nervous disorders for women — was com-plex. Dr. Graham had very specific ideas about the emotional needs of women.) Nina Fonaroff, whose association with both Graham and Horst was lifelong, saw their intimacy as a sharing of artistic lives.

Theirs was an extraordinarily powerful creative collaboration. There was a particular, personal and musical comprehension on his part of what she was and of what she was doing. It was not simply a matter of Louis supplying music for Martha's choreographic work. . . . His contribution was critical and catalytic: Louis was above all her greatest critic. There was an added tension in the air for everyone when Louis watched a rehearsal; his demands for rhythmical precision were fanatical. He could understand what was going on inside her — and other people's — work: he was a genius at this. It is hard to separate Louis and Martha at this time.[29]

He was able to temper her volatile personality; she seemed to rely on his attention and appeared to be the possessive one. It was obvious that Louis continued to flirt with other women. Martha had admirers of her own; a dozen red roses often made their way to the studio. Still, they remained devoted to one another.

Even as Louis prepared for his first concerts with Graham, other commitments earned money to support their cause and he was soon involved in a full array of freelance activities. With Denishawn still touring the Orient, he willingly returned to work under its banner, accompanying a March concert that featured Ronny Johannson, a dancer he greatly admired. Once back as pianist at the Denishawn studio and for Martha's classes at the Anderson-Milton School, he also accepted a commission from the dancer Ruth Page. She called the work *Two Balinese Rhapsodies (Religious Dance, Pleasure Dance)* and he played for its Cornell Dramatic Club premiere in Ithaca in March 1926. An assignment for the Ampico recording studio produced six records of musical selections that he had arranged to accompany Denishawn exercises. (Shawn theorized that Ampico pianos equipped with piano rolls were ideal for dance studios teaching his dances across the country. With the flip of a switch the roll moved the piano's ivories, reproducing pieces recorded by leading artists of the day.)

When Louis was in Rochester with Martha, Luening noted that "They gave much thought and energy to developing her dances and her first trio of dancers." He often met them for dinner at the Fern Restaurant or the theater as the semester progressed. "One reason [Martha and I] got on so well was because of my friendship with Louis . . . her constant companion." When the two musicians realized their similar backgrounds in vaudeville they became immediate friends. Louis accepted Luening as "an old pro" and welcomed him in the studio, where he watched the couple plot out new dances: "He helped her to form her fantasies and thought and to shape them in movement. He selected music, composed for her, and rehearsed her dances."[30] "He was kind of the censor at the time of who should write music for her."[31] Martha suggested that Luening submit music to Louis for consideration. "Louis didn't like the score much. He didn't go for it."[32]

The couple celebrated a quiet Christmas holiday in New York City working out program ideas and a rehearsal schedule for the next few months. For the first time in years, neither had performances to worry about. (Coincidentally, the Denishawn company, having just returned from the Orient, celebrated Christmas with dinner prepared by Betty Horst in San Francisco.) Graham's choice of a legitimate Broadway theater for her debut as a dancer-choreographer reveals her confidence in herself, and her daring. This was not to be another dance recital. It was something new and had to be presented in a different light. Succeed or fail, she was determined "to compete at the top."[33]

In developing materials for their first independent recital, Louis understood his potential influence as a nurturer of Martha's genius. She needed him and, in turn, he placed his future within the context of their creative life together. Nietzsche's view of artists "driving into heights and super-heights and into excesses of passion . . . toward a better, lighter, more southern, sunnier world," matched Louis's intention. Nietzsche also wrote that "their cramps are often no more than signs that they would like to dance — these poor bears in whom hidden nymphs and sylvan gods are carrying on — and at times even higher deities!" Louis saw himself as a "poor bear," with "a deep craving to rise beyond, or at least look beyond, ugliness and clumsiness"[34] in his work with Martha.

Margaret Lloyd observed that "Normal well-being revolted him — or so he said, particularly in relation to Martha. She, he believed, had been set aside for a special vocation."[35] She had enough energy and ego for both of them, and an unrelenting desire to make things happen. Taming Martha's emotional outbursts proved to be a constant challenge for Louis; he had learned to handle her angry ranting, usually by outlasting her stubbornness with his own. Having placed her trust in his judgment, Martha usually complied with his final decisions.

As a soloist Graham's presence on the concert stage was audacious. She was a "superb actress whose unpopular monkey face in a period of candy-box prettiness kept her out of the theater. So she turned dialogue into dance," Louise Brooks, the film starlet and former Denishawn dancer, reasoned. Brooks remembered Graham's dramatic flair in the early twenties: "What I would give to see her Hedda Gabler."[36] Shawn, too, appreciated Martha's intensity and theatrical flair. She had concentrated almost exclusively on performance and was plainly inexperienced at dance-making; now, she had to make choreographic statements of her own. If the photographs of Mary Wigman Louis brought back from Vienna had any influence at all on Martha, it was of a woman as dramatic soloist who commanded an empty stage independent of anything but musical accompaniment. Significantly different in concept from St. Denis's presence highlighting each work, it was clear to Martha that she must concentrate on choreographic content. It was Louis whom she trusted to guide her in the studio. She desperately needed his "outside eye."

Agnes de Mille wrote of Louis's intent to see that Martha find a condition of truth in movement as well as in philosophy: "He scolded and forced and chivied; the relationship was full of storm and protest. 'You're breaking me,' she used to say. 'You're destroying me.' 'Something greater is coming,' he promised, and drove her harder."[37]

Characteristically unwilling just to talk about a work, Louis demanded precision. "Show me what you've got," he would say. If the response was, "Something like this," he would wait out with stony observation the time it took to perform each movement phrase exactly. Until the dancer before him was disciplined enough to repeat each action in relation to his note-to-note accompaniment, he would insist, "Do it again, you are not accurate." Then he might point out weaker moments or suggest trimming of superficial material, with an intuitive sense about what "worked" and what did not. Louis disliked indirect actions. Turning or circling for no apparent reason bored him. "When in doubt, turn!"[38] he heckled. As a result few turns take place in Graham's repertory. Not satisfied until the movement was pared down "to the bone," he wanted to see the core of each action, its essential components free of meaningless gesturing. Like themes in musical composition, the choreographic process involved ordering, reordering, and manipulation of delineated materials.

During the rehearsal period the shaping and execution of the visible dance product was Martha's domain (she designed the costumes and lights as well). Louis's role was to find or write the music to support the dance ideas, all the while questioning the intention, timing, style, and quality of what he saw in movement as he performed in tandem at the keyboard. The creation of a new movement vocabulary was a difficult but necessary task for Martha alone. "[She] worked on technique. She discovered a lot of new movement with this philosophy of economy to get away from all flowing [movement]. She just stood still and did percussive things. She did dances on a dime. She developed a system of tucking under and moving the whole body more, but sharply. She worked out a lot of primitive-like, sharp, sculpted things."[39]

As Martha labored over movement choices, Louis might say, "Don't smile — your body is your expressive instrument, not your face," chiding her along the way, or "Dig deeper. The material is too thin," and press for attention to content as well as structure. Her frustration level ran highest as a concert date approached and she simply had to choreograph in order to have something to perform. When she was too tired to continue he might offer a few words of encouragement, such as "That's a little better," or a consoling "Not bad."[40] Then, he would play a smooth rendering of *The Maple Leaf Rag,* while waiting for the exhausted dancer to recover.

Martha's first concert in New York on 18 April 1926 consisted of eighteen short works, with three assisting dancers: Betty MacDonald, Evelyn Sabin, and Thelma Biracree (later replaced by Rosina Savelli), whom she had trained in Rochester. Al Jones, the producer of the *Greenwich Village Follies,* had "loaned" the 48th St. Theatre at cost (paid in turn by Steloff's "loan"). At the keyboard, Louis played his arrangement of music by Godowsky, *Alt Wein,* as well as his *Four Songs,* placed as interludes between dance works. Although he received second billing as concert pianist for Graham's recitals, Louis positioned his piano into the wings, where he could catch sight cues and assist the stage manager if necessary. Some of Martha's dances were eclectic in style, with the gentle skips, lyric scoops, and occasional Eastern accents drawn from her Denishawn training. But her new works — *Danse Languide* (a trio) and the solos *Desir* (Scriabin), *Deux valses sentimentales* (Ravel), and *Tanagra* (Satie) — began to explore more adventurous ground. If the *New York Times* mentioned Martha Graham's "interpretive dance . . . to modern music"[41] with only passing interest in the next day's paper, Louis and her small band of supporters were confident about Martha's future: "That was the start."[42] Daniel Mayer agreed, turning his attention from St. Denis to Graham.

During summer 1926, in contrast to the intensity of his work with Graham, Louis played for Denishawn's summer courses at Carnegie Hall and one given by Leo Staats, which gave him a change of pace and welcome extra income. He also began another important collaboration with the dancer Helen Becker, a beautiful, dynamic woman who called herself "Tamiris." But his first opportunity to perform with her seemed no more enlightened than had his experience with Denishawn's vaudeville-circuit act; they appeared at the Apollo Theatre on Atlantic City's boardwalk. "Tamiris was the Goddess of Light at the Electric men's convention. She wore a thousand-pound dress made of glass. She couldn't move."[43] The two managed to find the humorous side of a dismal situation, and as traveling companions on the train to and from Atlantic City their conversations were more metaphysical in nature.

She spoke about the kind of dancing she really wanted to do: "Louis could not understand my insistence upon calling my dances American. . . . To him it seemed paradoxical and inconsistent that I could speak of an American Dance and a Universal Dance in the same breath."[44] During this encounter Louis agreed to rehearse with her for the solo recital she planned to give. Over the next few years he enjoyed playing for the dynamic Tamiris whenever he could.

Graham, too, did not find many satisfying performance opportunities at this point, but she was managing to make herself known to the press. A newspaper feature article, "Martha Graham Warns Girls of Hardships in Dance Career," spelled out the ordeals of a dancer's life as "too hard and uncertain to be entered without a 'call.' . . . The modern dance is something far more complicated than cavorting about in chiffon robes, expressing joy or despair or springtime," and then paraphrased Louis's earlier analogy, "It is an integrated art in which the soul plays upon a disciplined body as a musician plays upon an instrument. But the musician, no matter how his soul is stirred, must have the technique for expressing his emotions. Beneath every art is a craft." She then described an incident that took place at one of the performances she and Louis gave that summer at Mariarden: "In New Hampshire during an unseasonably cold spell Louis Horst, my pianist, had to hold a hot-water bottle on his knees and warm his hands on it at every opportunity. We dancers in chiffon, of course, had no such aid. The audience was cold, too, I presume, but at least they didn't have to try to avoid looking cold."[45] Throughout these hardships, the article implied, Martha and Louis remained enthusiastic about their mission and were prepared for any challenge.

chapter four

1926–1929

"The dance has a tremendous

power; it is a spiritual touch-

stone." — E. Bugbee quoting

Martha Graham

For the next decade, Martha's and Louis's shared lives were filled with passionate moods and intense protectiveness, mixed with dispassionate denial. Although eighteen of their twenty-four-hour days were spent together, they separated to private quarters to sleep. Acquaintances knew that Martha and Louis were intimate companions who never shared the same legal address. "We never really lived together. But we were always together. We always rehearsed every night at the studio."[1] His own rooms were usually at a midtown residential hotel for short periods of time. "Hiking around, I didn't have any pictures or books much then. I lived in hotels . . . like the Wellington Hotel for eight months."[2] Content with his own bachelor quarters he confided that he "never did like seeing two toothbrushes in the morning."[3] Martha first kept a curtained cubicle for sleeping in the back of her 9th Street studio. Later she moved into modest quarters at 16 West 10th Street. Although Louis once informed a student that "Even Martha has pots and pans,"[4] neither cooked much except water for tea. Their meals together were usually of the Horn & Hardart Automat variety.

Others marveled at their odd combination of beliefs in free love and near celibacy, their austere daily living that consisted of rudimentary amenities in bare studios up too many flights of stairs. Whatever the condition of their intimacy, their love for one another defied simple explanation. Gertrude Shurr recalled, "Sometimes I'd see them walking hand in hand. On 57th Street or in the park. Martha always seemed so subservient. Even then, she had a little-girl look. She never even looked up. As an aesthete Louis kept

Martha on a pedestal and kept everyone away from her. He protected her — like a vestal virgin or concubine."[5] And Agnes de Mille wrote, "The first time I saw [Martha] off stage she was sitting in a New York theater in a melancholy which I had been told was her characteristic public pose. She held a single rose in her right hand which she sniffed from time to time. Louis Horst, to whom she did not address a word, sat stolidly beside her."[6] Their common mission unified every decision and everyone soon understood their fierce reliance on each another. Some colleagues sensed that Louis began to grow obsessive in his role as facilitator of her career. The dancer May O'Donnell confirmed that "he loved Martha very, very much and put his full energy into helping her develop her career,"[7] even at the expense of his own. Others envied her luck at being his "chosen" one.

Martha philosophized: "To those who can become as open-minded as children the dance has a tremendous power; it is a spiritual touchstone."[8] For Louis, Martha was his openminded child, who needed only taming. "She was a wild one. I was her ballast."[9] If in his own creative life he was content simply to arrange scores, his aesthetic preference for a "taut economy of means" became the constant creative theme he preached to Graham. It also described their near monastic personal life as a couple.

With her career as the focus of their energies there was little conflict between them. "Dance" and "life" became synonymous. Martha said, "Life does not have to be interpreted, and the dance is life. . . . Dance is not a mirror, but a participation, a voicing of the hidden but common emotions."[10] Many years later she said, "Perhaps we are all twins, we have both sides. . . . I know that unless I love [a] person very much, I [do not reveal] my savage side unless it's on the stage."[11] As seasoned performers, Horst and Graham had learned to save their most passionate expression for the theater.

The challenges facing Louis and Martha as they began to rehearse in fall 1926 centered on aspects of concertizing they had never worried about with the Denishawn organization. Making a new start meant not only taking responsibility for the entire production, but also developing a new audience. Months of concentrated work often culminated with a single performance. The next few years would take fortitude, conviction, and cunning — and above all a belief in themselves. Bolstered by their first successful venture, Martha and Louis were ready to proceed.

After a trip to California and a short visit with Betty and his mother, Louis moved into the top-floor tower studio of Carnegie Hall and returned to work as a pianist and music director for dance, taking all the work he could get to spare Martha the need to return to Rochester.

I had a rich technique in those days. I could see a dance, and then go. I could [sight] read like a flash. I'd read over [the score] two or three times by myself and I'd see it in the rehearsal. I'd remember the tempo and then I'd pick it up. Once in a while I'd practice on some of these things. [For the] Grieg Concerto I had to practice technical bits in it because it's a piano concerto. Some of [the] Scriabin they used was very difficult and some of Hindemith's things. Of course playing for Martha was different. I always played for Martha.[12]

When approached for concert dates, his answer was "Yes," if his schedule permitted, and he asked for $100 per concert from well-heeled requesters. Few paid that amount. More often he received an honorarium pending profit at the box office. Popularizing one's art for the sake of financial success was contrary to the revolutionary spirit of a true artist, he believed, and he was grateful when his various jobs paid enough to cover the month's rent along with any unexpected production bills.

Agnes de Mille had the distinct impression that Louis never spent much time practicing at the keyboard. He arrived at the theater an hour-and-a-half before curtain to fuss over difficult passages, "singing quite loudly to encourage himself. He sang throughout the recital and the alert ear could hear him through the playing. . . . Any delicately fingered passage he simply grabbed by the handful and tossed out of his way. He kept the beat and his beat was infallible, his pulse being in fact truer than the performer's."[13] He soon became indispensable to her.

Instinctively Louis guided dancers toward their best work in the studio by relying on his knowledge of contemporary music, and he willingly arranged or reorchestrated scores or wrote original ones for them. In concert his presence not only gave a chamber-recital ambience, but also freed the dancer from the hassle of recorded accompaniment, which in any case had not yet reached professional standards. Scratchy passages and skipped measures were common dilemmas for those who braved the off-stage technician's difficult task of changing phonograph records.

Louis also continued to accompany Ronny Johansson's recitals, and began to work with Michio Ito, a talented Japanese dancer who had performed with Martha in the *Greenwich Village Follies*. The pianist carefully observed the way Ito paid particular attention to the underlying dance rhythms in a Bach suite. In his classes in the studio below Louis's, Ito taught phrases in unison, canon, and with changes of rhythm and talked about symbolism, imagery, and the use of minimal thematic materials — ideas that found their way into Louis's teaching. "He was sort of a Dalcrozian dancer.

He tried to do things in rhythm and yet in a Japanese style — interesting, but very limited. He was an important figure at that time because he was also looking for a modern expression."[14] As Ito and Johansson fed Louis information, he would then share it with Graham.

But it was the Daniel Mayer organization that became the major source of his income. Mayer hired Louis to conduct a "full dance orchestra" or accompany at the piano twenty-one different programs, ranging from song recitals to virtuoso concert work during the 1926–1927 concert season. Dance artists under his management included Adolph Bolm, Maria Montero, and Doris Niles, who gave performances at Carnegie Hall and toured regularly. For the next two years Louis also worked as a musical director for shows such as John Murray Anderson's *Edison Follies* in February 1927 at the Hotel Astor and later his *An Entertainment,* and *Dancing Shoes* for the New England Shoe and Leather Exposition held in New York in July, for which he wrote the theme song. This commercial work saved Martha from similar banalities, so that she could spend time in the studio by herself.

On 28 November 1926, six months after their first concert, Graham presented a second New York recital at the Klaw Theatre. The premiere of *Three Poems of the East* claimed to be Louis's first score especially composed for the dance. The complete program was again choreographed to short, contemporary scores for piano, with only her *Baal Shem* to a piece by Ernest Bloch inclined toward more abstract handling of dance materials. At the next recital, at the Guild Theatre on 27 February 1927, the dances were still reminiscent of Denishawn.

If critics were not overly enthusiastic about this "graceful" girl who "made pretty pictures" and "lacked power," she began to define her own persona as a performer. Free from strict ballet technique and in her use of contemporary music, Martha represented a definite departure for young artists who came to New York to study dance. Martha Hill, who would begin her professional career as a performer with Graham and soon become a leading force in the development of twentieth-century dance in her own right, was one of them: "I was looking for an expressive medium. When I first saw Graham [at the Klaw in 1926] I was bowled over. It was instant conversion. I immediately went to study with her at the John Murray Anderson–Robert Milton School of the Theatre."[15]

It would take another season for Graham to develop a more distinctive style, but noticeable changes were already beginning to appear in her movement vocabulary. Louis may have considered Martha his best student, but she was also his most problematic. Her work continued to be a proving ground for both of them. As she sculpted her body with more angularity,

Louis began to insist that she remove any transitional or unnecessary action. Martha told an interviewer that "like the modern painters and architects we have stripped our medium of decorative unessentials. Just as fancy trimmings are no longer seen on buildings, so dancing is no longer padded. It is not 'pretty' but it is much more real."[16]

Martha pulled away from Denishawn still more dramatically after St. Denis and Shawn grumbled that they were not pleased with their renegade offspring carrying on its tradition "without consent." Doris Humphrey, who remained appreciative of the performing and teaching opportunities Denishawn had given her, observed the hostility Shawn displayed toward Martha and Louis in their new venture:

> The Shawns, I'm ashamed to say, are jealous of Martha. It's disgraceful, and as Louis knows the bitter things Ted has said about her, he hasn't been near them. So there's a breach wide & deep that may never be spanned. They think Martha should mention Denishawn on her programs, and in her interviews — and that is the fly in the jam. She considers that she has broken away from everything they do, and is individual. (Mr. Shawn having emphatically pointed out to her before she went away that she had no right to any Denishawn works.) So there it stands. I'm much more in sympathy with Martha & Louis and have looked forward to seeing them for ages. It was rather difficult at first, because they thought all of their old friends in the company shared Ted's viewpoint, and it took aggressiveness on our part to assure them of our friendship.[17]

In a brief renewal of friendship with Martha and Louis, Doris had earlier invited them to visit her in Westport, where she was staying in Denishawn "camp" dormitories. After a weekend of reminiscence and discussion of Doris's contemplated defection from Denishawn, she described the couple in a letter to her parents: "[Martha is] . . . intensely feminine, not a flaming obvious flower, but a night blooming thing with a faint exotic perfume. . . . He believes in equality and freedom of the sexes, but dies of jealousy, and says no man can love a woman who is unfaithful to him. He believes that there is no happiness in love, and that art is the only fun that lasts, and in the next breath says that half an hour with the one you love is the greatest ecstasy! He's a hopeless romanticist and sentimentalist — full of Neitche [sic] in his brain and romance in his heart."[18]

Louis and Martha were teaching and rehearsing together while headlines dwelled on Lindbergh and his monoplane's historic flight to Paris in an astounding thirty-three-and-a-half hours. Taking dance classes with them that hot summer of 1927, Martha Hill found Louis to be a "sophisticated, mature musician who had returned from Vienna. I remember him sitting at the piano, and Martha romanticizing, building a poetic little frame around things we were doing in dance. If she went too far off the track in this direction, Louis would call a halt to that."[19]

Graham was often depressed with the laborious rehearsal process. "You can't give up," Louis told her, as she struggled with a new solo. "There's nothing else you know how to do!"[20] Walter Terry later commented:

> Louis saw more in her than she had yet found in herself. He recognized genius in her, and it was up to him as musician, composer, teacher, friend, and confidant, as well as lover, to help her to release what she later called "divine discontent" in a torrent of creative energy. . . . She had discovered that she did indeed possess the power to speak — and eloquently — through movement, of her deepest feelings. . . . She was not entertaining the public — she was disturbing them. And that was her intention.[21]

In the fall Graham opened a studio of her own. Ardent students at the Martha Graham School during its early years remembered "a movement barre, a number of set exercises, and 'the calls,' "[22] which were the beginning of "a sort of contraction and release feeling of going forward and falling back. This was done hanging on to the barre. We did very little on the floor. There was not a lot of percussive movement then."[23]

For an interview for *The Dance Magazine,* Martha mused about the importance of structure: "Out of emotion comes form. We have form in music as the reflection of the composer's emotion. There is a corresponding form of movement, a dynamic relation between sound and motion. One can build up a crescendo either with a succession of sounds or with a succession of movements." In the same article she also stressed the need for content: "Any great art is the condensation of a strong feeling, a perfectly conscious thing."[24] But clearly Martha was struggling to find a balance between form and content as she approached her "long woolens" period, and as a result her 1927 work *Revolt* was severer in style (five months after Kreutzberg's *Revolte* premiered at the First German Dancers' Congress). When Louis demanded simplicity, she searched for deeper sources of meaning without melodrama. Even as he watched over her artistic progress, he also attended to organizational details and fought for appropriate press coverage in order to attract a broader audience. While he took responsibility for her public relations, she handled the artistic concerns of production.

If Graham's recital work had not found critical attention earlier, her

Little Theatre concert on 22 April 1928 created a stir. Newspaper inter-
viewers quickly latched on to her pressworthy declarations, such as, "Ugliness may be actually beautiful if it cries out with the voice of power"[25] — a
startling revelation for a dancer who one year before was dancing with
Eastern attitudes, saris, and leopard screens.

Her collaboration with Louis for this concert resulted in the solo *Fragments: Tragedy — Comedy,* to a score for flute and gong that they later
claimed to be the first example of a dance score written after the choreographic work was completed. *Fragments,* he explained, was the result of her
desire to use vibration as a dramatic force, with the flute translating it into
clearer melodic form: "Inasmuch as the *Fragments* were an expression of the
Greek theatre, the old Greek modes were employed as a base for the flute
phrases."[26] They reworked the 1926 trio *Three Poems of the East* as a solo
and called it *Chinese Poem,* and presented *Immigrant: Steerage — Strike,* her
second attempt at social commentary, along with *Poems of 1917,* with its
strong political overtones.

Louis still found ways to play for everyone who needed him: "[I was]
just dashing from one place to another — always rehearsing and playing,
often two concerts on one Sunday."[27] Now living in Carnegie Hall's "Studio
121," he accompanied virtually every dance artist on the New York concert
scene, including Doris Humphrey. A touch of reserve had always been
present between Humphrey and Graham during their early career at Denishawn, and it was Louis who continued to act as the common denominator
between factions as their contrasting styles began to emerge. Appreciating
Humphrey's beauty as a performer and admiring her sense of craft as a
choreographer, Louis did not stop badgering her to leave the Denishawn
company:

> Doris was running the studio at Carnegie Hall. I tried to talk her into
> leaving, but she said, no, she wouldn't leave. "Martha is wrong and Miss
> Ruth is right. I'm going to stick to Miss Ruth." I kept after her and
> Pauline [Lawrence]. Finally Pauline told me, "You win. She said last
> night she was going to give a concert and do what Louis said." She was
> always more lyric than Martha — windblown, you know. But she was
> strong, but not the dark color. Blond, light color. Martha was darker.
> Doris was like a violin.[28]

Humphrey may not have been his "cup of tea," but Louis did value her
artistry. For a concert on 24 March 1928 at the Little Theatre in Brooklyn,
featuring the premiere of Humphrey's *Air for the G String,* Louis played a
Bach gigue and Ravel's *Pavane* (a work he had recently heard the composer

play at Carnegie Hall) for Humphrey's dances. Three weeks later he conducted a small orchestra for a performance at the John Golden Theatre for "Doris Humphrey, Charles Weidman and Students of the Denishawn School," in their gradual separation from the main company. Very much a woman who knew what she wanted, Doris had begun to draw her materials from natural impulses, away from musical visualization and dependence on the melodic line, to Louis's delight. He again marveled at her ingenuity when he accompanied the first Humphrey-Weidman Company appearance in concert at the Civic Repertory Theatre on 28 October 1928, in which he played Gershwin's Three Preludes, programmed with Humphrey's innovative new dance in silence, *Water Study.*

If these choreographers seemed to handle the mounting competition between them more graciously than their dancers, it was Louis who continually reminded all of them of the need for different approaches. For example, at one point Gertrude Shurr told Louis that she planned to leave the Humphrey-Weidman Company (with which she danced from 1927 to 1929), to study with Graham, a situation that was fairly typical in this small circle of performing artists. Louis scolded, "Don't you dare leave Doris now! She is in the middle of preparations for an important season and she needs you."[29] She took his advice, but did eventually venture into Graham's classes before joining that contingent in 1930.[30]

Another artist with whom Louis was still working, Helen Tamiris, had told him about wanting her dances to provoke social consciousness for her first solo concert, Dance Moods, scheduled by the Mayer management for the Little Theatre on 9 October 1927. The results were a far cry from the Atlantic City electric show Louis had accompanied. Like Gershwin, whose music she used, Tamiris chose to express the tempo of American modern life with speed and vitality. Although Louis was mildly sympathetic to her objectives he worried about her use of "low" art ideas. One reviewer perhaps sensed his ambivalence by saying that he accompanied "with sympathy and with orders," mentioning that he gave stage-managing cues from the keyboard, as was his habit.[31] "Horst again proved himself the most desirable of dance accompanists,"[32] according to another reviewer, Lucile Marsh, but a writer for *Musical America* gave still another perspective on his performance manner as an assisting artist "who performed behind the scenes and refused to emerge even for his share of the applause."[33] Although Tamiris had accepted his usual suggestion of music by Debussy and Scriabin for her second program on 29 January 1928, a jazzier style was evident in her *Prize Fight Studies* to the beating of piano strings and *20th Century Bacchante* to music by Louis Gruenberg. This trend troubled him, as did the manifesto printed in her program, stating that the "aim of dance . . . is simply movement with a personal conception of rhythm."[34] Tamiris and Horst had a gradual falling out, disagreeing on more than just musical choices. They did not work together again after this performance, but retained a cool friendship.[35]

One freelance assignment led to another. Louis also began in December 1927 to work as musical director for Ruth Page,[36] having written a score for her the previous spring. She wrote that "while [Horst] worked with you sympathetically, he was very severe. While I was 'creating' he would sit at the piano patiently repeating the phrases while reading a book or looking out into space. But when I was finished, he always had constructive comments and helpful suggestions. He was not only a critic in the real sense of the word, but he was the most sympathetic accompanist I've ever known. His first touch of the piano keys put you into the right mood."[37] Page sometimes "did quite modern dances,"[38] Louis remarked, thinking back on their collaborations. Page and Horst also worked with Edwin Strawbridge and were paid exceedingly well. Louis later said disparagingly that "Strawbridge was a rich boy from Philadelphia. He'd been dancing around in a sort of exotic, erotic, I mean aesthetic . . . yes, oh—aesthetic, you know."[39] Throughout his life, Louis could never quite come to terms with any artist whose career relied on independent wealth.

Years later, Louis disclosed the virtues and quirks of some of his favorite dancers at that time. One was the Russian dancer Adolph Bolm. Bolm had left the Ballets Russes and established a company, Ballet Intime, in America, trying desperately to keep afloat with a few weeks of touring and occasional dates in Manhattan. "I was very close to Bolm in those days. He didn't give me a nickel. He'd get a Metropolitan [Opera] conductor—an Italian [to conduct] and I had to run the stage, because he couldn't get stage hands [to work for him]. He tried. He'd say, 'lift the curtain,' and they thought he meant drop the curtain. He got so exasperated."[40]

By 1928 Louis was overwhelmed with commitments, usually attending several rehearsals a day with a wide variety of concert artists, continuing his work with Doris Niles, accompanying Hans Wiener (the German "modernist" who later changed his name to Jan Veen) as well as Ruth Page in performances with Edwin Strawbridge, touring with the Humphrey-Weidman Dance Company and again with Ballet Intime. Another job placed him as musical director for the New York Public Library Staff Association's revues for the next two years, beginning with their production of *Keep Stepping*. Throughout this hectic schedule Louis was still accompanying Graham's technique classes at the Anderson-Milton School and at her studio on West 10th Street.

Louis thrived as the indispensable pianist and was able to move to a more expensive pied-à-terre at 149 West 57th Street. "I looked over Carnegie Hall. At night I used to see the world like that. I used to tell guests, 'I'm living at the center of the world.' All these people going to concerts! This was to me the center of the world."[41]

If Louis's life shunned involvement in the workaday world, other artists, faced with the difficult conditions of the late twenties, began to take a more social than philosophical stand. Some in this small band of contemporary dancers found themselves caught up in left-wing activities in support of labor reform and social justice, using their dance voices for sectarian concerns. Not particularly interested in making outright political statements, Louis felt that artists should transcend the ordinary and not proselytize social ideas. "Art is art," he told Martha Hill. "It was all right to do these things, but they represented a different use of dance."[42] However, he did perform with Martha in fund-raising rallies for causes such as union organizing and settlement houses when he thought the work would increase her exposure in the art world. (In the mid-thirties Louis also accompanied Martha's performances in concerts for Spanish Civil War relief and for several WPA projects.)

Wrestling with an unpopular, and to some, elitist viewpoint, both artists were nevertheless willing to state their opinions, when asked. "I feel very deeply about certain political issues,"[43] Martha said, but she believed as Louis did: dance needed its own political support. Ways must be found to guide the politics within the field of dance itself. Dancers should not waste their time at politicking but rather direct their energies to their own expressions in choreography. "One only tries to keep it [the propaganda] within the range of art and not make it completely colloquial. . . . The minute you start to preach you are not dancing. Your material must be sublimated to form and stylization or symbolization into a work of art. Until that takes place, it is only self-expression," Louis stressed.[44]

Louis later recalled this period as one when "most artists were a little 'pink.' We had organized groups such as the Workers' Dance League, students were dancing about things such as 'Poor Spain,' 'Poor China,' or the 'Naughty Capitalist.' They scorned the ballet because it had connotations of imperialist Russia. This was a time of revolution."[45] In contrast, Louis praised the unpretentiousness of Martha's and Doris's work: "They would do things on a bare stage. Costuming and lighting were at a minimum. The accompaniment was kept simple too—never being more than a piano or a small ensemble of instruments. Dancing made its own theater."[46]

After the exhausting spring season of 1928, Louis returned to San Francisco. He noted in his journal: "June 27. Breakfast at Palace Hotel—

May, Ernest, Betty, Mama" (afterward underlining Mama and adding "last time" as a reminder of his final meeting with her). He then headed for Steamboat Springs, Colorado, to fill the position of music director at the Perry-Mansfield Dance Camp, a popular place for student dancers seeking summer study.

The mountain air and tennis courts added refreshing vacation bonuses to Louis's work as dance pianist and lecturer. His first lecturing assignment was a music appreciation course, which made his position at the camp its first of "aesthetic stature," as he put it. "Edna McRae taught ballet and there was tap and step. They had mostly 'second shelf' teachers. . . . I just went there and turned off my aesthetic buttons . . . turned them on again when I left."[47] While at the camp he composed incidental music for a student production, accompaniment for dance exercises (published as *Rhythmic Design*) choreographed by Portia Mansfield, and a score for Charles Weidman's *Japanese Actor: XVIIth Century,* which soon was shown at New York's Civic Repertory Theatre. Martha visited twice for short stays. The directors appreciated Louis's presence among the staff of their outdoor "dancing and horses" camp. As the easygoing "professor" of dance music, he was asked to return to Perry-Mansfield for the next five years, and again in 1946.

After his respite in the Rockies, Louis returned to a teaching position at the Neighborhood Playhouse School of the Theatre — one that would give him a small but secure income for the rest of his life. Originally funded by the Lewisohn sisters, whose extravagant productions with the Cleveland Orchestra at the Manhattan Opera House in the mid-twenties had become their trademark, the Neighborhood Playhouse had flourished as a settlement house on Henry Street in lower Manhattan since its establishment in 1915. Irene Lewisohn and Rita Wallach Morgenthau were the directors of the settlement's new School of the Theatre, located on West 56th Street. They also hired Graham to teach technique classes. The couple would thus complement their acting program and be on staff to perform in Playhouse productions Irene Lewisohn called "orchestral dance dramas." Graham had already appeared under her direction in performances of Debussy's *Nuages* and *Fêtes* in May.

"Irene said I was so helpful with Martha, she offered me a job. I helped Martha from a practical standpoint, coaching her and all, so Lewisohn asked me to teach. Of course, I probably would have drifted into teaching anyway, but she brought it up."[48] Louis accompanied Graham's technique classes along with his own sessions and acted as musical director for student productions and showcases. "I was sort of a specialist. That's not bragging. I was the only one that worked with the dancers. 'Who do we get? There's only one man who can do it!' There was me! So I started a college course in choreography."[49]

Unsure of how to begin, he talked over possible pedagogical approaches with Irene Lewisohn. "I started with music forms, but I had no idea of teaching composition . . . but suddenly to get it down into a structure, I thought I'd begin with the old forms because they were dances."[50] Dancers needed rudimentary compositional skills, he reasoned, knowing the problems that plagued dance rehearsals. If, for musicians, "pre-classic" pointed to the period before Haydn and Mozart, for dancers it simply meant "before ballet." Wigman had used these materials successfully in her *Suite in Old Style* and *Dance Suite,* choreographed between 1920 and 1923, and Louis was well aware of these studies in the use of various pulses and meters. Combined with some of Ito's ideas, the suite gave a convenient structure for lessons and ingeniously offered actors a chance to explore different historical styles. Conveniently, the dozen authentic forms divided neatly into the appropriate number of weeks of classroom study.

Using methods learned from trial and error with Martha, Louis began to teach within the context of his work as her musician. Anna Sokolow gave the following account of his first course at the Playhouse: "He introduced us to the world of culture—something none of us knew about. How to go to concerts, how to go to museums—everything that feeds or inspires you. He made us realize that to be the artist you have to have the inspiration from the culture."[51] He later reasoned that this was necessary because "the early modern dancers thought it was enough to revolt against the ballet and barefoot dancing—no form—and then for awhile we had a lot of 'revolting' dances, but they soon got to work on that, and this is one of the reasons I felt inclined to teach."[52]

If 1926 to 1929 were years of fermentation and growth for Martha's work, it was also when Louis developed his special pedagogical style. As they worked at refining concert ideas they inevitably tried out the same materials in the classroom. Students could experiment all they wanted in practice sessions, but when they entered his classroom, completed assignments were expected. Louis usually rejected most of what he saw, asking the student to change, edit, or reorganize certain sections on the spot, the rest of the class nervously watching—an ordeal that could take a few minutes to a half hour per student. Only when the entire class had finished the assignment to his satisfaction was he ready to go on to the next. He admired the ease with which aspiring actors would take hold of an idea and work it out physically, giving a fresh perspective to the use of motivation, intention, and theatricality in dance.

Sokolow explained the Neighborhood Playhouse approach: "With Graham we learned modern dance technique, and with Horst we began to study, and I mean study, choreography."[53] Students and then Graham company dancers—Sophie Maslow, Jane Dudley—were among the diligent whose lives were changed by those first classes at the Playhouse. After a year of study Sokolow, too, joined Martha's group. She also became Louis's assistant at the school, strongly contributing to his early success as a teacher.

Both Martha and Louis saw the need for establishing a dance technique that trained style and strength into her dancers as she set more rigorous sequences in her classes. He noted down the exercises and began to compose music for them, helping her with phrasing, meter, and tempo. Graham created sequenced exercises to build technical proficiency, much as a pianist practices scales, and then etudes to increase virtuosity. Louis used the framework of a sarabande or an allemande to create more cohesion in an exercise. He also composed a melody and a set of variations that he played continuously. Ralph Taylor, one of Louis's few lifelong male friends, could still hum the tune after fifty-eight years.

Through repetition Louis's sparse musical handling wedded to Martha's movement so completely that she never worried about counts or sound; that was Louis's domain. "It's a matter of musical timing," she said upon reflection. "As a dancer, you must not follow the music, you are the music. It's an emanation of the body."[54] But in fact, Louis carefully attached appropriate meters to specific exercises, also choosing suitable music forms such as A-B-A or theme and variations—compositional devices he had used with Portia Mansfield. Martha was able to "be" the music because Louis was there to give sound to her action.

Because Graham tended to be most interested in performing, she struggled to create movement that suited her own body rather than focusing on classroom technique. Her self-contained floor exercises warmed her back and stretched her thigh muscles, followed by some foot exercises. For the remaining portion of each class longer movement phrases were tried out for possible inclusion in her new work. She quickly learned that a structured class-plan permitted assistants to take over when she and Louis had other commitments—an arrangement that Irene Lewisohn heartily approved.

Louis's admiration for theater, talented directors, and well-written plays made his teaching association with the Neighborhood Playhouse a pleasurable assignment, and he shared in the teaching of students destined to become prominent actors and directors. Already inclined toward theatricality Graham immediately responded to the challenge of working with these professional colleagues. A sturdy relationship with the Playhouse was established, giving the couple a regular, assured salary. Louis soon became the solid man of music whom everyone trusted, an integral part of the smooth running of the Playhouse, loved by students and appreciated by the staff.

Ralph Taylor recalled, "I used to go with Louis to various concerts. He knew I was very much involved in music and he led me along the right path. I began to understand that Tchaikovsky was not the be-all and end-all of music," and why Louis confessed to favoring the "purer" forms of theater and dance to dramatic staged productions, which might prove disappointing.[55] Gradually, theater concepts derived from Louis's Playhouse experiences crept into his dialogue with dancers. He enjoyed working with actors — who sometimes turned into professional dancers for Martha's company — because they constantly tested the potential for abstracting ideas through dance. Still, the most primal of art expressions as he saw it — pure dance — pleased him more.

Horst was a man on the go during the 1928–1929 season, working with the greatest number and variety of dance artists of his career. Beginning with rehearsals with Humphrey and Weidman for their October concert, he then prepared for another tour as musical director for Ballet Intime. Bolm, now director of the Chicago Opera Ballet, chose Agnes de Mille as a replacement soloist for Ruth Page for what was billed as his last annual tour. De Mille wrote about the "once great Bolm, the ill-assorted group of dancers and the near-empty houses,"[56] but painted a tender portrait of Louis: "A very large man, in appearance a cross between Silenus and a German Micawber . . . [he] always sought to give the impression of a satyr, but he seemed to me from the first fatherly and kind. . . . He carried a music case and bag with one dress suit and a supply of paper-bound detective stories in it."[57] She was amazed to find that, like her Denishawn predecessors, Louis knew the best hotel or restaurant no matter what town they were in. She recounted a dialogue between Bolm and Horst after only forty-five tickets had been sold in a Macon, Georgia, theater that seated four thousand: " 'Do you think that the Pittsburgh management will ever pay what they owe?' " " 'No,' said Louis, looking up from his detective story, 'I don't.' "[58]

A cryptic man in some situations, Louis could also be a charming conversationalist when the subject was dance, de Mille noted: "As an antidote for this *Cherry Orchard* atmosphere, Louis Horst talked of Duncan, of Mary Wigman in Germany, and of a young dancer, Martha Graham, who he believed would one day be good; he talked for hours and hours. . . . The long talks he had with us worked like yeast in our creative thought."[59] After Ballet Intime, he accompanied de Mille in a program of her own work, which included the three solos she had performed with Bolm. A later program, at the Martin Beck Theatre in New York, featured a new Percy Grainger score, the beginning of Louis's practice to interest other composers in writing for his dance colleagues. When de Mille again presented a concert with Louis, for the MacDowell Club in January 1929 in honor of Mrs. Calvin Coolidge, he arranged a thirteenth-century manuscript, scored for piano and voice, for the occasion. His score for her *Civil War Songs* on that program was "arranged by the writer into a potpourri with the aid of bugle calls, drum rolls and good old-fashioned vamps. After a stirring climactic fortissimo finish, the verse of the last song was repeated pianissimo as the curtain fell."[60] De Mille's idiomatic style, using ballet as its base, was popular and theatrical. If not particularly fond of her work, he respected her intelligent use of indigenous materials, from medieval and baroque to American folk, and enjoyed working with her. De Mille reciprocated: "[Horst] was a darling and I loved him, caustic, difficult, and astringent. I think he liked me very much. He did not admire my style or my way of work, but he could see plainly that it was successful."[61]

At age forty-five Louis began to look for other ways to help the cause, and considered the state of dance writing. Frances Steloff's Gotham Book Mart had become a thriving haven for artists, and Louis and Martha enjoyed its homey atmosphere, browsed the shelves regularly, met other artists at the store's salon evenings, and even helped giftwrap books at Christmastime. Steloff could always be found at her desk in the "Mystics, Philosophy" section, where Louis greeted her on each visit.[62] He noticed the increase of little journals for new writers that Steloff always stocked along with *The Dance Magazine,* and together they talked about the need for dance journalism.

Beginning with Mary F. Watkins at the *New York Herald Tribune,* critical writing about dance in Herbert Hoover's America had begun in earnest. But other points of view were desparately needed. Walter Terry wrote of the pressure exerted on those few who were willing to review dance at that time: "Miss Watkins . . . told me that many of the moderns would come to her and beg, on their knees, for special attention. She recalled that she was immune to their pleadings but wholeheartedly behind the cause of all dancers when they were at their best in their pioneering efforts."[63]

Another facet of Louis's career began formally when he accepted a monthly assignment for *The Dance Magazine.* He jotted in his notebook: "Feb. 20.[1929] Accepted charge of "Music Page" of Dance Magazine." The editors asked Louis to take on a column called "The Music Mart," although his only writing experience had been "The Musician Comments" for Denishawn's 1925 periodical. This opportunity positioned him as a dance advocate and as a "music for dance" authority for a growing number of teachers who were interested in the latest available recordings and sheet music. The new dance movement needed advice about music for classroom and recital work, and he was happy to give it.

The May issue featured his article "Exceptional Selections from Recent Dance Events Discussed." Louis wrote six more articles in 1929 under the "Music Mart" banner, covering the current activities of de Mille and Tamiris and giving suggestions for musical scores. His critical eye and ease with words must have encouraged the editors to give him the opportunity to write more freely. His article "Discussion of the Musical Selections of a Young Dancer," voicing support of modern dance as an art form, typically embodied a discussion of Graham. His intense favoritism toward her work appeared in a variety of thinly veiled ways, for example, "Martha Graham firmly believes that the greatest dances are conceived in the idea, and in the course of her experience had discovered that her finest dances were created in this manner: the music being composed or adapted to interpret the idea instead of the dance interpreting the music."[64] Louis not only incorporated his ideas into these columns, but managed to use words such as "great" and "finest" in his writing about Martha.

In another article Louis translated the German preface of the Universal Edition of *Musik für Tänzer* (a collection containing works by Casella, Prokofiev, and others), describing the interaction of dance and music and demanding free counterpoint of movement with music. Although the tradition of composers writing scores set to ballet scenarios was well established in Europe since the seventeenth century, recent collaborations such as that of Picasso, Massine, and Satie in their 1917 work *Parade* were making significant contributions to the concept of music for dance. Few parallels could be found in twentieth-century America. Louis continued to glean ideas from Germany's dance musicians and dancers, led by Mary Wigman's "fanatic sincerity." The German influence was definitely the most important movement to watch. Even Shawn admitted Wigman's powerful effect on American dance: although "decidedly ugly in form," her work was a "valuable and necessary contribution to the dance as a whole."[65]

Louis first played for Harald Kreutzberg at a special matinee, when Kreutzberg came to New York with Tilly Losch in Max Reinhardt's 1928 production of *The Miracle* at the Century Theatre. "We rehearsed in Martha's studio. That's how Martha and I got so friendly with them, and I played their first concert. It was a tremendous hit. There were big write-ups at that time."[66] (Years later, Losch recalled being very upset by the fact that although Martha did loan them her studio, she did not leave them alone. Saying, "Go ahead," she would sit there and watch them.) Kreutzberg's appearance caused excitement among American dancers, some of whom had only read about Germany's "expressionistic" dancer and his "tender graciousness, noble elegance and distinguished musicality."[67] His abstract dancing, distinctive costuming, and professional theatricality were the stiffest competition Martha faced because they were most akin to her own developing style. As musician and confidant for both of these contingents Louis found himself in an uneasy position. On 20 January 1929, for example, he accompanied an afternoon concert for Graham; that evening he played for a 9:00 P.M. performance by Kreutzberg with his partner Yvonne Georgi.[68] Kreutzberg received praise for his "stark, angular, elegant lines"[69] as the "ambassador to this country of the Wigman principles."[70]

Louis wrote about the handling of music by these "German visitors" in his column for *The Dance Magazine,* referring to Friedrich Wilckens's music for *Revolte* and *The Angel of the Last Judgment.* "Although constructed on a sound and interesting rhythmic basis, these compositions are essentially dramatic, graphic, objective, [and] contain no sustained melodic line." Of the use of Satie's third Gnossienne for a duet, *Persian Song,* Louis quietly reminded his readers that *Trois Gnosiennes* had been used frequently by American dancers, including Martha Graham for her "well-known" *Tanagra.* Rather than praise Georgi's *Mazurka,* he also told his readers that all modern dancers had Scriabin on their programs. The Germans' approach to music was not really different from that of most American creative dancers whose ideas were "conceived first and then the music is composed jointly with the dance."[71]

Mention of Louis's German heritage diminished as his pro-American stand became more obvious; creating a pure "American" dance rapidly became his personal battle cry. But privately he savored the "unity with variety" notions he had gathered from Wigman and from his Goetschius primers, badgering his colleagues to follow these dicta, but toward originality. A self-typed document found among Louis's papers translates a fragment of her writing. Headed "The Idea" and "The Theme," it begins, "The danceable idea one generates always from a heightened life feeling [and] manifests itself in a number of small, intimately connected movement parts (motifs)," and continues, "The intrinsic parts of a dance composition are the theme; its development and variation; structure (of the whole); dynamic, nuance, ornament. Structure is systematic arrangement. The structure of a dance grows out of the demands of the theme."[72] These notions he soon applied to his own teaching.

But for Louis, a more subtle influence in the wide array of cultural crosscurrents was the work of the Spanish composer Federico Mompou. His music gave the dancer "space" in which to move, Louis felt. It enhanced movement without dominating it. The magical qualities of Mompou's *Cants Magics* suite intrigued him, replicating in sound the wondrous primitivism of Chagall and Picasso. Playing the piece as accompaniment for Graham's solo of the same name for the January Booth Theatre concert, Louis had been struck by the music's simple patterning of a few notes. For the next concert Graham gave at the Booth on 14 April 1929, he repeated a few bars from an old French song, producing the same quality for *Heretic*, a collaboration that would herald the arrival of a more definitive style. Leaving timed, long pauses between sections to suit Martha's attacking gestures and loose-hair swings, he allowed no dynamic change from repeat to repeat as the simple melody reinforced the unison walks of her newly formed group of women. By the seventh repeat, insistent and grave, the solo figure ended the work lying prone on the floor, her raised fists visibly losing their power and becoming limp. *Heretic* was Graham's first attempt at using a large ensemble of dancers; her occasional setting of movement on a trio of women to offset her solo performances had not inspired a sense of ensemble dancing.

Louis's musical choice was the precursor of a minimal style fifty years ahead of its time and so was Martha's use of a group of women. In retrospect she confessed, "I wasn't trying to shatter anything—I only sought to build. I wanted life to pass through me as best it could. And I felt I had to find something that was true for me to dance about."[73] The work represented a significant new direction for Graham and Horst. He had encouraged Martha to work as boldly as the German dancers who had caught attention in the States, and he wanted his score to enhance the choreography's drive, allowing the movement to speak for itself. Claiming "the austerity of *Heretic* [as] a product of a time when she was herself regarded as a choreographic dissenter," Louis said that although they encountered "scorn and opposition," it was his firm belief that Martha had created a work of "unusual variety and scope."[74] Mary F. Watkins, on second impression, would call the work "a tremendous, almost overpowering emotional achievement."[75] John Martin, too, would retrospectively praise *Heretic* as "tremendously dynamic . . . one of the finest compositions of the entire Graham repertoire."[76] At the time of its first production, however, admirers were scarcer than dissenters.

Touring was to become an important part of Martha's and Louis's work together as concert artists, but in 1929 the only dates they managed to secure came through personal contacts at the Bennett School in Millbrook, New York, and Smith College in Northampton, Massachusetts. Martha put together a more cost-efficient solo program, and its appeal began to attract a special audience. These "educated" viewers were a far cry from Denishawn's vaudeville audiences. The Humphrey-Weidman Company also began to find isolated dates for which Louis willingly conducted. After a New York City concert at the Guild Theatre on March 31 that premiered one of Doris's finest works, *Life of the Bee* (accompanied by Louis and Pauline Lawrence, who blew into combs covered with wax paper), the company traveled to Philadelphia for a performance at the Academy of Music.

The last letter Louis would receive from his mother arrived while he was on tour. Shortly before setting sail on a cruise to South America, she wrote (in German) complaining of a constant cough. On a brighter note she said that her financial situation was secure. If he was concerned about his mother's failing health it was not apparent in his actions. He increased the dizzying pace of his concert work — his way of avoiding conflict. He noted in his diary that on 10 March 1929 his mother died on a steamer off the coast of Central America and was buried at sea. "A peasant woman given a burial at sea! Can you imagine?" he remarked to a friend. To comfort Louis, who fell into an unusual state of melancholia over his mother's death, Martha presented him with a puppy. They dubbed the brown dachshund Max (pronounced with a German "a" — Mox). Man and dog became inseparable.

Louis returned to his "working" vacation at the Perry-Mansfield Dance Camp — the kind he continued to take every summer for the rest of his life. As musical director for the eight-week session Louis taught Music Appreciation: The New Relation. In her book *Dancers on Horseback: The Perry-Mansfield Story*, Lucile Bogue describes Louis's boundless energy: "Tennis was his game, and when he was not at the keyboard or with a class, he was on the courts. He was always accompanied by his lively little dachshund, who doubled as a ball retriever. The only difficulty with this pleasant arrangement was that the dog refused to relinquish the balls and raced around the court with the overweight Louis puffing along behind in futile chase. But the Camp's greatest laugh was at the dachshund's custom of trotting along the paths under the belly of Socrates, Kingo's [Charlotte Perry's] Great Dane. The little dog had found a fine moveable shade from the bright Colorado sun."[77] Martha visited the Dance Camp at the end of the season. Louis's single journal entry that summer marked her arrival. "She went [to Santa Barbara] and on her way back she stopped off at Steamboat Springs for a day or two and then we went home together."[78]

When Harald Kreutzberg and Yvonne Georgi returned in autum 1929 Louis was at the keyboard. "She did some solos herself. They did solos and duets. Kreutzberg didn't speak any English. I had to translate everything. I played about forty concerts for him, and on the road for three or four weeks."[79] Gertrude Shurr was at Martha's studio when Louis played rehearsals for Kreutzberg and Georgi: "It was amazing. May [O'Donnell] and I would sit in the other room and we'd listen. . . . Louis would play music that was loud and ferocious, and then all of a sudden so soft. I couldn't wait until the rehearsal was over. I rushed over to Louis to say, 'What did they do in the loud music?' and Louis would say, 'Georgi never moved on the loud music. She only moved on the quiet music.' Oh, I was so mad!"[80]

Kreutzberg had a profound effect on many others, including José Limón, who later exclaimed, "What I saw simply and irrevocably changed my life. I saw the dance as a vision of ineffable power."[81] Even Louis saw this concert as a highlight of that dance season. If Gertrude and May were not privy to what went on in rehearsals, Martha was filled in with detailed descriptions after each session. She would soon refer to the German dance as "nearest to us of all, dangerously near."[82] Her own work was now strikingly similar in style and content to that of Kreutzberg.

A few days after Kreutzberg's concert with Georgi, on 24 October 1929, "Black Thursday" at the New York Stock Exchange shook the nation and a downward tumble of America's economy began. Yet artists working at the end of the twenties in New York survived without much change in their daily lives. In fact, some of them believed that the economic depression opened up opportunities to perform in Broadway theaters, as producers happily rented their "dark nights" to dance groups for the extra cash. "As artists, our way of life didn't change. In ways it was easier for us than most. It was much more exciting than now, partly because we're so blasé. But this was new, and it was a vibrant time."[83]

Ten days after the crash, on 7 November 1929, the opening of the Museum of Modern Art in the Heckscher Building at Fifth Avenue and 57th Street (its location until March 1933 when it moved into a five-story limestone townhouse at 11 West 53rd Street) was a great social event for New York's artist community. The museum and the Whitney Eighth Street Gallery became regular haunts for Martha, Louis, and their students.

Louis's frugal existence with Martha dwelt almost exclusively on their art-making, according to Shurr: "All their energy, it seemed to me, was spent on either rehearsing or teaching enough to get money."[84] They lived modestly, with few expenses save an occasional good meal. Nevertheless, Louis saved the largest sum of money of his lifetime during this period, recording $5,736 in his account. Others on the vaudeville circuit had bought houses or invested their earnings and lost them in the crash of '29; Louis had simply saved his money. He maintained a balance of $2,000–$5,000 for the rest of his life.

chapter five

1929–1932

"At the crossroads."

— *Martha Graham*

oncert dance reached its pinnacle in Germany's Weimar Republic when Robert Musil's book *The Man without Qualities,* the film *The Blue Angel,* and the Brecht-Weill collaboration for the opera *The Rise and Fall of the City of Mahagonny* stirred its artistic climate. The dance theorist Rudolf von Laban had recently been appointed ballet master at the Berlin State Opera. In contrast, early twentieth-century American dancers — Loie Fuller, Isadora Duncan, Ruth St. Denis, Ted Shawn — had had to struggle for recognition in the United States, where vaudeville, variety shows, and musical comedy reigned. Martha wrote in a carefully penned essay, "Seeking an American Art of the Dance":

> As a result we have had a dance of "appearance" rather than a dance of "being" — instead of an art which was the fruit of a people's soul, we had entertainment. Interest in the dance as an art of and from America, is new — even to dancers themselves, fettered as they have been, together with the general public, to things European. . . . Although she may not yet know it, America is cradling an art that is destined to be a ruler, in that its urge is . . . creative rather than imitative.[1]

Remarkably, it had taken Louis and a handful of his dance colleagues less than a decade to erase their vaudeville past and place their art in the concert hall. It was Louis's intention that this new dance should be as honest and spartan as possible. His stance was that modern dance must not be a popular art. The endeavor must remain as purely conceived as a poem, he said repeatedly. He seldom approved any sacrifice of integrity and continually discouraged dancers from going to auditions, no matter what monetary rewards were promised.

With the exception of German exponents in expressive dance, Louis acknowledged that choreography was still a subordinate theater art in which the arrangement of ballet steps dominated, and he took on the challenge of changing that attitude. He understood why Igor Stravinsky's 1910 score for *Firebird* defied choreography, and why intention was lost through Diaghilev's collaborative models. Even Lincoln Kirstein had to admit that "Beginning with *Petrouchka,* Stravinsky did not compose music to accompany the dance, but to direct it."[2] Music should enhance and sustain the dancer's medium rather than control it. Choreographers must create their own vocabularies to lead rather than follow musical accompaniment.

While ballet's penchant for frivolous subject matter and lack of substance disturbed Louis, Martha's confrontations with the ballet world created a more perilous threat. "It is a question of purpose, an attitude toward itself as an art, rather than exploitation of any given style or form,"[3] Martha soon learned, after surviving historic encounters with famed Diaghilev Ballets Russes choreographers Michel Fokine and Leonide Massine.

Armed with translations both literal and figurative of German artists' philosophies, Louis found himself in a position of authority. Half amazed, he also learned that he was an organizer who could generate productivity. In a life measured by seasons and now semesters, once settled into the Hotel Great Northern at 118 West 57th Street, with its special $21-a-week rate for theater people, he looked forward to the challenge of his fall 1929 teaching commitment at the Neighborhood Playhouse. The school's catalogue listed his course as Music Applied to Movement for the study of the "origins of musical forms and the development by the students of rhythms in individual movement and original dance patterns." Using Arbeau's 1588 book *Orchésographie,* Desrat's *Dictionnaire de la Danse,* Ardern Holt's *How to Dance the Revived Ancient Dances,* and John Playford's *The Dancing Master* as primary sources, he first instructed his students to investigate and reconstruct authentic steps of these early dances.

Anna Sokolow, a student then, recalled that "He played the music [of Blow, Handel, and Bach] and analyzed it to a point — the rhythm, how many bars to the theme and so on. We had to learn to listen to it that way. He didn't [have the] answer. We had to find out for ourselves. Then he had a rhythmic approach where we had to analyze the form and structure of the music, making us aware of how important it is for the choreographer to be musical."[4] Gertrude Shurr added, "You could work with the counts lyrically or dramatically, or with social content, like a tone poem, just use the music as accompaniment, or discard it."[5]

During this period Arnold Schoenberg began to teach fundamentals of music composition in California. He often quoted Brahms and Goethe: " 'A good theme is a gift of God' and 'Deserve it in order to possess it.' "[6] Toward their separate goals, Horst and Schoenberg took these Teutonic principles from their German predecessors. In a manner "both simple and thorough," Schoenberg taught the three-part song form, theme with variations, and various rondo forms, with assignments designed to construct themes, motives, and phrases to show "the greatest number of methods of solving problems and explaining them systematically. . . . Only acquaintance with a wide range of possibilities gives the student enough freedom to meet the unique problems which each individual composition poses," he believed, asking for "certain aesthetic essentials, such as the clarity of statement, contrast, repetition, balance, variation, elaboration, proportion, connexion [sic] transition — these and many others are applicable regardless of style or idiom."[7] Louis may have deviated to the extent of teaching actors and dancers rather than musicians, but other aspects of his pedagogy were nearly identical.

Having to devise a new course for his returning students at the Neighborhood Playhouse, Louis "just brought them modern music. I'd bring in and we'd do Bartok for a month and Hindemith. I read a lot about modern painting . . . and developed my modern forms."[8] By grouping the cyclical phases of art history styles and trends, as curators were beginning to do, he compared the visual images in art with dance by analyzing the various elements of composition in painting. To the study of primitive as a background of modern art he added the linear style of Egyptian art, which became the resource for his "archaic" dance study. He sent students to the Etruscan collection at the Metropolitan Museum, and then in the classroom they reproduced the angular lines on their own bodies, moving from one precise design to another. As a musical parallel he chose Erik Satie's *Trois Gymnopédies* for accompaniment; its use of Greek rather than tonic and dominant modes, as well as its slow tempo markings, created an unusual sense of linear tension.

At the Playhouse, voices and bodies were trained through group instruction. Professional actors and directors who, like Martha and Louis, also happened to teach conducted their classes in an intense environment. Using a conservatory approach, the students' individual needs were developed within the context of classroom teaching. As a trained musician guided by master teachers, Louis taught as he had learned, coaching on a one-to-one basis: "I would say to the actors, 'Yell with movement, or whisper with it. Men, you must speak physically, not only orally.' "[9] He then devised specific compositional assignments that demanded invention as well as practice.

Now a familiar figure in Manhattan's dance studios as well, Louis smoked his cigar in the hallway between classes, exchanging jokes with the dancers as they played with his dachshund, Max. During more sober moments he preached Nietzsche's "glorious prophecies . . . for an untrammeled dance" of "strong, free, joyous action." He spoke of Isadora Duncan as "almost as misunderstood as Nietzsche, [she] revolutionized the world of the dance and all arts which touched the dance,"[10] amused his rapt audience with stories about Miss Ruth, and commented on the fresh relationship between dancer and musician he was exploring with Martha. Under the piano in an open valise during classes, rehearsals, and sometimes even performances, his well-behaved companion (the only obedient dog he ever owned) curled into a ball and slept through everything.

In his monthly magazine column Louis summarized the "vital" developments "as exemplified by the German school and, more recently, here in America," as reaching "heights of abstraction."[11] In 1929, when Martha Hill returned to the city after two years of college teaching, she saw a complete change in Graham's work toward a powerful new abstraction. John Martin, too, observed the "passion and protest" that burned "with the slow and deadly fire of the intellect," noting that her work dealt "more and more in essences. . . . She boils down her moods and movements until they are devoid of all extraneous substances and are concentrated to the highest degree."[12]

It seemed that as Graham's reputation grew, Louis tended to remove himself from the limelight, Hill observed when she began dancing in Martha's group: "Louis, as the male, was the organized one, whereas Martha's femaleness of being charming was a little bit wanton, and going her own way, with Louis pulling her back."[13] From the perspective of a half century, Agnes de Mille declared that of all Martha's advisers throughout her long life, Louis was the "most sane, never lending himself to the vagaries and hysteria of spite, vanity, or paranoia. Emotionally he was clean and openhearted."[14] Selflessness, calm nerves, and perhaps his maturity kept most situations he found himself in manageable.

In fact, it took an inordinate amount of energy to keep up with his pace. Martha Hill often found him practicing at the keyboard when she arrived at the studio. The demanding scores he played during the 1929 season would have been a significant undertaking for any pianist: selections from

Serge Prokofiev's *Visions Fugitive,* Alexander Gretchaninoff's Sonatina in G, and scores by Paul Hindemith, Tibor Harsányi, Darius Milhaud, and Julien Krein for Martha's programs as well as music by Ernst Toch and Aleksandr Scriabin for Hans Wiener's "movement chorus," and Richard Strauss's symphonic poem *Ein Heldenleben* for a Neighborhood Playhouse production. *Heldenleben*'s cast included Graham and Weidman in the pantomime and dance sections; Louis called their performance unforgettably beautiful.

De Mille described the pianist's manner during performances: "He arranged the instrument in the wings so that he had a clear view of the stage, hanging his coat over the back of his chair and playing in waistcoat and shirt sleeves. When everything was over, he put on his coat for the bow at the end, and then took it right off again and packed it."[15] Although he regularly concertized with de Mille, Page, and Strawbridge, accompanied technique classes, taught, and made *The Dance Magazine* deadlines, his daily schedule always ended in late evening rehearsals with Martha and her company of women.

In the studio Louis soon matched Martha's angular designs, achieved through percussive force from the torso, with equally jagged, percussive rhythms at the keyboard. She used two parts of speech, according to the dancer Bonnie Bird, "verbs and adverbs."[16] The spatial considerations so basic to Wigman's movement did not interest her. Martha searched instead for axial actions — arching, spiraling, whipping, and pulling against gravity — for dramatic and emotional effect. "The floor is a direction," she rationalized. "When you are very upset . . . you have a sinking feeling inside you. So as a dancer I showed on the outside what was happening on the inside — my whole body sank or fell to the floor."[17]

For a while the group rehearsed in Edith Isaac's apartment. Isaac, the editor of *Theatre Arts* and one of Graham's first supporters, had written, "Only real genius can withstand the rigors of the life. If this is true of the painter, the poet, the novelist, it is doubly true of the dancer, who must use himself as the material for his own experiments."[18] She offered her town house on Central Park South for Graham's rehearsals in luxurious surroundings convenient to the Carnegie Hall studios. During this period Lillian Shapero joined the company after being recommended by Horst, whom she had met while taking Ito's classes, and Dorothy Bird came from the Cornish School. According to Hill, Martha approached each session with the "spirit of experimentation." As a group, they sought "inner feelings" and improvised with "sounds, words, intensities of emotion, and qualities of energy. . . . Once movement possibilities were explored fully, Graham abstracted them to an essence and gave them form."[19] Hill recalled working on movements based on an idea suggested by Graham: "She started probably eight or twelve different things—very exciting for us because she'd let us improvise—we'd play around with these ideas. Finally, come January, Louis said, 'Here! We've got a date at the Guild Theatre, Martha. You've got to set one thing and finish it. Now, come along, which thing are you going to do?'"[20] Martha complied.

"If any one in dance could raise money for their art, it was Martha,"[21] Hill said, thinking back on Graham's early success at cultivating backers. Gertrude Shurr agreed, adding, "Once Martha was going to meet Otto Kahn (with Doris and Tamiris) to ask about money. Martha didn't even have a coat. I had a cousin that was a furrier, and he gave me a little fur coat that I loaned her!"[22] Just before Thanksgiving 1929 Martha gave a solo concert for the MacDowell Club dance series in Manhattan and assembled a demonstration for a Jewish benefit, the Junior League, and various art clubs and high schools. In a fund-raising effort, she then used these materials for private showings for interested backers and booking agents. One of these took place at the Roerich Museum, attended by Leopold Stokowski, his wife Evangeline, and the artist-designer Nicholas Roerich. Roerich and Stokowski were preparing for a spring production of Stravinsky's *Le Sacre du Printemps* for the Philadelphia Orchestra and although they did not think Graham had enough experience to handle the choreography they wanted her for the principal role of The Chosen One. Graham accepted without hesitation, appreciating the chance to perform with such an illustrious group. But more crucial to her personal aims, she needed the income to produce her own work.

Clearly, more performance opportunities were needed for these modern dancers if America "cradled" an art destined to rule. De Mille calculated that the cost of a self-produced concert was about $1,200 before rehearsal or costumes expenses. A more conservative estimate, according to the concert manager Frances Hawkins, was that $900 would pay for theater rental, accompanist, management, advertising, printing, and stagehands. By the early thirties the only dancer who could cover expenses with ticket sales was Martha Graham.

It was Helen Tamiris who felt that, as recitalists, they must join forces to create a producing unit for modern dance. Louis was her co-founder of the first Dance Repertory Theatre for modern dance, a "first attempt to organize and bring before the public the American dance in its various aspects. It was a very vibrant period—very historical because we tried to get together. It kept me busy! I was playing for all of them, going from Martha Graham's studio to every other."[23] Bessie Schönberg, then dancing with Graham, observed that although it was Tamiris who gave stimulus to those productions, she could not have succeeded without Louis's help: "He was trusted by all. . . . I don't think anybody would have danced without Louis playing. He was very important."[24]

When the choreographers — Humphrey, Graham, Tamiris, and Weidman — planned the week of shared concerts, scheduled for Maxine Elliott's Theatre 5–12 January 1930, skepticism ran high. Humphrey confessed that "It has seemed necessary for us to incorporate, and of course I hate that idea because organization has come to be such a hateful thing. They simply organized the life out of Denishawn. And besides I haven't much faith in Martha Graham. She is a snake if there ever was one. In spite of all misgivings, it is the best thing to do — the thing is to be ready for double crossing."[25]

But Doris and Helen knew that Martha's participation was essential. A newspaper article had already suggested that with the exception of Graham, this band of modern dancers lacked "showmanship." Even Martha, "artist as she is, could not fill Town Hall to standing room capacity, for she has not this quality. Her work means just about as much to the layman who sees her for the first time as the pure form of a Cubist, if that,"[26] the critic believed. This prevailing attitude had to change.

As musical director of the series (a de facto title; he played for each group anyway), Louis was especially helpful not only in convincing the somewhat reluctant Graham to participate, but also, as John Martin noted, because he was the only pianist these dancers trusted: "Strange as it may seem, the same Louis Horst is called into service by about 3-quarters of the recitalists in New York." And Martin added slyly, "To protect themselves from each other they have thus appointed him as musical director of the organization."[27] Since he had composed two works for the program he asked that the Dance Repertory Theatre program identify him as "Composer — Pianist," a title he preferred from then on.

Louis had little competition as one of the few male authorities in music for this new American dance. An efficient conductor for dance, his inclination to take charge, ability to keep an accurate tempo, and insistence on seeing the same thing twice helped the scattered, understaffed choreographers who not only performed, but also acted as costume and light designer, rehearsal director, and general manager for their own work. He understood this new breed of dancer, and he saw each performance through to its last chord. Then, hurrying to another rehearsal or performance, often he would not bother to wait for a curtain call before he was out in the street hailing a cab. Although Louis's talent as a conductor was only "serviceable" and the quality of the performances by the musicians who played in his orchestra sometimes not very good, he was "an extraordinary pianist and gave the romantic impression of a Brahms or a Liszt," the musician Ruth Lloyd later remarked.[28] In his journal Louis jotted down his long list of commitments in association with the Dance Repertory Theatre, ending with "Jan. 12. 46th Birthday. Too ill with flu to play final concert of D.R.T." Even this true believer in the cause bowed under the pressures of the series.

Soon after, Graham expressed her view about the venture:

When the Dance Repertory Theatre was formed . . . there arose intense criticism of the esthetic purpose of the organization. This criticism was made blindly, not in realization of the fact that the very freedom existing, the lack of similarity, and the frank pride in that lack is its safeguard artistically. The Dance Repertory Theatre was established as a theatre where the dance as an art was the focal point. . . . It has produced and been produced by five or six individuals distinctly American in type, . . . It has stung a public into protest and curiosity, . . . it has created the need for dance critics on all the leading newspapers; it has fired musical organizations.[29]

If this group of personalities benefited from the joining of forces, it was Graham who fared the best with the press. *Heretic* from the previous season now received excellent reviews. The *New York Telegram* reported that "cheers and bravos at the fall of the curtain [applauded] . . . the astounding quality of her dancing and her composition," and rhapsodized, "with the assistance of a group of ten, there are those transcendent evocations which bear with them the mark of greatness more unmistakably than any accolade of mere personal opinion could bestow upon them."[30]

For Louis, the highlight of the series, on 8 January 1930, was Graham's new solo to music by Kodaly, *Lamentation*. He called it her "dance of sorrows" and the "personification of grief itself."[31] Delighted with the dance, he wrote about her swaying from side to side at the opening as the kind of "sublimation of a natural movement" he most appreciated. In the same way that some theorists have placed the Bauhaus at the root of Mary Wigman's dances as early as 1920, so could they place it at the core of *Lamentation*. However, Louis and Martha now looked to another aspect of their philosophic guide. Louis had read Nietzsche's belief that "the primitive mind is a one-track mind," and noted that the primitivists used "symbols as the equivalents of the natural, and devise conventionalizations (the faces of Modigliani, the stick figures of Klee). . . . These conventionalizations lead the modern artist to simplicity and unity."[32]

In comparison with *Lamentation* the other premiere (on the January 12 program), which had taken months of rehearsal, resulted in near disaster. *Project in Movement for a Divine Comedy,* a group work based on Blake's illustrations of Dante's *Inferno,* was performed in silence. Although Louis later credited *Project* as Graham's "first and only dance completely without music,"[33] dancer Bessie Schönberg said that in fact a "conductorless" orchestra was supposed to accompany the piece: "When we got together, it didn't work. It was too late. The only thing to do was to let it go on in silence. . . . John [Martin] the next morning in the review . . . spoke of the wonderful chromatic fall of the group. You see, we couldn't go down together because we had to [have a] cue."[34]

A week after Dance Repertory Theatre closed, Louis, barely recovered from a severe bout of flu, joined the exhausted but elated Martha on a train ride south for performances in Georgia, Alabama, and Mississippi. After this brief tour of three college campuses, Louis was back in Manhattan to play his arrangement for de Mille's premiere of *Julia Dances.*

Although Graham's ill-fated *Project* had been criticized by the *New York Herald Tribune* as "dangerously close to a modernist's Delsarte"[35] and was soon dropped from the repertory, the experience further convinced Louis that in order for music to frame the dance rightfully, it must be composed after the dance materials were set. He also realized that what Graham needed for accompaniment was very different from what he felt was right for de Mille. With characteristic savvy he had learned to suit the individual style of each dancer with whom he worked. De Mille's choreography was definitely balletic, with a sanguine sweetness he matched in his scores for her. "We hardly ever performed these pieces more than once,"[36] de Mille admitted, and Louis, an agreeable collaborator, had no particular interest in preserving the work either. He did, however, appreciate her talent: "Agnes was the comedienne of the dance, doing light things. She was always trying to get a new approach to it. . . . She had [this] one facet of modern dance that was important."[37]

After a return performance at the Bennett School, Martha began an intensive period of artistic battling under Leopold Stokowski's baton in a performing experience that would mean a great deal to her spiritually — the planned *Le Sacre du Printemps* with the Philadelphia Orchestra. This first American staged performance of *Sacre* was to be paired with Schoenberg's *Die Glückliche Hand* (with Humphrey and Weidman as featured dancers) for the benefit of the League of Composers. To be presented in April 1930 in Philadelphia and at New York's Metropolitan Opera House, it was decided that Leonide Massine would re-create his original chore-ography.

Excited about this opportunity to star in the major event of the season, but anxious about her group, Martha asked that her dancers also be hired. Behind-the-scenes battles with Massine, who argued over tempi with Sto-kowski and style with Martha, were constant. She had her own ideas about what created a primitive look. (The desire to be primitive, a "function of fin-de-siècle imperialism," appealed to "strong egos and domineering minds," according to the writer Robert Hughes.)[38] Massine, in turn, was insulted by the arrogance of a dancer who questioned the validity of his acclaimed 1920 masterpiece. Graham related that half-way through one rehearsal "he asked me to resign because he said that I would be a failure. And then I said, 'Did Mr. Stokowski say that?' And he said yes. So I said, 'Well, I'll ask him.' And so I went to him and Stokowski said, 'I don't understand you. What are you talking about? Do you want to quit?' I said no. So I stayed and I finished the performance but I did do exactly as he [Massine] said."[39] According to her dancers Graham gave a "charismatic" performance while "standing still"[40] for a great length of time before the final sacrificial dance.

Louis compared the event with *Sacre*'s first momentous performance in Paris, except that this time, "It cost $15 a seat to see Martha Graham!" He philosophized, "It was modern in the way Matisse was modern in painting, or young Picasso at that time. It hadn't taken in what I call the freakish aspects of modernism — the avant-garde, the real bizarre."[41] Martha called this production a turning point in her life: "Somehow one identifies oneself with a central figure; you perform a sacrifice, whatever it is, and whether it's your life or whether it's giving up the extraneous things of your life for a purpose — for the necessity — it's a sacrificial act."[42]

That spring Louis had his own, if less dramatic, panoply of professional activities. Among them he "conducted trumpets backstage" for *Pagan Poem*, Irene Lewisohn's stage version of a symphonic poem by Charles Martin Loeffler, after Virgil; played in the orchestra for her *New Year's Eve in New York* production with music by Werner Janssen (both featured Graham and Weidman); and accompanied recitals throughout the season given by de Mille, Wiener, Jean Börlin (a Swedish dancer), Humphrey and Weidman, and Strawbridge. Strawbridge evidently relied on Louis for more than accom-paniment. "I had to tell the stagehands everything." Responding to a review that mentioned his "uncommon power and understanding," he quipped, "Well the curtain wouldn't have gone up without me!"[43] The Humphrey-Weidman Company's lecture-demonstration, which included a new score by

Dane Rudhyar, received a scathing review from the Cleveland *Plain Dealer,* but their pianist fared better. The review, "Modernism runs away with Dance," ended, "It must be said of the pianist Louis Horst, that while he had some pretty terrible music to play, he played it extremely well."[44] Good reviews or bad, Louis thrived in a dancer's world. In fact, he was delighted that the threat of "modernism" was now evidently visible in dance.

When Martha accepted a ten-week contract at the Cornish School in Seattle, Louis played for her classes for the first five weeks before his return to Perry-Mansfield. Louis's recollections of playing for Martha for a special performance celebrating the school's fifteenth anniversary centered mainly around his dachshund: "I had Max with me and he sat right at my feet on the stage, so Martha took him out for one of the bows. He didn't mind, and he didn't howl when he heard music."[45] While in Seattle, Louis carried out promotional chores on Martha's behalf, arranging interviews with the press, suggesting to students that they must study with her in New York City, and strengthening their association with Nellie Cornish, director of the school.

A writer for the Seattle *Post-Intelligencer* called Graham "one of the country's foremost exponents of modern expressionism in the dance," and quoted her as saying, "Through the creation of theatres exclusively for dancing, the art is coming into its own and an American style is being perfected."[46] In the one brief season that had passed, Martha had realized some of these artistic goals and had emerged as a major figure in the field. At the end of their separate assignments, Martha, who had been visiting her newly remarried mother in California, met Louis for their first adventure together in New Mexico's Indian country.

The trip had been prompted by Dane Rudhyar, who considered Graham the major influence on "the entire field of the modern dance in America" (to Humphrey's chagrin) and would speak on her behalf whenever possible. The *Plain Dealer*'s culprit "modernist" composer had written a note to Mabel Dodge Luhan in Taos, introducing Martha as "a fine dancer" and a "marked Mongolian-Amerindian type . . . planning very interesting things on her own account."[47] Martha had once mentioned to Rudhyar that she was moved by Luhan's article on the Southwest, "A Bridge between Two Cultures," as a source for a "theatre of the new culture."[48] Graham was convinced that "a clear accent" had to be placed on what she called "the consciousness of country . . . something akin to a folk condition of truth from which to begin. Once this narrow but firm base was established emergence could follow."[49] Writing poetically about the Indian's "intense integration" and "sense of ritualistic tribal drama," Graham loftily proposed that the answer to the problem of the American dance for "individualists who point the way is, 'Know the land' — its exciting strange contrasts of barrenness and fertility. . . . From it will come the great mass drama that is the American Dance."[50]

In an all-out effort to know the land the couple began their study with fervor. Louis wrote in his journal, "Met M. [in] Albuquerque. Visited Pueblos at Isleta, San Felipe & Santa Dominigo; then drove to Santa Fe, N.M. for the Fiesta. Saw Indian Dances at Armory. Trip to Taos. Left Santa Fe." Although their sense of mission toward a "neo-primitive" style was avidly pursued at this point, they had not actually considered drawing ideas from the American Indian as a part of their cultural heritage. But when they visited the religious sect of the Penitentes in the Sangre de Cristo Mountains, this unforgettable experience provided a new inspiration. Kin to the Aztecs, the subject of Shawn's *Xochitl,* the mysterious Penitentes, with their incongruous mix of Hispanic Christianity and Southwest Indian thought, fascinated them. Winthrop Sargeant wrote that they found fresh impetus: "A new mysticism crystallized, and was to furnish [their] future work with a central core."[51]

Back in Manhattan for the 1930–1931 season, Martha found an apartment at 46 East 9th Street. Her teaching and rehearsals continued at what "we called 'the dancer's building.' Tamiris lived there and the puppet creator, Bil Baird, lived on the top floor with his wife," Ralph Taylor recalled.[52] At one end of Martha's studio a curtained area served as a dressing room for her dancers, with sleeping quarters with bare necessities one floor above. According to Taylor, who was her only male student at that time:

> She lived like a pauper in that brownstone. She had one of those shower units with no curtain. I used to rush at the end of class to the shower before twelve girls got there. Even that didn't help sometimes. I remember being in the shower one day, and in walks one of the girls. "I'm awfully sorry Ralph. You'll have to get out of the shower. I have a date." I'm standing there wondering where I can find a fig leaf! That was the kind of life we led then.[53]

Satisfied with hotel-living, Louis's studio apartment had the luxury of a grand piano, a bed, and a respectable address for lessons and music rehearsals. With little time or interest in total relaxation, he did have a particular fascination for the history of America's wars. He attended auctions regularly, looking for Civil War memorabilia and American stamps and coins for his collection. He studied maps of Revolutionary War battlegrounds, even tracing the exact fields on foot whenever he could. But baseball was Louis's major preoccupation in summer months. He listened to every game broadcast on the radio and scheduled outings to the ball park to see his favorite team, the New York Yankees, with whomever would join him. Occasionally it was Martha: "She saw Babe Ruth hit a home run!"[54] "He was endearing and fun," Martha remarked, adding that they also went to bantamweight boxing events and track meets. "He liked anything that was physical, that had to do with the vivacity of the moment."[55]

Louis's passion for action also revealed itself in his love of mystery stories. Although Martha and Louis lingered over their art books, and he occasionally delved into his volumes of American history while she read poetry and the writings of Carl Jung, the bulk of his fast reading centered on pulp thrillers.[56] He propped them up on the music rack and read them between dances or cues. If he read thrillers in private, in public he discussed the latest exhibition, or poet, or music review. (He and Martha regularly clipped articles and filed photographs from the Sunday *New York Times* for future reference.) And when he talked of books in the classroom, he referred to art books.

The couple regularly attended music recitals on the lookout for usable scores, afterward going for a meal at the Carnegie Tavern. "Once in a while she'd be down and she'd want to go to a movie alone. She'd come out [of the movie] and ring me up. I'd meet her someplace and everything would be alright. We always went for breakfast at a French place on 13th Street."[57] Together they went to more formal occasions, often attending Edith Isaac's supper parties to meet illustrious guests.

The day after Christmas 1930, Martha and Louis were invited to a special tea in Mary Wigman's honor at the Plaza Hotel, an important event for these dance professionals. Favorably impressed, they would soon be less enthusiastic about the competition they foresaw when Sol Hurok, Wigman's theatrical agent, announced the opening of the Wigman School of Dance in New York City with Hanya Holm as its head. (Hurok did not consider Graham a marketable artist until 1946, when he finally agreed to arrange a national tour for her company.)

During the next years Wigman's Laban-based dance style became a point of contention as they all struggled for more exclusive control of critics and performance opportunities. Martha's sensitivity to the competition of German dance artists grew as the press plagued her with questions such as, "How much or how little [have] Miss Wigman's innovations influenced you?" Pressed by an insistent interviewer, Graham wanted to answer that question once and for all: "Mary Wigman, through her greatness as a person and as a dancer, has given us all an added courage. The comparison of the dances, I am afraid, between Mary Wigman and myself must be left to others.

The modern dance in America, however, was firmly grounded in its own way before Mary Wigman came to this country. . . . The American dance today is in no sense German," adding as an afterthought, "Neither Doris Humphrey nor Charles Weidman nor myself have ever been to Germany."[58]

But Louis had been to Germany, and his enthusiasm for its expressionist artists was well known. Ralph Taylor commented, "They couldn't ignore this tremendous thing that was coming out of Germany, but Martha was a very original being. Her work was quite essentially different, and grew out of the fact that this was America and that was Germany — the same thing as if a composer like Shostakovitch is compared to our American composer Copland."[59]

One of the surest ways to prove separation from past influences was to claim a new inspiration. At this point in their careers these mature artists had absorbed a variety of ideas from other sources. "We had duller art in the twenties. Nothing at that time you'd call avant-garde. They were still sticking to the towline — the ship — they didn't divert from the ship and go off in a . . . new tangent. But [in the thirties, it] was a complete new thing."[60] If congenial to Wigman's dance of expression, and genuinely interested in supporting her theories at first, Graham and Horst soon realized the importance of dissociating themselves from her ideas. Although John Martin continued to praise Wigman's heroic stature and "likened her works to great sculptures of antiquity suddenly breathed into movement,"[61] within the New York dance community resentment toward anything German was becoming more evident.

Graham's work, now energized by the strength she found in the rituals of the Southwest Indians, was totally unrelated to Wigman's Gestalt theories. Martha preferred the angularity of the body, the cupped hand, the right angle of the elbow, adopted from Native Americans and entirely divorced from German dance in which, according to André Levinson, "emotion determined form," and expression alternated "between agonized ecstasy and a bitter romantic irony."[62] Graham's newest methods for creating movement were more closely bound to the paintings of Georgia O'Keeffe than to the arcs and fall-rebound actions of Doris Humphrey. Louis recognized that "it was the naive but powerful simplicity of primitive people that provided the desired vigor and directness. . . . Primitive art has been by far the strongest distinguishing influence for all the moderns."[63] In this, Martha was no exception.

It can be argued that her new inspiration was not entirely original in concept. As early as 1925 Ted Shawn had visited some of the same pueblos in New Mexico and wrote about them in his diary. Shawn's 12 January 1925 entry reads: "Visited Pueblo of Isleta. . . . Most wonderful dance — about 60

Indians in full regalia performing dance ritual to persuade the sun to re-turn."[64] Although some discussion among Denishawners must have taken place about Ted's visits, directness was a persistent leitmotif in Louis's think-ing. Louis drew Martha into the aesthetic aspects of Native American art, rather than suggesting that she replicate it, as Shawn had done. Once authen-tic materials were understood, a freer approach was applied—just as Louis had done with pre-classic dance forms. Martha had begun to focus on the abstract motifs of this art in her search for native subject matter. Her earth and airborne images would be matched by Louis's concern for breath and chanting, strict repetitive structuring.

On Louis's visits to art galleries around town, including Stieglitz's "291" on Fifth Avenue, he watched for new painters. He admired, and collected over time, the work of Arthur Dove, Marsden Hartley, George Grosz, and John Marin—artists who sought fresh ideas and aimed to be "characteristi-cally American." He respected these painters' "back to go ahead" theories and their concern for a "native" expression in an "abstract spirit." Ideas developed by the anthropologist Franz Boas, one of the first to insist that primitive works *were* art, interested him, as did Picasso's "magical inherent power," so much like tribal art in style.

Impressed earlier by Friedrich Wilckens's rhythmic percussion and un-rhythmic melodies for Harald Kreutzberg, and Hans Wiener's use of the drum, Louis began to consider the piano a more percussive than melodic instrument. Together he and Martha discussed each volume on primitivism that came into print, filling notebooks full of references; as Martha translated these ideas into danced ideas, Louis translated them into sound scores. Looking back he wrote, "Paint went onto the canvas straight from the tube; music became more percussive; the dance moved with a conscious awkward-ness; writing grew more terse, more abrupt."[65] He had long relished the innocent qualities of Erik Satie and Paul Klee's "child-cult" primitivism, art that was functional and "above all simple and direct."[66] Martha redefined that expression as "divine awkwardness." The Southwest Indians walked from their hips, Louis observed, with little articulation above the shoulders: "The hands and feet tend to remain clumsy and not useful . . . far removed from the careful technical delineation and intent of the ballet dancer whose every movement is carefully selected and precisely approached."[67]

Stravinsky had earlier claimed the "vivid qualities of primitive art" for a new aesthetic and Massine's Russian mode of primitivism was absorbed by Martha as she worked in *Sacre*. Louis's collection of Bartok's compositions based on folk motifs pointed him also in this direction. The American Indian gave the couple an indigenous American root they needed for inspiration.

Martha's new choreography for her chorus of women, *Primitive Mysteries,* used accented, flexed-foot walks like the repetitive steps in a Southwest Indian circle dance. The spatial designs were as angular as the patterns of the Two Grey Hills Indian rugs the couple collected while in New Mexico. "Come down into the earth with your heels!" Martha coached her dancers. "Walk as if for the first time."[68]

Casting herself as the solo figure, she divided *Primitive Mysteries* into three sections — "Hymn to the Virgin," "Crucifixus," and "Hosanna." The three parts represented the solo dancer's "joy, tragic grief and exaltation." In Louis's support of Graham's choreographic intention his music had to "enrich" the dance and not influence its creation in any way: "Dance is an independent art, and its motivation should be the feeling of the choreographer, not of the music. . . . *Primitive Mysteries* was a dance without music." First he notated the counts, adding:

> I took the flute and oboe and had them play in unison on the pentatonic scale throughout. No drums. In the interludes between each one of these phrases I used religious chords on the piano, and I used [different] kinds of scales and melodies. I never studied authentic American Indian music before I wrote *Primitive Mysteries* . . . I didn't need to. There isn't one authentic Indian note in that score! . . . It was a revolutionary score. The simplicity [was] the thing of it, because I never heard a score like that. It was something I got from the dance.[69]

Louis wanted the music to be as poignant as the chief's chant at the start of a ceremonial dance. He then alternated episodes of modal harmonies and broken, rhythmic melody to suggest the contrast of Catholicism and paganism intended by Graham.

He replied to questions asked by a Juilliard student about his preference for woodwinds, "The tone of the woodwinds seems to be more expressive of the character of the modern dance — the strings remind me of the court ballet," and about his use of dissonance, "The combination of modern movement and diatonic scale melody produces a sentimental effect. Besides, who writes in the diatonic scale today?" Using the pronoun "she" years before equal rights outcries, he continued, "We are now at a period where the dancer dominates — as she should — and has grown to be absolutely independent. She does the dance and creates the rhythm for it. She then gets a composer to write the music upon the form she has created. Naturally this will make the music secondary. The music is the frame to the picture. It is only an assistance to the dance, but that assistance is very important."[70] Walter Terry, however, gave Louis equal credit as "an explorer and experimenter like Martha herself. . . . The music for Martha's *Primitive Myster-ies* . . . sounded new and avant-garde, but the structures were solid and proven."[71]

But it was Graham who received final acclaim for the work as a whole, whether Louis had mentored the project or not. To answer the question "What is the procedure in creating your dances?" she reiterated Louis's words, confirming her dependence on his ideas:

> The dance comes first. In all cases except two or three dances in my present repertoire . . . the dance has been finished in its entirety; its rhythmic patterns and tempos set before the music is written. The composer then comes, sees the dance performed and builds his music structure on the dance's rhythmic pattern. I think that it is important to state that the dance does not interpret the music; the music is a setting for the dance.[72]

For Louis *Primitive Mysteries* achieved his description of a good score as one that "should have the transparency of primitive music so you can look through it and see the dance."[73]

The composer David Diamond later observed that "The composer of dance music must have the whole work in mind," and called the music for *Primitive Mysteries* one of the most flexible dance scores of recent years. He analyzed its construction: "He has seen the big phrase of the line and move-ment of the dance and has adapted it to his type of musical movement so that both work together."[74] Shrugging off such compliments, Louis had an honest opinion of himself: "I am no genius. I just took a few ideas and . . ."[75] This admission hints at his self-effacing nature, subservience to Martha's work, and reluctance to interfere with her deserved success. But his influence was soon felt as other composers followed his formula for working with dancers. One of them was Wallingford Riegger.

Louis became a composition student of Riegger's for a brief period. Be-fore long Riegger found himself composing scores for dance as well: "I went backstage to become one of a line waiting to shake [Graham's] hand. . . . She asked me to consult with her about music for a new dance, *Bacchanale.* When I arrived at her studio I found to my surprise her dance group assem-bled and ready to perform for me the already completed dance." He imme-diately admired her ability to abstract ideas: "I became party to nearly the first attempt at writing music to a dance already composed — I say nearly for at this time Louis Horst was writing music for *Primitive Mysteries.*" It seemed to Riegger that every gesture had an organic element, never for-malized: "She is a true apostle of the 'modern' in doing away with the fripperies of a bygone age, stripping art down to the essentials. If this process has taken place in the other arts, it was Graham's world contribution to accomplish it in the dance."[76]

In the weeks preceding the opening night of the second Dance Repertory Theatre season on 1 February 1931, Louis had received word of his brother-in-law's death and had himself fallen ill while accompanying de Mille at a private party in Delaware (Martha had to go and get him). But he was there at the Craig Theatre as music director for the first downbeat, and the gifted choreographers around him were the benefactors of the seeds he had talked of sowing in his letter to Miss Ruth from Vienna five years earlier.

His remembrances of this period were vivid: "I was just a boy of forty-seven. . . . Doris opened the series with *Shakers*. Pauline learned accordion just enough so that she could get the chords to sound like a poco organ — the little organ they used in country churches, and she sang the blatant hymns. I'd be standing back there, and occasionally I'd say, 'Amen,' or 'God bless you!' Then she'd hit a high note and I would say, 'Hallelujah!' " Helpful as he was throughout the series, the closing bill on Sunday, February 8, originally planned for the evening, had to be rescheduled as a matinee because of a conflict in his schedule: "I had to go over and play for that old Strawbridge!"[77]

This second series of concerts established a kind of artistic supremacy among the participants of the small dance world, with *Primitive Mysteries* its unanimously acclaimed masterwork. In a way the premiere signaled a kind of cultural colonialism for dance, with New York City as its capital. Insofar as Dance Repertory Theatre made an impact, it was Graham who reaped most of the benefits. One critic wrote that "Of all the modern dancers at that time it was Graham who dominated the scene and exerted the greatest influence, if for no other reason than that she was the most glamorous figure and the strongest performer."[78] Of Martha's two premieres to specially composed music *Bacchanale* received little attention, while *Mysteries* was immediately labeled innovative and original. They had created their own *Le Sacre du Printemps*.

Later, Louis's recollection of the Dance Repertory Theatre seasons was one of seeming equanimity, but without doubt the highest praise was reserved for Graham. He pronounced matter-of-factly that "after Wigman . . . the members of the newly organized Dance Repertory Theatre (Martha Graham, Doris Humphrey, Charles Weidman and Tamiris) are accepted leaders."[79] (His omission of de Mille is interesting here.) Although Louis had managed to apportion his rehearsals with each of the five choreographers, tempers flared and the tight rehearsal sessions were difficult because each company presented premieres as well as repertory pieces on programs that changed every night. But again, in the irreplaceable pianist's mind the series was a success:

> There was really repertoire. There were no jealousies. There was competition, yes, but no jealousies. . . . John Martin was particularly enamored by Tamiris's physical power. You know — the attraction as a woman. She was of the people — always to the left, and did protest dances, things like that. Tamiris made *Sound of Liberty* using Negro spirituals. Not much subtlety but a lot of vim, vigor, and enthusiasm. . . . Doris was of the more classic — doing Grieg concertos. Doris and Martha were more in one line. Martha was more dramatic and Doris was more purely choreographic. They were always going in one way together, but in their own way. . . . Martha didn't bother much with the rules of composition [as] Doris did. She didn't need them with me around, naturally. She always had shape to her things.[80]

Unfortunately the mixed reviews for Dance Repertory Theatre's joint concerts further eroded the already fragile relationships among the dance artists themselves and dampened any thoughts of continuing this cooperative venture. Marc Blitzstein's sharply worded criticism recounted factors that led to the demise of the second (and last) of the series. He wrote in *Modern Music* that Tamiris — whose generous notion it was to establish these programs in the first place — possessed "a definite lack of intelligence. . . . However, Martha Graham was the dancer-choreographer to get excited about. . . . Graham is fanatical, which is good. . . . She goes deeply into mysticism with an intensity at once ferocious and brooding. . . . Even her lighter dances adhere beautifully to this fixed path." He continued, "I liked best the *Primitive Mysteries*. . . . It was perfect in conception and perfect in projection."[81]

Blitzstein noted acidly, "Everybody stepped pretty generally on everybody else's toes. . . . What critical acumen survived traveled in the direction of comparisons. One evolved a whole set of them: Humphrey treats choreography as music, Graham treats it as plastic, Tamiris is most of the things de Mille is not, and a great many of them are bad."[82] The returns at the box office were excellent, but an irreparable schism had developed among the artists themselves. As a result these choreographers chose competitive independence once and for all. The brief idealistic hope for a united front ended abruptly.

Another dance event in 1931 provoked a great deal of anger and controversy. John Martin and Louis served on the advisory panel for a lecture series that the composer Henry Cowell had designed to help promote modern dance. Cowell, already established as an internationally known figure in music, had begun his long association with dance—one that had many ties with Horst—as pianist-composer for Humphrey's *The Banshee,* premiered 15 April 1928 at the John Golden Theatre in New York City. His 1919 book, *New Musical Resources,* and his journal *New Music Quarterly* founded in 1927 reiterated his belief in experimentation of sound. As a composer and friend, he continually entertained music's potential when paired with dance.

Martha and her group were, of course, on Cowell's series, held at the New School on West 12th Street. During the usual discussion following their lecture-demonstration, a confrontation between Graham and an audience member who turned out to be Michel Fokine erupted. Louis reported that "the renown[ed] ballet authority [said] 'Miss Graham, you must admit that this modern dance is ugly,' and she answered with hasty disregard, 'Yes it is, if you're living in 1890.' Fokine went there with the idea of heckling her," he believed,[83] and on Martha's behalf he was insulted and enraged.

A New York Russian-language newspaper, *Novoye Russkoye Slovo,* published Fokine's angry letter in rebuttal, a translation of which, "A Sad Art," appeared in the May 1931 issue of *The Dance Magazine,* much to Louis's chagrin. Fokine argued that Graham's philosophy for dance was unnatural and ignorant of dance history. Forced to defend their ideas in an artistic arena they had so recently claimed, Martha and Louis grew militant. She said, "I didn't know I was talking to Fokine," adding decisively, "We shall never understand each other." To this Fokine replied, "I understand and love art of all the nations, no matter how remote, and of all the times. It is strange that I should not be able to understand the art and theory of Miss Graham."[84] In Martha's defense Louis insisted that Fokine had misunderstood Graham's meaning when she described the special movement quality she considered necessary, even in a formal bow.

Spurred by the Fokine incident, an all-out battle was about to be waged between the ballet world and its allies and the modern dance contingent led by Graham and Horst. Louis had long believed that this new form of dance needed its own set of philosophies and goals. As a professional he had maintained unbiased relations with ballet choreographers, but his sympathies were clearly for the moderns. Critics who favored ballet as their chosen dance idiom were in the majority, and Martha had made enemies of both Massine and Fokine, who saw her as a rebellious and difficult imposter.

Edwin Denby, who would soon become the poetic darling among dance writers, struggled to accept Graham's "highly intelligent pieces" and her "particular genius," although he himself had a German performing background rather than a traditional one in ballet. As he saw it Graham used "heaviness and oddity [in] a complete system of her own. . . . Miss Graham's gesture lacks a way of opening up completely, and her use of dance rhythm seems to me fragmentary. It does not rise in a long, sustained line and come to a conclusion. I find she uses the stage space the way the realistic theater does, as an accidental segment of a place; not as the poetic theater — as a space complete in itself. And I do not feel the advantage to dancing in these qualities of her style."[85]

Reactions such as this were prevalent and increased Louis's concern that Martha would continue to be misinterpreted. One critic who felt that "the whole activity was episodic and without cohesion," said so in a *Dance Magazine* article, only to receive an angry letter of protest from Graham and Horst, in which they banned the reviewer from their performances. The reviewer replied in the August 1931 issue of the magazine:

> Miss Graham is permitting herself to grow peevish. It is a bad sign. I was deeply honored when she notified me that I was not to be permitted to enter her theatre. How could she ever expect me to deny myself the pleasure of seeing her? Try and keep an old newspaper man out of anywhere he wants to go. . . . Nor is Miss Graham the only one to grow peevish. There is a gentleman [pointing to Horst as the only male presence in Graham's company] who is angry with me. [I fear for] the welfare of the dance as a virile masculine expression.[86]

Perhaps a more accurate appraisal than some realized, Martha did demand an ascetic atmosphere, which some observers saw as verging on martyrdom; she surrounded herself with her group of dedicated women. Louis *was* the only male on the scene, save a few irate boyfriends and husbands of dancers who waited in the wings. But others were very excited by the female dominance of her dance company. "This female fortress had an Amazonian look. . . . Quite wonderful. The girls were substantial," Ruth Lloyd recalled.[87]

Typically, Louis had been diplomatic in his vigil over Graham's image, but this time references to his "harem" vented full-blown anger. *The Dance Magazine* had begun in any case to lose favor in the modern dance community. Its editors, in an attempt to stay afloat during financially difficult times, were fostering "yellow" journalism with a more flamboyant, gossipy style of reporting. Furious because his cause was now receiving the brunt of the criticism, Louis dropped his association with the magazine and concentrated instead on his busy schedule of composing, conducting, and performing.

Along with the growing number of New York concertgoers, who appreciated this vigorous new dance scene, other voices made themselves heard as well. One European writer offered his view that Graham and Horst had little cause to worry about their battle with European dancers. Musing at Wigman's American success, *Der Tanz* critic Joseph Lewitan complained that "It would not be the first time that something becomes fashionable in America as soon as it is 'passé' in Europe, and that one is 'crazy' over there for things that have outstayed their welcome here."[88]

A busy schedule of other activities occupied the couple that spring. They traveled to Scranton, Pennsylvania, for a performance at the Century Club in March and then toured for a week with Blanche Yurka's production of *Electra,* for which Louis was musical director-composer and Martha choreographer-dancer for the dance sections. He conducted the Cleveland Orchestra for a Neighborhood Playhouse production and accompanied Ruth Page and her company in performances of *Story of a Soldier,* staged to Stravinsky's *L'Histoire du Soldat*—one of his favorite scores.

With "original" dances choreographed by members of Martha's group for a New School course, Arts Related to the Theatre, Louis put together his first of many lecture-demonstrations. In his usual pedantic style his journal entries mention only dates, places, and practical duties: "At Wash., D.C. Rehearsals for N. P. Production of Bloch Quartet at Library of Congress. Gave light and curtain cues for N. P. Production at Kaufmann Audit," and he noted a weekend trip to the country with Martha to visit Portia Mansfield and "Kingo" Perry.

In June, after a special showing of Martha's dances to Cecil B. de Mille at the Heckscher Theatre, the couple left New York for California. Graham stayed in Santa Barbara, while Louis visited briefly with Betty and May and then traveled to Colorado on his own. At the Perry-Mansfield Camp that summer he composed eighty-one short "musical settings," planned for September publication by Fischer and Company as dance accompaniment for the classroom. He also organized his weekly music lecture-demonstrations.

At the end of the summer Martha and Louis returned to Santa Fe and the Indian environment they loved, this time as guests of Mary Austin, an early authoritative writer on the Native American. Her books—*The Basket Weavers, The American Rhythm,* and *Earth Horizon*—spoke of the "pulse of emerging American consciousness" drawn from the Zuni and Oraibi-Hopi Indians, whose culture demonstrated the "new earth" from which the American dance must grow.[89] Martha and Louis had been inspired by her words.

Austin placed her charming cottage at their disposal and arranged their daily visits to the neighboring pueblos. Louis's journal began on 30 August 1931: "Met M., Visited Jemez and Zia Pueblos, To Acoma Pueblo. Saw Ceremonial Dances and Religious Procession. Also visited Lagune Pueblo. Trip to Tesuque, Santa Clara and San Juan Pueblos. Also Puye Cliff Dwellings. To San Ildefonso Pueblo for 'Butterfly Dance.' To San Domingo Pueblo for part of 'Pine Dance.' "

In a letter to a friend Martha confessed that her life was changing: "The first night I arrived here I saw an Indian blanket, a Navajo — in a window. It was woven in natural colors of the sheep, white and brown and black — in stripes. On the ground of it were two crosses — one at each end — in red. It means — 'at the crossroads.' It was very prophetic — I was at the crossroads." She goes on to describe the dance ritual they attended at the Santo Domingo Pueblo:

> I arrived when they were dancing. I heard their voices and I rounded the corner of an adobe house in a narrow street, to enter the plaza — and saw them — one hundred men in a straight line — dancing and chanting. . . . The chanting was low, deep, intense. The faces of the men pure and fanatical and beautiful as gods. They danced in perfect unison — for no one. They danced to generate the magic for rain, good crops, and fertile land and people. There were about six visitors — that was all. It is difficult to describe — but nothing I have ever seen or dreamed of equalled that great communal dance ritual in earnestness, intensity, faith in the eternal recurrence of natural phenomena — such savage ruthless awareness of life. It was the most pure holy ceremony. There was not only great soul — but the sense of form was also moving. They are so wise and such great artists.[90]

Martha's introspective references are singular and intensely personal. For Louis, his experiences in the Southwest would be the happiest moments of his life with Martha — ones that he never tired of recalling.

Upon their return to New York they found waiting a letter from Lehman Engel, another composer interested in collaborating with dancers, requesting a meeting with Martha. "After several months of fruitless pursuit I was at last given an appointment to meet her and her accompanist, Louis Horst, at the latter's apartment. At the designated time, I rang the doorbell, received no reply, waited an hour, then went away." Weeks later another appointment was kept. They listened intently to his music and promised to collaborate. Engel, a Juilliard student whom Louis affectionately nicknamed "noisy sunshine," called the experience "among the sublime moments of my young life."[91]

Engel began his work with Martha under Louis's influence, which Ruth Lloyd described: "Louis tried to get anybody that wrote for Martha to have the same feeling about it that he did. He was very stern and rather difficult, but he managed to get Lehman to write a different kind of music than he ever wrote for anyone else."[92] Engel's own account confirms this:

> Martha created most of the choreography in advance of my seeing anything. . . . I would comprehend an overall mood, write down the counts, notating phrases or accents or climaxes or places where we agreed there should be silence. . . . Then [she would] dance to it, counting and listening at the same time. Here she felt there were too many notes. (I would thin them out.) Here the music should sustain while she moved, or the music should move rapidly while she sustained. Always there had to be complementary interaction. Much of the most concrete work was done in the final week and even on the day of performance — in an atmosphere of terror.[93]

Engel described the charged atmosphere before the Guild Theatre premiere of *Ceremonials* on 28 February 1932 in much the same way others had described the charged prelude to *Primitive Mysteries:*

> She decided that the girls' costumes were not "right." She herself sat on the floor and cut, fitted, and pinned together new ones for the waiting seamstress. The next morning, she had a bad cold, and several of her girls were ill from exhaustion. At the lighting rehearsal in the theater, Louis spoke so sharply to her that I feared she might collapse. I spoke up, begging him to be less harsh. He smiled, confiding that at these times Martha might "fall apart" if he let her alone. He had found that by quarreling with her, making her fight back, she kept her spirit and energy up and would not then stop.[94]

Louis put it another way, "When she's down, she gets what the Irish call 'the glooms,'"[95] for which he had found various cures. The finished work was a "fun dance," according to May O'Donnell: "The piece wasn't a religious dance, except it did have a ceremonial quality. . . . But it was a much freer dance than *Mysteries.*"[96]

Lehman Engel's playful influence was the exception rather than the rule at Martha's studio. Tension had become a normal condition in the creative lives of these artists. The rigors and controversies of the past five years had produced varying degrees of success. Graham approached her thirty-eighth year more mature, yet continually moody and self-doubting. Louis dealt with her temperamental outbursts with resolute calm, and privately and artistically "governed" her. She later confessed, "When the music is finally there, it's just as though I hadn't done anything. I have to start over and do what the music says."[97] As musical director Louis assumed final authority in all musical matters, as he had with the Denishawn company; in their personal life as well she usually did what he suggested.

De Mille described an incident after a long rehearsal of *Ceremonials*. Having dismissed her dancers, Martha disappeared into her sleeping quarters. Wanting to speak with her, Agnes waited for almost an hour before Louis suggested that they might go to her:

> In the center of the bed was a tiny huddle in a dressing gown. The only visible piece of Martha was a snake of black hair. Every so often the bundle shivered. Otherwise there was no sound from that quarter. Louis droned on through his nose, "Now, Martha, you've got to pull yourself together. . . . You can't do this. I've seen you do this before every concert. You're a big enough artist to indulge yourself this way, to fall apart the week before and still deliver on the night. But the girls are not experienced enough. You destroy their morale. You tear them down. They're not fit to perform." . . . Without showing her face or moving, Martha whimpered, "The winter is lost. The whole winter's work is lost. I've destroyed my year. This work is no good." "It is good, Martha," said Louis persuasively. "It is not good. I know whether it's good or not. It is not good." "It may not be so successful as "Mysteries" — whimpers and thrashings — "but it has its own merits." . . . "One cannot always create on the same level. The Sixth Symphony followed the Fifth, but without the Sixth we could not have had the Seventh." . . . "One cannot know what one is leading into. Transitions are as important as achievements." "Oh, please, please leave me alone," begged the little voice.

Martha refused to budge, and after dressing both himself and Max for a brisk winter walk he complained to Agnes that it was just not worth the struggle with Martha:

> "Every concert the same. . . . She's put us all through the wringer. She destroys us." "But, Louis," I said, pattering after and peering up and around his coat, "she is a genius." He snorted. "Would you consider working with anyone else?" At this he stopped. He slumped down layers of himself to a thickened halt. "That's the trouble. When you get down to it, there is no other dancer."[98]

Ralph Taylor witnessed similar scenes. "Louis was a strict task master. He wouldn't let anybody get away with anything, including Martha. He'd get Martha so mad. She'd get her Irish up, and the nearest thing that was available she'd grab and throw at him. I was there in the studio one time when she grabbed the flower pot and threw it at him. She missed him by inches. . . . Louis accepted it very quietly. He'd walk away or he'd leave."[99] Louis himself admitted that "She'd kick up scenes and I'd always have to go [to her] and say, 'Well, what's the matter? Is there a funeral here?' To snap her out of it."[100]

Graham's anxiety over *Ceremonials* may have been well founded. The work was her most structurally complex to date. Its three sections and two interludes, again exploring motifs from the Southwest, relied on her dominant presence center stage. She had inspired her devoted ensemble of women with her stunning creativity and had taught them not to separate the technical and intentional aspects of the movement. Deeply inspired by Graham's artistic vision they "breathed as one." Recalling their intense relation to the couple on a personal level, Bonnie Bird remarked, "We were their children."[101] For Louis as father figure, "taking care" of Martha and her dancers had become a top priority during this difficult 1932 winter.

Politicians' pledges to remove bread lines had little effect after several years of deepening depression across the country, yet artists managed to continue their frugal existence with little concern for material needs. The women who constituted Martha's group were drawn in consultation with Louis from her best students. They found part-time teaching to pay for their rent and went home to their families for a square meal whenever they could. "We didn't have enough money to go to the theater or take trips much. But socially, one could still have a rousing good time."[102]

The dancers' consensus was that Louis understood all when he offered stern advice "about how we could get a lot of lovers and become much more freed artistically by shenanigans like that. He recommended it. He hated virgins and said so."[103] He strongly believed that artists should live together and knew that Martha had her share of admirers. Nevertheless, among these many women Louis belonged to Martha, and she relied on him emotionally and financially. Ralph Taylor recalled "a time when I went into this small room to get dressed and I knocked a book off of a chair. Out came a receipt for a dress for $125 from one of the important department stores. At that time $125 would be like $10,000 today, so I know Martha did spend money on herself. But for her money had no value, of course. . . . I'm sure Louis supported Martha's endeavors financially. Very much so."[104]

When the Graham company performed at the National Theatre in Washington, D.C., on 22 January 1932, *The Washington News* printed a photo of Horst as composer of "music especially designed for Martha Graham. [He has written compositions for] all others." At this point, "all others" included Weidman, Humphrey, Bolm, Page, St. Denis, and Shawn. Returning to the Guild Theatre for a performance on January 31, the company then traveled to Florida and South Carolina for concerts during the first week of February. Preparations for a lecture-demonstration at the New School and a second Guild Theatre performance on February 28 added to the physical strain. Louis left to perform with Ruth Page in Havana in the middle of February, then returned to accompany Humphrey and Weidman for their March concert at the Guild and arrange music for de Mille's *Orchesography* for a MacDowell Club performance.

This jumbled schedule undoubtedly interfered with the flow of rehearsals for Graham's offerings for the second Guild concert. Although she did not produce the anticipated sequel to *Primitive Mysteries,* the company's repeated performances of that work sustained critical attention. After fulfilling concert dates at the recently established Washington Irving High School Dance Series and at Jordan Hall in Boston, Louis and Martha again presented their Neighborhood Playhouse students in a program of dances.

Still, his calendar of events showed other concerns: "Feb. 1–2. Max gone all night. Miss Deerfield found him. Guild Theatre, Feb. 28. M.G. Mar. 6. De Mille, 13, Doris Humphrey, 20, M.G., 26, M.G. Apr. 3, M.G. Apr. 21. Alla and Lani [puppies] born to Mädl [Martha's dachshund]."

The prior fall Martha had applied for a grant from the John Simon Guggenheim Memorial Foundation, a process no doubt strengthened by her collaboration with Aaron Copland, the most promising composer in New York. Copland had been agreeably surprised when she asked for permission to use his new Piano Variations to accompany a solo, *Dithyrambic.* "Martha had heard someone play it at a modern concert, so she made an appointment with Aaron Copland at his apartment. . . . She asked if he minded if she used it. 'No, I'd love it, but you mustn't cut it.' The whole thing was sensational. I didn't particularly like the dance, but it was a real tour de force and made a terrific impression."[105] Copland's response was that he "was utterly astonished that anyone would consider this kind of music suitable for dance. It was my introduction to Martha's unusual and innovative ideas. That season we were much talked about and praised, although her choreography was considered as complex and abstruse as my music."[106]

Martha received the Guggenheim Fellowship in spring 1932—the first ever given to a dancer-choreographer—on the merit of her significant innovative work. She made arrangements to use the $800 grant for three months of study, beginning in Mexico. Louis helped to organize an itinerary. He planned to accompany her for six weeks of vigorous sightseeing before returning to the Perry-Mansfield Dance Camp. They embarked aboard the *Morro Castle* on June 18. Typical of Louis's lifelong preoccupation with record-keeping, his chronology identified Graham's "Guggenheim" activities as they sailed to Havana and on to Mexico. They visited Aztec ruins, churches, temples, monasteries, and pyramids as well as Agricultural and National Dancing Schools. In Mexico City they had tea with the composer Carlos Chavez.

At the end of July Louis returned to Steamboat Springs, while Martha visited her mother. They joined again on September 1 to revisit the pueblos of New Mexico. His journal describes with the same orderly notation the ceremonial dances they saw; it was evident that this briefer excursion dwarfed the Mexican one: "M. arrived. Visit to Pueblo of Laguna (Met the Stokowskis). To Acoma Pueblo for ceremonial dances. At Albuquerque, N. M. Saw Midnight ceremonial dances at Isleta Pueblo. Corn dances at Leta Pueblo. At Santa Fe, N. M. (La Fonda Hotel.) Fiesta. Saw 'Los Matachines' dance. To San Ildefonso Pueblo for Corn Ceremonial Dances. . . . Sept. 12. At New York City. 63 E. 11th St."

Louis savored every aspect of his vacation in New Mexico with Martha — one that reinforced his passionate enthusiasm for everything "Indian." His intense love of Native American culture did not so much mold his attitude toward the arts as confirm it. His inclination for a simple, "lean," duty-bound life found its parallel in the adobes he admired, giving strength and purpose to his daily life. From now on he would draw his romantic vision from the cultural roots of the Southwest.

chapter six

1932–1936

"We were famous as a

team." — Louis Horst

A s pianist-composer and teacher, Horst's lived experiences served as his resource; to the dancers surrounding him, his omnipotence was assured. He had blended the high standards of his early classical training with his work in raucous West Coast entertainment houses and the theatrical extravaganzas of Denishawn, and developed confidence as a Renaissance man out of this eclectic background. After years of vaudeville and concert tours nothing surprised him: he had "seen it all." He had lived through thousands of performances and been a still center in the vortex of dance history. He had seen Pavlova dance and cheered on baseball's San Francisco Seals. He had nursed St. Denis's and Shawn's every choreographic whim, surviving their disasters and successes for ten years. Although this way of life was plagued by endless train rides and untuned pianos, it fulfilled his need for variety.

Having witnessed the influx of German dance expressionists, Louis had literally translated their ideas into a working method for Denishawn's rebellious "children" and seen their growth as American artists safeguarding his theories of musical accompaniment. This background allowed him to support their maverick ideas without preconception, and he saw to it that those ideas got "on the boards." In conversation he continued to mix sophisticated with mundane remarks, and offered perceptive, acutely poignant observations, to the delight of his colleagues.

The corpulent musician was now forty-eight years old, and enjoyed his emerging reputation as mentor. He had gained admiration in theater, music, dance, and education circles as a teacher as well as concert pianist. Many were awed by his uncanny ability to attract beautiful women; his position as confidant to the exciting Graham contributed immeasurably to that aura. Students felt privy to inside information when he made passing references such as "Martha once said . . ." with an authority that let them know he was speaking firsthand. While his sense of mission continued to lead others in an all-out effort for dance as a bona fide art form, Martha was to be its chosen head. It was no longer necessary to take a stand, as he saw it. When asked for a public statement, the notion of score-writing for dance and the Graham name usually entered the conversation.

Louis functioned in each role he undertook with efficient good will. He had little cause to complain — he was doing what he wanted to do. His status had even begun to stir remarks from abroad; the London *Star* quoted Agnes de Mille saying that she considered him "to be the most dominating personality in the present dance renaissance in America."[1] And the figure he "dominated" was Martha Graham. "We were famous as a team. It got to be Martha and Louis for everything. . . . We always went together."[2] Anna Sokolow echoed him: "Louis and Martha were together. Always."[3]

Of the two, it was Graham who secured a firm position in the American theater. Robert Sabin wrote in retrospect, "Until the middle 1930's [Graham] . . . adhered, by and large, to an austere style in which every element was . . . stripped to [its] bare bones. Then, having created a technique that she could use with security in any framework, and having purged herself of the superficial pettinesses of the past, she was ready to come more closely to grips with the dramatic and theatrical aspects of dance."[4] He gave Louis credit for insisting on that "austere style" that gave "security in any framework."

In return Louis enjoyed his position of unchallenged rule in Graham's all-woman company. Privileged and in the company of artists like himself, who had escaped the humdrum of ordinary lives, Louis had a tendency to procrastinate when it came to work that required solitary concentration, such as composing or practicing. His activities were self-governed — a state few of his contemporaries managed to attain. He enjoyed relative good health and was able to keep in perspective the constant tensions created by deadlines, performances, and conflicts among personalities.

Although content with his prominence as a one-of-a-kind musician, Louis hoped that others would join this new profession he had helped to fashion:

> I should say broadly that I am a musician who is interested in music insofar as it is related to dance, and not dance insofar as it is related to

music. . . . Just as there are virtuoso pianists, and pianist accompanists who developed with the concert singer, so with the dance there will develop the composer-accompanist. . . . Music . . . serves not only to limit, to accentuate, to confine, to deepen the dance choreography, but specifically to discipline the very plastic instrument of the dancer. The body is not the simplest of instruments. Music is only in a manner of speaking, a frame . . . it enters more directly and is much more a part of the composition. The only relevant question is . . . "Is music good for the dance?" In Germany such compositions go under the general heading of Gebrauchsmusik, functional music. In the composing of music for dance, it should be specific music for a specific choreography, to begin and end with it.[5]

In the same interview, Louis summed up the logic behind his later establishment of a dance periodical and his concentrated support of choreographic efforts. It was crucial for potential choreographers to know principles of composition; it was time to pronounce the validity of dance within the academic world:

Modern dance as yet has no literature that is not historical or inspirational. We have histories and polemics and panegyrics and poetry, but no studies in form, composition, etc. It is very easy for the musician to procure all sorts of theoretical works, but the absence of this same type of material in dance literature has caused me to use music as form examples (parallel examples) . . . for anything but formal compositions. In a sense we are returning music to dance from which it originated.[6]

As Martha's musical director Louis began to influence other composers in a "ruthless and demanding and utterly patient" way, asking for scores that displayed "the right melodic inflection or rhythmic nuance," according to the composer Norman Lloyd.[7] Having played some of the earliest performances of scores by Edgard Varèse, Ernst Toch, and Arnold Schoenberg, Louis gained the respect of those interested in the modern dance as a potential outlet for composing. Gradually these composers would go their separate ways, but while they were under Louis's guidance Graham profited from their talents for the next few years. "They were of a different ilk," Ruth Lloyd said, "seeking awards and prizes. They had their own composing business to uphold and they managed to have more influence on the dance world than people in Louis's time." For all Louis's outward reverence for innovators such as Schoenberg, he never really embraced their methodologies in his own musical writing. Lloyd conjectured, "Maybe those advanced theories never made sense to Louis in terms of sound. He really favored the diatonic for dance."[8]

Louis had become a seminal figure in the establishment of choreography as an artistic endeavor, and sharing the bill with Graham as her musical director, concert pianist, and composer, his career was at an apex. Together they had ascended in art circles by creating their own kind of concert performance: modern dance was not to be a popular art; the artist must not compromise. Graham's work, through his determination, must continue to use technique to abstract content. He monitored her movement patterning with fierce concern for good form. Development of materials must include handling themes with repetition as well as fragmentation, in compositions that must be "sensibly matched, evenly balanced" where "the form is good."[9]

In his classroom he used these objective means to achieve a subjective end, methods that his surviving texts do not illustrate. Schoenberg was using in his own teaching atonality as a means of ridding romantic notions of melody from his system of precise ordering, away from the organizing factor of a tonal center. This means echoed those of his painter friend, Vassily Kandinsky, who refused to abide by "traditional" techniques on canvas. (Some people agree with the writer Robert Hughes that today's avant-garde has become "swollen in excess claims for itself." If he were alive today Louis too might agree, but at the time he doted on theories of abstraction as the structural foundation for art-making, and intellectually, at least, believed that rules were made to be broken.)

Louis enjoyed the pronouncements of Klee: "One must know a great deal and be able to do a great deal, while creating the impression of its being innate, instinctive. . . . Modern art is a free art and refuses to live within any boundaries."[10] Like Klee and Schoenberg, Louis knew a great deal and taught a great deal to preserve and inspire freedom through modernism. If for him there were distinct differences between concepts of modernism and avant-gardism, he still upheld the Utopian view of "Tomorrow's world — today," to be heralded as the New York World's Fair motto in 1939.

After their return from the New Mexico Indian fiestas, Louis and Martha resumed their full schedule and prepared for another concert season. The most productive and emotionally satisfying time of their "turbulent and delicately balanced relationship"[11] would continue to the end of the decade. Ralph Taylor marveled at their working partnership, recalling their late-night preparations for three out-of-town engagements.[12] These were tryout dates for the program to be presented at the Guild Theatre on 20 November 1932. The composer Hunter Johnson, who saw one of those out-of-town performances, remembered that "Everything about her struck me as being . . . intense and concentrated. Her mind, her emotions, her body, her motion, the spareness and starkness of her dance motion, everything about her . . . was of terrible intensity and originality at that time. It was unlike anything I had seen before."[13]

Graham's new work for this program was *Chorus of Youth — Companions,* to a new score by Louis. Referring to the "sheer driving power of her personal art," John Martin wrote, "Martha Graham opened her New York season at the Guild Theatre with another of those stirring performances which her audiences have come to expect . . . [filling] every seat in the house and bringing forth more than once, whole-hearted cheering."[14] May O'Donnell appeared with the company for the first time in this work: "It was a little less stark than the primitive pieces like *Primitive Mysteries* and *Heretic.* But it was a transitional piece. Of course that was a period of political unrest. . . . Martha wasn't really basically political but she had a sense of that and she would incorporate in her works much of that feeling. At the same time it was still pure dance. . . . You had to contribute. . . . She was very astute. . . . She watched us very carefully."[15] Martin's review did register a formal complaint about the awkwardness of the title, but then praised *Chorus* because "It dares to go so far from the precincts of abstraction as almost to have a plot. . . . Here for the moment, Miss Graham has turned her back on the primitive and ritualistic and has recaptured something of the mood of her 'Adolescence.' Louis Horst has composed a delightful musical setting, which was played by a small orchestra under his direction."[16]

That fall Louis received his share of complimentary notices, one critic calling him the "pianistic patron of the dance,"[17] a phrase Martin changed to "the perennial pianistic patron saint of the dance," adding, "Louis Horst knows more about dancing than dancers."[18] He was not above receiving unfavorable notices, such as those for concerts with Ruth Page and with Sydney Thompson, a singer he sometimes accompanied (this unfortunate evening not only reminded him of the fickle nature of the theatrical world, but also dampened his reputation as a vocal coach and accompanist).

Martha was invited to perform with her group in the "inaugural" program for Radio City Music Hall (an honor of mixed blessing for those who remember the chaotic circumstances surrounding the occasion). Louis wrote "original music especially created" for the resulting work, *Choric Dance for an Antique Greek Tragedy: A Chorus of Furies.* Returning to a music hall environment brought Louis's career full circle, but with a difference. Rockefeller's 6,000-seat theater in mid-Manhattan represented the epitome of showmanship as presented by "Roxy" (Samuel L.) Rothafel. With this invitation, modern dance came of age. With its art deco flamboyance, revolving stage, giant orchestra, and ability to show motion-picture films, Radio City Music Hall synthesized the glorified American vision of entertainment, in which dance had now joined.

The opening-night bill on 27 December 1932 also included Ray Bolger, Harald Kreutzberg, and the Wallendas in their high-wire act. Martin was again there to praise Martha's work and report that *Choric Dance* "proved an extraordinarily fine piece of work; in fact the only number that did justice to the magnificent stage upon which took place some four hours of first-night effort."[19] But the Graham company did not reach the sacred "boards" until after midnight of that over-scheduled opening night. By then the house had emptied of all but the staunch few. Ralph Taylor's wife, Sidney, was in the Radio City performance, but he had to admit, "Some critics the next day said they all looked like little ink spots. The stage was so tremendous. It didn't extend itself very well."[20]

Although the opening of this extravagant palace for the lively arts created much ado, audience turnout was unexpectedly poor. With over 200 performers, including the corps de ballet, full orchestra, and the famous line dancers, entrepreneur Rothafel (who suffered a heart attack days after the opening) was forced to scale down his production. Graham was dropped from the bill, but her stubborn supporters, who believed that she must be represented in this new artistic enterprise, continued to arrive each evening for the run of the show. Martha Hill recalled, "We diehards made a point of calling the box office to place a ticket order for a theater party. I'd ask when the group would be performing. To the answer, 'Martha Graham isn't on the schedule,' in protest I said, 'Graham isn't on? Well then, cancel!' "[21]

Louis had learned to take such catastrophes in stride. It was all part of the business. Within two weeks the Music Hall's bill featured a movie and a shorter stage show, a formula that spelled the demise of the already faltering vaudeville theater, but filled the 6,000 seats of Radio City Music Hall for years to come.

Theater notables were attracted to Martha's latest references to ancient Greek theater. One, who would prove to be an invaluable friend, was Katharine Cornell. She had sought Louis's counsel in the past, but this time she asked the couple to work on the production of André Obey's *Le Viol de Lucrèce* in January 1933. The Stage Alliance used their talents in a production of *Six Miracle Plays* at the Guild Theatre the following month.[22]

In the midst of profound global conflict, communist sentiment was building among dancers and heated arguments divided political factions. The complexion of the arts was affected by the rallying of manpower in the face of war and the influx of leading German artists who settled in the United

States. Incredibly, the dance press still continued to dwell on the earlier Graham-Fokine confrontation at the New School. Furious that the event had escalated into outrageous proportions, Louis sent an angry letter defending Martha to the editor of the *Literary Digest,* in hope that it would squelch the argument once and for all. It read in part:

> In the May 29th issue of the Literary Digest you quoted from Fokine's version of the now famous controversy between him and Martha Graham. . . . I resent rather particularly the in depth publicity that has been given to Fokine's theory of Miss Graham's work and his quotations of her views of the classical ballet, because they are untrue. Mr. Fokine, who was once a great and daring radical in the world of the dance, has now become so reactionary that he distrusts and fears the modern dancers and is, either consciously or unconsciously, willing to twist Martha Graham's remarks and to misquote her to prove her a fool. I have been advised [to bring] a case for a libel suit against him for his misquoting her, but, partly because of the long and tedious process of law, and partly because Miss Graham does not desire the publicity, I have refrained from bringing the suit for her. But I was terribly annoyed at finding the whole matter brought up again in the Literary Digest. . . .
>
> Martha Graham is pretty shy of publicity and I am always forced to tone down any effort on my part to get her the recognition that is due her, but in the heat of my anger that Fokine's misrepresentation of her should be broadcast by the Literary Digest, I am writing to convert you privately, as I know the Digest does not enter into public controversy.[23]

Louis enclosed a folder of press comments on her work and invited the editor to see for himself that there was no "dark soul" or "cult of hatred" present in her work. *The Dance Magazine,* too, had presented its own "dark soul" theory about Graham in its pages. Perhaps overly sensitive to this recurring criticism Graham tried to balance her repertory with lighter, more dancey themes. Louis himself broadened the spectrum of his scores to include lighter instrumentation, for example, adding the cello, clarinet, and baritone voice in *Chorus of Youth.*

In the spring Louis finished the score for the May 1933 Guild Theatre performance of Martha's completed work *Tragic Patterns — Three Choric Dances for an Antique Greek Tragedy,* with new sections, *Chorus for Supplicants* and *Chorus for Maenads,* added to the *Chorus for Furies.* Swamped with work, he learned that it was far easier to adhere to a prescribed teaching format, as Graham had done in her technique classes, in order to reduce preparation time. Louis began to follow a stricter schedule of assignments for his students and tightened his teaching syllabi. These were influenced by his current work with the musically astute Doris Humphrey on her *Pleasures of Counterpoint,* for which she requested asymmetrical rhythms in an assortment of 7/8, 5/4, and mixed meters.

Anxious to choreograph, May O'Donnell began to study with Louis. "I could see immediately that it was a difficult prospect. He was a musician, and he also knew the trend of the times. . . . He wanted something very clean . . . not overdecorated. Trying to get back to basics because it was part of the trend of the whole art experience at that time. . . . And he was very severe . . . very astringent . . . full of subtraction. You had to subtract a lot of notions like, 'Oh, look Ma, I'm dancing.' He made you think."[24] When Marian Van Tuyl encountered Louis in 1933 she found that "He was convinced that study of the 'rules' of form was essential in order to be able to break them for purposes of expressiveness. Otherwise, it would be like a musician discovering the 'C' scale at sixty!"[25]

After returning to Perry-Mansfield for the month of July 1933 to teach his course Survey and Use of Music in Relation to the Dance, Louis met Martha in Santa Fe, where they began their five-week vacation. As guests staying first with a Mrs. Black, then Mary Austin, and finally Mabel Dodge Luhan, they traveled to every pueblo that held a ceremonial dance. Louis's presence became known to the local press, and a reporter dubbed him the "greatest authority in America on the modern dance and music."[26] His journal noted:

Jemez Pueblo for Corn Ceremony. To San Domingo a few days stay at Mrs. Black's house on Atalaya Hill. (and to a Dr. Barton for eye-operation), a trip with M., Bob & Ethel Walker, Jim & Ellen Loeb to see the "Sunset Dance" at Picuris Pueblo. (staying at Ranchos de Tres Rios. — To Picuris Pueblo for Ceremonial Foot Races and Deer Dance. Return to Santa Fe, via las Trampas, Las Truchas and Chimayo. To Santa Clara Pueblo for Corn Dances. To Zia Pueblo for Ceremonial Dances. To Taos Pueblo, (with M. & Mary Austin) via Chimayo, Cordoba and Las Trampao. Visited a Morada at Cordoba — Staying with Mabel Dodge Luhan. Trip to Walpi. (Ariz.) with M., Bob & Ethel Walker. Saw Antelope Dance. Staying at Indian School. Saw Hopi Snake Dance. Also sunrise race. Aug. 23–24–25. Attended Inter-Tribal Ceremonial, before returning to Santa Fe, for the fiesta at the beginning of September. Then watched the Procession to Cross of the Martyrs, leaving Santa Fe on Sept. 5th.

By coincidence, May O'Donnell and Gertrude Shurr stopped at Flagstaff on their way back east from Sacramento. Hearing that there was to be a trip to Walpi the next night, they rearranged their itinerary in order to attend the snake dances. Shurr related:

> At four o'clock in the morning there were eight cars waiting ready to go over the desert. At daybreak they made a big circle, and had breakfast. At Walpi we climbed up the stairs way up on the top mesa to wait for the dance. . . . Meanwhile [the Indian dancers] were busy combing their hair, washing everything. It was hot. I fainted. After the Snake Dance, Louis and Martha invited us to Santa Fe where we stayed with them in a house belonging to the author Mary Austin. In her front yard was corn growing — all the planting was corn. Behind it was a trail. We'd hear bells of little donkeys as they'd go all the way up, and children would come back with firewood on the donkey's back.[27]

Louis mentions Austin, who died later that summer, in his chronology. Martha and Louis treated their unexpected co-workers with good humor, but insisted that they be on their best behavior: "The bathroom must be left exactly as you found it," Martha solemnly instructed.[28]

For Louis, the fall schedule was patterned much like the previous one: teaching at the Neighborhood Playhouse; accompanying Martha's November concert. Ralph Taylor described the political atmosphere at that time as very agitated:

> Martha's [work] became more and more interesting to the intellectuals. There were pressures of all areas of the intellectual groups in New York, all tending towards magnifying this marvelous communist theory and communist life, and communist never-never land to the point where people were inevitably caught up. . . . Martha got involved indirectly in some of these things, giving performances and making speeches about the rights of man and all that. . . . Louis hated the communists. He was very contemptuous of all their efforts. We very much shared political views. He was very liberal in the old-fashioned liberal tradition that harked back to the socialist tradition from the German migration before the 1900s.[29]

Louis continued to enjoy the camaraderie of a group of men who often met to play cards, joke, talk politics, and inevitably to rehash the state of the arts and Martha's "bad" press. Ralph, who had helped to found the Socialist Party in New York and was a natural organizer, prodded Louis to elaborate on his idea of a monthly publication devoted to modern dance. Together they enticed Lehman Engel, Paul Love, Martha's brother-in-law Winthrop Sargeant, and another dancer's husband, Cook Adolph Glassgold — a museum curator, painter, and technical expert on printing and design — to serve with them on the first board of editors for the periodical, to be named *The Dance Observer*. Samuel Loveman and Martha Hill were enlisted as contributing editors.

This small magazine, established by friends of dance, became the "sorely needed" voice of the cause. The week after Louis recorded background music for a project with Katharine Cornell at World Broadcasting Studios, his journal noted December 14 as the date of the "first meeting of staff of dance magazine." His other notes included, "New Year's Eve. Small party at M.'s apartment," and as usual a mention of his birthdate: "Jan. 12. and 50th Birthday." He described 9 February 1934 as the "coldest day ever recorded in N.Y.C. 14.3 below zero." While he prepared Martha's February Guild Theatre concerts, he did so assured that she would now receive appropriate criticism. His journal documented with some pride, "First issue of 'Dance Observer' Feb. 1934."

Although Louis's apartment became headquarters for the editorial staff, *Dance Observer*'s official location was a post-office box in Madison Square Station. Ralph helped by offering space in the basement of his perfume factory in lower Manhattan for a filing cabinet and storage. The first issue of the magazine established its general format — twelve sheets with a feature article dealing with some aspect, activity, or point of view the board thought worthy — but reviewing concerts was its central focus and purpose, and probably the main reason the magazine sold copies. A handful of ads for books, announcements of studio dance classes, news items of upcoming events, and a college dance department listing completed the format. Generally Louis, Paul, and Ralph covered the concert scene, while feature articles on the relationship of music to dance were written by Riegger, Cage, and Cowell (who had just completed his first composition for Graham, *Four Casual Developments,* which had its premiere at the Guild on 18 February 1934). Other series addressed a variety of topical issues, including articles on costuming for the modern dance, although it was the political arena dancers who dominated the feature articles for the next few years.

With a natural inclination for order Louis prepared paste-ups, proofread, and sought out and accepted monthly ads that just about paid the monthly printing bill. He pressed Martha's dancers, his students, and assistants to work between rehearsals and on Saturday mornings, sending them off to sell ad space and type labels and bills. Louis returned corrected galleys to the printer, picked up and delivered the 200 to 500 copies to the post office

for mailing, and dropped off the rest at newsstands and bookstores fre-
quented by dancers. "The only ones that got paid were the printer and the
post office," one volunteer said.[30]

Others helped when they could, but except for the brief respite the
combined July-August issue offered, Louis assumed all the major duties of
the publication. Baird Hastings, a writer for the magazine, said, "We were
delighted to be published in the little advocate sheet for dance. Louis saw
what had to be done, and then saw a thing to its completion. It was a
privilege to work for him."[31] Martha Hill commented, "Evolving out of the
failure of *The Dance Magazine* and coinciding with the first Bennington
summer, Louis had wonderful soil on which it could start because we had
students from all over the United States."[32] Few predicted that *Dance Observer* would provide a monthly beacon of support to college dance departments and studios across the United States for years to come. Although Louis
gradually assumed the role of editor-in-chief, this herculean effort was shared
by others who vowed to cover the New York dance scene with the same
enthusiasm and fairness.

One of the first works to be reviewed in *Dance Observer* was Martha's
exuberant *Celebration*. Louis scored the work for trumpet and drum, filling
the air with sound. According to Norman Lloyd, Louis rewrote many times
to arrive at the final version, which "was sparse, dissonant and highly
melodic." At heart a sentimentalist, Louis struggled to keep sentiment out of
his music: "Romanticism was to Louis an epithet that stood for all that had
gone wrong in the arts. It was synonymous with overblown, and Louis
preferred understatement."[33]

A welcome contrast to Graham's other works, the piece found its place
as a program-opener after the February 1934 premiere. May O'Donnell
related, "It was sensational because we jumped the whole time. I think [the
critics] had been waiting for a breakthrough."[34] Gertrude Shurr felt that
Martha's intention was to get the dancers off the floor: "No one did a
jumping dance like this before. We had to do it one hundred times. It was
wonderful!" She remembered Louis at the keyboard during rehearsals: "He
absolutely knew the movement. If you did the least little thing wrong he
noticed. Our rehearsals were always like a performance. You didn't dare
mark. With Louis you really had to perform for the muscular memory — the
physicality of the movement. In *Celebration* we had to perform it all the time
so that Louis could get it into his bloodstream too."[35]

In the spring Louis was finally introduced to Arnold Schoenberg at a
party and invited him to attend Martha's upcoming concert at the Guild.
Schoenberg had never seen modern dance, according to Ralph Taylor:

"There was Martha doing what critics called 'pretzel bending' movements, and Schoenberg turned to Louis and said, 'Is that dancing? I always understood dancing was, Dum-dum-dum, Dum-dum-dum (singing a waltz). But this?' Louis said it so scornfully, too, as if to say, 'How little he understood!' Modern dance of all the arts was closest to music. You'd think Schoenberg would have been close to these ideas. Anyone who wrote *Verklärte Nacht* and then comes up with dance being ump-pah-pah has got a cockeyed idea of what it was all about!"[36] The incident confirmed his hunch that Louis's vision was not shared or even understood by this important music theorist—a disappointment that dispelled Louis's notion of the Germans as leaders of the avant-garde. Still confident, Louis was determined to forge ahead with less-sanctioned theories of "functional" music.

Having shaped semester courses at the Neighborhood Playhouse, Louis and Martha entered the liberal arts arena in the spring 1934 term at the invitation of Marion McKnighten at Sarah Lawrence College. Lasting friendships evolved. Marion and Louis, both January-born, often celebrated their birthdays together at Marion's and her husband's Bronxville home, to which Louis always brought a jar of fancy S.S. Pierce marmalade. Joseph Campbell, a professor at Sarah Lawrence, also became a loyal friend and convert to their cause, and soon married their most gifted student and dancer, Jean Erdman.

As Louis's teaching reputation grew, contracts to teach his course at Teachers College and Barnard College of Columbia University followed. Believing in the importance of support from the ranks of higher education, he was generous with his time and energy, always preparing a final demonstration of his students' best work, to the sponsoring faculty's delight. These teaching situations often provided added income for members of the performing group, who were used as assistants, easing Martha's and Louis's loads.

Since many of the company dancers had studied choreography and wanted to create their own dances, in May they encouraged Louis to create a separate performing organization that he formally named The Producing Unit. At the time Martha believed in the concept of dancer-choreographer as strongly as Louis supported that of musician-composer. She insisted that her dancers study choreography with him as rigorously as they studied technique in her classes. Bonnie Bird, Sophie Maslow, Anna Sokolow, and others avidly tried out their choreographic ideas; Louis critiqued their dances, rehearsed the group, and sought performing opportunities for their endeavors. Anna gradually took the Unit's mission under her own wing.

The opening of the School of the Dance at Bennington College in

Vermont[37] that summer of 1934 would have a vital impact on the development of a mainstream American modern dance. For Louis, Martha, Doris
Humphrey, Charles Weidman, and Hanya Holm, Bennington was a great
influence on their emergence as leaders in the field. Envisioned by Martha
Hill, then on the faculty at Bennington in addition to New York University,
the idea was to gather the most talented practitioners of the new dance in the
hospitable environs of the exclusive, very liberal college for women at Bennington. In this endeavor she had recourse to the organizational talent of
Mary Josephine Shelly and a willing president of the college. The first summer the directors set up schedules for each of the artists that complemented
their choreographic work. With space, production expenses, and comfortable room and board in the Green Mountains of Vermont, everyone was
delighted.

A willing assistant in the design of the curriculum, Louis agreed to serve
as a founding member of the newly created board. Although he enjoyed his
summers at Perry-Mansfield in the remote beauty of Colorado, he appreciated the opportunity to continue his work with Martha at Bennington. His
work as a musician for dance and teacher of composition balanced the
concentration on dance techniques, Hill reasoned. She also hired Ruth and
Norman Lloyd, her colleagues at New York University, as staff musicians —
the trio of musicians would be able to encourage others to become dance
accompanists. The Lloyds were especially pleased: "Everything that we did
in our dance-music career started from Louis," Ruth said. "At the time, he
was the most important person involved in music for the dance."[38]

The first year the students were mainly physical education teachers,
America's most ardent dance enthusiasts. They soon made Louis one of their
favorite representatives for dance. As a guest teacher in their own schools, he
was able to convince their students and colleagues that dance was worthy of
serious study. There were also rising dancers. Sybil Shearer vividly character-
ized the first-season faculty:

> [Louis was] major-domo throwing cold water on most choreographic
> projects. . . . Looking back on my relations with all those dedicated
> people, I know now that they were romantic, too, although it was the
> last thing they were ready to admit. There was Bessie Schönberg, de-
> lightful with her long nose and pale, freckled face, explaining in her
> German accent that only Martha Graham could make her so excited;
> Norman Lloyd and Gregory Tucker put life into the dancing with their
> music, and Dini ("one-note") de Remer played for agonizing stretches,
> while Pauline Lawrence gossiped in the hall. There was Hanya Holm

with her decorative speech, Doris Humphrey wearing a butterfly skirt, and Martha Graham in her mandarin coat. Charles Weidman was rebounding, and José Limón was following suit. . . . Mary Jo Shelly was distributing orange juice. Dancers were everywhere stretching; in a way it was like the Foreign Legion recruited by Martha Hill from the gymnasiums of America.[39]

Gertrude Shurr reminisced, "There were some that studied mostly with Doris and Hanya, or Hanya and Martha. I was Martha's practice teacher. May O'Donnell was Louis's assistant. Everybody was working in their own studio. We put on a demonstration that was fantastic. Everybody was flabbergasted. It was wonderful!"[40]

Ruth Lloyd described Louis's talent:

I remember walking on the grounds at Bennington and hearing this marvelous piano playing. It was Louis playing Copland's Piano Variations. It was wonderful to hear the way he did it. He was an extraordinary pianist. His rather small hands were alive with music. They say he never practiced. Well, he didn't really practice. He would look at things and they would come into his fingers. He was very much attached — his mind, his fingers, and he listened and danced all the time. He was a dancer. . . . There are some people who are a quick study, and obviously when you're rehearsing, you have to play it. When he played for performances he was always more involved with the dancer than he was with the music. When you rehearse a dance, you get to know the music, and he knew it all by the time he played it. There's a difference between knowing the music and practicing it.[41]

Others were not as impressed by Louis. Hanya Holm spoke of the "green jealousies" at Bennington, saying that she did not consider Louis a friend.[42] He treated her rudely on the very first day of the session, she disclosed: entering the Commons dining hall she sat next to Louis, hoping to start a friendly conversation in her native German; he refused to speak to her, got up abruptly, and stormed off. Whether his tolerance for European dancers had reached a low ebb or he was simply in bad temper, Holm decided then and there — Louis suffered from a big ego. It was an opinion she continued to hold. As for Martha, "[She] always had that isolation thing. . . . And Louis created that little Garden of Eden. And if you have so many protectors, then you finally don't join any more."[43]

Louis was also the preferred accompanist in chamber music ensembles at Bennington; his steady, focused reading of any score was appreciated. Serviceability and appropriateness were by now prerogatives in every musical situation for Louis. As a composer, just as in his conducting, his main concern was to control a danceable tempo, nurturing the strong melodic flow over the solid, identifiable rhythmic structure. Clearly defined phrase lengths, beginnings, and cadences were absolutely necessary. Along with this, whether he was composing or conducting, the quality of the music had to be "transparent," giving lift to the dancer. In an era in which many conductors had little facility at sight-reading and often had to simplify scores, these skills were at the root of Louis's success. He still spent composing time on development of rhythmic ideas, with interesting results: "There might be three fours, and then within that four three's. I've done it with some of Martha's things. She might move in five bars of four and I'd write four bars of five to it."[44] He found that simple chord clusters added weight between essential silences and gave his music a feeling of contemporaneity. Generally he now kept melodic invention to a minimum.

As artists Martha and Louis enjoyed the freedom that emerged from years of imposed self-discipline. They had learned to address each problem — whether artistic or routine — with exacting concentration and candor. But Louis's particular ability for cold analysis was very different from Martha's emotionally driven vision. It may have been his most valuable asset as a professional, but it often devastated those who loved him most. His pale blue eyes detected actions that lacked honesty. Martha relied on qualities and "essences," allowing her intuition, and Louis's analysis, to guide her.

Although Louis's official capacity was music director for Martha, he also assumed the unofficial position of general manager for each concert. Marketing and managing often exceeded his musical duties. Few others were willing, or able, to take on these additional pressures. If Louis had no competition it was most likely because no one else wanted the job. The lecture-demonstration format served as a vehicle for attracting concert organizers without access to adequate theaters, funds, or audiences for a full-scale concert. These "lectures" could easily be presented in dance studios or gymnasiums in conjunction with a master class in dance technique. Graham could be booked as soloist or with her company. In addition, Louis was available to give a master class in dance composition or appraise student dances. This scheme informed new audiences and paved the way for return visits.

John Martin, now dance-series coordinator for the New School, invited Martha to speak about making dances, as she had earlier for Henry Cowell's series. An excellent extemporaneous speaker, her words were illuminated by her dancers' movements and Louis's accompaniment in a smooth, well-designed program. In February 1935, Martha and Louis presented the "demonstration" portion of her lecture for the Conference on Modern Dance at Teachers College, Columbia University, and then traveled to Washington, D.C., to repeat it for the National Conference of the Progressive Education Association. Martha gave solo performances with Louis at the keyboard for the remaining dates on the tour, dancing in Pennsylvania, Connecticut, Illinois, Missouri, Ohio, and Nebraska before heading back east to Massachusetts. Although their touring schedule was exhausting, they made good use of their time on the rails from one place to another: they discussed a new work, Louis wrote snippets of the score, and at each stop they tried out movement ideas.

Back at the Guild Theatre in April 1935 Martha premiered the resulting work, *Perspectives of the Plains*. A dance in two sections conceived as an "American" statement, Lehman Engel wrote the score for the first part, *Marching Song*. Louis's music for the second part, a solo for Martha, was called *Frontier*. She envisioned a set for this section and asked her talented seamstress's son, a sculptor, to design one for her. It was Isamu Noguchi's first work for the theater; his sister, Ailes, later joined the company as a dancer. Martha explained that "the dance *Frontier* came from our discussion of the hold, as an American, the frontier has always had for me as a symbol of a journey into the unknown. Traveling to California by train, the tracks were to me a reiteration of that frontier. When at last I asked Isamu for an image of those endless tracks for my dance, he brought me the set for *Frontier*—the tracks now the endless ropes into the future."[45]

Inspired by the great expanses she saw as they crossed the States, Martha created a work of genius—a true American statement, Louis felt—which became her signature work. Only eight minutes long, the dance was structured in simple theme-and-variations form: starting upstage center, arm and leg raised, she progressed forward for each variation, returning to the fence only to come forward again: Louis's simple melody for piano framed without interfering with her intention.

The couple returned to Bennington in July 1935 for a second summer. On the first day of registration the school's financial success was assured, much to the relief of the directors. The enrollment—144 students—had doubled in one year, many students returning for a second session. Each artist's teaching schedule again allowed for rehearsal time with their own company, which sometimes caused friction in the ranks. Humphrey and Graham soon became polar opposites in the eyes of the students. Petty animosities flared among their assistants and company dancers as they vied for salaries, rehearsal space, and student allegiance. Only the presence of Holm helped to diffuse the emphasis on one style or the other; unperturbed, she forged ahead, offering a third style from which dance technicians could draw.

Martha created *Panorama* over the six-week session. In a workshop format she cast thirty-six dancers, then discussed ideas for a set by Arch Lauterer and mobiles by Alexander Calder. Norman Lloyd wrote, "Sometime in the first week, Louis asked me if I would be willing to write a work for Martha. Actually, Louis was supposed to have done it, but he must have realized the time was too short. I was young and willing, if not able!"[46] His wife added, "When Norman was writing *Panorama* there was a special communication, special wires between Martha and her composer. . . . But Martha always had an intermediary and that was Louis. Norman had to come home and sit in a tub of tepid water. He was so charged, excited and scared as hell!"[47] Martha Hill remembered Norman taking his first draft to Louis: "Louis said to him, 'Look Norman, you wrote this to Martha, not for Martha.' He put in it everything he knew."[48] The composer then set out to pare down the forty minutes of music. The *Theatre Arts Monthly* critic agreed that although the work was clearly experimental, "vigorous, bold and beautiful in design and execution," it was incomplete.[49] The *Herald Tribune* called it too frequently "irrelevant."[50] Otto Luening suggested:

> There was never enough time to get this dream of hers focused. And the first performances were never very hot. But they never stopped at the first performance. I remember John Martin would come up and say, 'Well, this piece of Martha's just didn't come off. It ought to stay here and expire in the Vermont hills where it was born, because it just wouldn't get anywhere.' That's where John made his mistake because Louis and Martha would go back to New York and shine up those pieces and sometimes they'd come out as major works. It was a slow process where Louis would help to get this thing on a conscious level for Martha."[51]

As time went by it became increasingly apparent that there were not only technical polarities between Humphrey-Weidman and Graham but also financial ones. Even though Doris and Charles were producing some of their finest work to date, they found it impossible to rent a Broadway theater on a regular basis, as Martha did. Their most lucrative assists came intermittently from work in a Broadway show, much to Doris's dismay. They taught in their studio-theater on West 18th Street, a loft that also served as their rehearsal and performance space, with no steady income except an allowance from Charles Woodford (Doris's seafaring husband). Month-to-month financial crises were handled by Pauline Lawrence, as usual. (Pauline's energies would turn to promoting José Limón's career after her marriage to him in 1942.) Graham and Horst, on the other hand, had organized their lives more cohesively in order to have a more stable environment in which to work. Although both companies had little remaining cash for performance fees, Graham and Horst did manage to find other ways to support their dancers, landing teaching jobs or assistantships for them with increasing regularity.

More problematic in terms of artistic continuity, the Humphrey-Weidman Group repertory had become increasingly diverse in subject matter. Often needing large ensembles their company seemed to be in constant flux. In contrast, Martha's loyal group of women seemed committed to her cause with cultlike fervor. To miss one of her rehearsals was sacrilege. Once in the studio, Martha demanded slavish discipline, full devotion, and professionalism, and received it.

In the fall Graham received an invitation from the Ministry of Propaganda for the Third Reich to perform in one of the cultural programs for the 1936 Berlin Olympic Games. The letter was signed by Rudolf von Laban. She declined. Alarmed by rumors of harsh treatment of the Jews, Martha publicly attacked the Nazi government's policies and refused to take part in the games. This outcry was in part fired by her dancers, several of whom were Jewish and all of whom were politically active. Her letter of reply to the ministry was published in the *New York Times*:

> I would find it impossible to dance in Germany at the present time. So many artists whom I respect and admire have been persecuted, have been deprived of the right to work for ridiculous and unsatisfactory reasons, that I should consider it impossible to identify myself, by accepting the invitation, with the regime that has made such things possible. In addition, some of my concert group would not be welcomed in Germany.[52]

American athletes participated without reservation — Jesse Owens won three gold medals and shared a fourth at these Olympic games — yet by publicly stating this disparaging view of the political happenings Martha further severed her association with Germany's modern dance movement. It had been rumored that Kreutzberg and Wigman were favorites of the Third Reich. This event strengthened Martha's image as an "American" artist in the public eye and served as a final mandate against all German influence.

During the winter Martha worked on an ensemble piece, *Horizons,* in four sections: "Migration (New Trails)," "Dominion (Sanctified Power)," "Building Motif (Homesteading)," and "Dance of Rejoicing." *Horizons* had a score by Louis that he did not think much of, and decor by Alexander

Calder. First performed at the Guild Theatre on February 23 the work presaged others of the type, but no one was very happy with it. At the time, it received little attention; what little it did get was not good. According to Louis, one reviewer wrote, " '*Horizons* . . . was a poor dance and poor music score.' It was kind of a failure."[53] Rereading the 1936 newspaper clipping in his scrapbook years later, Louis could not help but agree.

Spring 1936 marked Martha's and Louis's first cross-country tour. The "trans-continental," as Louis liked to call it, was only of Martha's solo works. As they traveled from place to place Louis would contact the local papers, follow up their press agent Frances Hawkins's preliminary press releases, and arrange for interviews with Martha and for performance reviews. A *Los Angeles Times* reviewer quoted Graham as saying about Louis, "He really dances with the dancer, although he weighs 250 pounds and doesn't move from his piano bench."[54] This tour, helped by Merle Armitage's work as booking agent for the western concerts, not only served to introduce Martha's work, but also paved the way for tours by the full company. Dates were usually arranged with the help of a personal contact in each community—a former student, an avid fan, or simply a concert manager with no particular interest in dance. For Louis, it began a succession of important personal contacts across the country that would help to proclaim Graham America's visionary in dance.

They presented concerts at colleges, art clubs, and occasionally concert halls. Most were poorly equipped for producing dance. Few sponsors realized the hardships of performing on tour—the constant travel, little sleep, and little time to eat a balanced meal. As Martha made up, unpacked her costumes, and warmed up for the performance, Louis positioned the piano in the wings stage right, next to the stage-manager's desk. Here he could signal curtain and lighting cues to whomever was in charge backstage, close enough to do it himself if necessary. One incident particularly impressed him:

> At the Ethel Walker School (one of those snotty, strict all girls schools), a man took our bags, and we entered a dark theater. No one was there to meet us. The head didn't come. No one asked us if we needed help. It was something awful. Martha and I just had a great laugh over it. I've never had such rudeness. Someone brought us sandwiches and coffee before the performance. Afterward, Martha was getting her makeup off and they turned the lights off on us. I yelled, "We aren't finished undressing and packing yet!" Finally we snuck out of the place. We felt like thieves! We went to the train station and caught a night train back to New York City.

[In another place] they didn't even turn the lights on, and the review says about me, ". . . skillful hands, sensitive ears, and sympathetic response. At the same time coordinated in pace, rhythm, phrasing and every dramatic modulation of the dance." In other words, I was good in those days.[55]

Another review from that tour by "one of the best critics in Boston — Horace T. Parker — a world renown[ed] name — an old timer, who wrote all of his reviews in long hand, and signed [them] H. T. P."[56] pleased Louis: "No dancer has brought to Boston as discerning and responsive a musician as Louis Horst."[57]

One performance, at the Fredricksburg Women's Club, did not go well. Its members were from the oldest families in the South. "Martha actually didn't get a hand, and I played two solos and got quite a lot of applause. That's what they knew about dance. Martha said, 'They should bill you as the star.' By that time she was so disgusted she wouldn't have opened the curtain at the end even if they had applauded. But I didn't hear any. I only heard applause for me, because I stepped out and took a bow. Martha teased me all the time about it!"[58]

Then, after what Louis called an "old home" week in California, the couple opened at Colorado Springs Fine Arts Center and gave performances in Chicago and Oxford, Ohio, before returning to New York. The successful tour left Martha with increased prominence as a leading force in modern dance, and Louis with reviews that called him America's "number one musician." As for their financial arrangement, "In a place like Columbia, South Carolina, we'd get $300 or $400 a concert. Altogether, we'd get $1,000. Probably our expenses would be two or three hundred — railroad, and all that. That would leave $800, and we'd divide it. Playing in New York, we just divided the money."[59]

One incident in spring 1936 illustrates Graham's sure position as a leading dance figure and the softening of Louis's attitude about ballet. He had long admired Lydia Lopokova, Russian star of Diaghilev's Ballets Russes, creator of roles in Massine's *Parade* and *La Boutique Fantasque* and Frederick Ashton's *Façade,* and praised for her Swanilda with the Vic-Wells Ballet. "Louis was in love with her," Martha Hill remembered:

Lopokova was married to the economist Maynard Keynes, and when Columbia University bestowed an honorary degree on him he made arrangements to bring his wife. The only thing she wanted to do in America was to meet "la Gra — ham," and so I helped arrange it. Martha, Mary Jo Shelly and myself joined Lopokova for high tea in her suite at the Waldorf-Astoria. She was a lively soubrette type who spoke fine English. Martha and Lydia were poles apart as artists, yet sisters. When the ballerina asked, "You dance to an orchestra?" Martha replied, "No. I have a pianist." "And you have costume designers and seamstresses?" "No, I make my costumes myself." Lopokova was amazed. It was an historic meeting that pointed out the great differences, yet the similarities, between these two great artists.[60]

At forty-two, Martha was at the peak of her physical strength as a dance artist. Louis, in contrast, carried a considerable potbelly and smoked continuously. Her success depended on his ardent encouragement; Louis thrived on her need of that support. The impressionable young Ruth Lloyd suspected that everything was generated by Louis and that he never let his feelings interfere with the discipline of Martha's work. But since he was always somewhat paternal toward the Lloyds, they were perhaps the first to sense some emotional strain between the couple. Martha had long since accepted the conditions of their intimacy and absorbed the philosophies of Nietzsche and Schopenhauer, but now she was delving into the writings of Freud, Jung, and Eastern cultures, advising her dancers to read the *Bhagavad Gita* along with Nietzsche's *The Birth of Tragedy*. Louis, more inclined to be influenced by trends in the visual arts, was nevertheless a good listener and a match for Graham's inquiring mind.

Throughout his years as Martha's constant companion, Louis always flirted with the ever-changing roster of youthful actresses and dancers, taking every occasion to be with an ingenue of his choice. Louis did not need much, according to Gertrude Shurr, "A pinch of the knee was all!"[61] But Anne Douglas, and many afterward, spoke of the romantic and physical nature of their particular friendships with him. Ralph Taylor knew that "Louis was a womanizer. There were many women, but let's not exaggerate that. He led a very active life, and in order to carry on with women, you need time. He wouldn't let anything interfere with his work, and so on, but there were young women, particularly ones that threw themselves at him. I remember a letter I saw from Martha. One line struck me. It said, 'To Louis Horst, whose bed has always been his throne.'"[62]

After the successful cross-country tour and spring season commitments, they returned to the West Coast, this time to relax—Louis to visit his wife and friends, and Martha to spend a few weeks with her mother. On the train ride back east that he had grown to love, he worked on preparations for his six-week stint at Bennington—a full session. He taught dance composition with Martha Hill and directed a new program in music composition for dance — ten students enrolled, but only four qualified after an initial screening. Dance technique was taught by the various artists in two-week sessions, with May O'Donnell assisting Martha's section. Martha had no commitment to produce a new work and instead presented two solo concerts of the ten pieces she now performed on tour. Louis conducted an ensemble of five instrumentalists and a singer for the retrospective evenings. The final concert of the season offered one of Humphrey's finest group works, *With My Red Fires*, from the *New Dance* trilogy.

The critic Walter Terry surveyed the Bennington campus population:

Two hundred of them. And all of them students of the dance. Boys and girls from 28 of the states. . . . Here is to be found an organization devoted entirely to the dance in all its aspects. Under the tutelage of a faculty consisting of 38 members, the students study many types of the modern dance both in technique and choreography; courses in dance history and criticism; staging; costuming; musical composition for the dance; the use of percussion instruments in the dance; and a study of the basis of dramatic movement.[63]

Louis was now director of the Music in Dance program and, with Norman Lloyd, created a course that focused on principles of accompanying and composing, which by 1939 developed into a major course of study for composer-accompanists. Their fellow composers — Cowell, Engel, Luening, Riegger — bolstered this notion with enthusiastic support. The dancer Mary Anthony portrayed all of them in her description of Cowell: "In constant anticipation of the reward of being joyously alive. . . . He either wore the same suit or had many versions of one suit — all a little too small so that they fit him like a mould. His coat was always closed by one button that seemed about to pop off at any moment. His pants gave an unplanned comic effect because he spent so much of his time sitting crosslegged . . . that when he stood up straight they bulged forward at the knees."[64] These gentlemen around dance who came to Bennington enjoyed one another's company, often socializing at the local pub. They called themselves the "Housatonic Falls Fellas" and spent a good deal of the time joking and making up "terrible puns." Luening, then on the Bennington College music faculty, said: "We had the Hoosick Tunnel Marching Band, which was anybody who thought he could play an instrument. We would just raise hell. We'd do a lot of improvisation. Louis would join if there was any room at the piano."[65]

chapter seven

1936–1941

"Out of emotion comes

form." — Martha Graham

n fall 1936, after a move into a first-floor studio at the Hotel des Artistes on West 67th Street, Louis worked intensively with his Producing Unit to prepare for upcoming lecture-demonstrations. Using a refined version of his earlier New School lecture, he designed the program as an amusing but informative introduction to the art of choreography — a format he would present for the rest of his life. He also used it to encourage the choreographic careers of his dancer-students. At a Sarah Lawrence tryout, Louis told his audience, "At first, dancers who broke away from the classic forms thought that self-expression and emotion were enough, but all emotion and no form results in bad taste, whereas all form and no emotion leaves a base which must be built upon."[1] He then took his position at the piano to accompany movement studies analogous to melody, rhythm, and harmony — dissonant ones to dissonant sound — and spatially designed dances to the whole-tone scale.

Louis had organized the year before a Symposium on Modern Dance for the Work Projects Administration (WPA), which had been held at the YM–YWHA on Lexington Avenue and 92nd Street. (This project launched myriad dance activities at the Y over the next decades, with Louis figuring importantly on the advisory committee.) Now receiving word of government sponsorship through the WPA, Louis negotiated for rental of the Y's Theresa L. Kaufmann Auditorium and presented the lecture-demonstration to a discerning New York audience.

In the musical arena of the mid-thirties, major orchestras included the Boston and Philadelphia Symphonies, with others gradually joining the ranks: the NBC Symphony on radio, the New York Philharmonic, the New York City Orchestra at what is now City Center. The "golden-age" conductors dominated by Dimitri Mitropoulos, Fritz Reiner, Leopold Stokowski, Arturo Toscanini, and Bruno Walter — all age-peers of Louis — would gradually be usurped by the next generation, like Leonard Bernstein, who took the podium to promote new works. The old-guard committees, which made the major decisions in the music world, pressed younger talents into closer allegiance. Groups such as the League of Composers and the Pan-American Association were formed, with the Composers Alliance and the Copland-Sessions Concerts promoting new American music.

New York's new breed of musicians were impressed by Aaron Copland's facile, open style and the range of his endeavors. Henry Cowell's decade of lectures at the New School for Social Research and his journal *New Music Quarterly* were well appreciated. Other American composers, such as David Diamond (who as a youngster had seen Martha in rehearsal at the Eastman School), Virgil Thomson (who also became a reviewer for the *New York Herald Tribune*), and Paul Bowles gained status as composers in the late thirties. This group, adept at writing criticism as well as music, would far outdistance older leaders in their versatility. In comparison, Louis had his independent journal and a composing style of his own, "understated, clear and specifically wedded to the dance," according to Norman Lloyd.[2] He had found a place apart from the mainstream music field in which to prosper.

The saddest entry in Louis's early 1937 journal pages noted the death of his beloved Max; four days later he recorded one of the high points of his life: "Feb. 26. At Washington, D.C. Played for M. G. dances at White House after dinner, which [I] attended." Martha's emergence as an important woman artist had begun to register in the minds of national organizers. She represented the new American spirit, and would continue to place herself in the heroic mold of a leading American when, a year later, she presented *Militant Hymn* from *American Document* for the Preview Pageant of the New York World's Fair. But in early 1937 her greatest honor — and Louis's — was a request to perform at the White House. For the occasion she reworked her *Dance of Rejoicing* to Louis's score based on a Southern hill shout, to be performed with *Frontier*. The invitation came from Eleanor Roosevelt in response to earlier prodding by the group's diligent press representative and manager, Frances Hawkins.

The President's wife had attended a fund-raising lecture-demonstration as Rita Morgenthau's guest and afterward met Martha. Impressed, she wrote about it in her syndicated news column "My Day." Frances then offered her tickets for the upcoming premiere of *Chronicle*. Although she declined she later wrote via the Neighborhood Playhouse asking Martha if she might perform a few dances at the White House (after Sydney Thompson, the "diseuse," delivered several recitations) for a birthday celebration honoring Mrs. Henry Morgenthau, Jr., Rita's sister-in-law. "I do not know who travels with you on these occasions," Mrs. Roosevelt wrote, "but I am quite sure I can put you up for one night, and perhaps one friend."[3] Louis's official invitation arrived as Miss Graham's "friend" and pianist.

Louis recounted this event to Jeanette Roosevelt, granddaughter-in-law of the President.* Yet on this thrilling visit he nevertheless worried about proper White House decorum. The couple departed in a snowstorm on the half-hour late train from Grand Central Station's "depot six." Driven to the White House by limousine, they entered through the front door, much to their delight.

> Good thing the President was a Democrat, otherwise we would have gone through the side door and been served dinner in a hallway with the servants. [They were escorted to their chambers to dress for dinner.] Martha's was the Lincoln bedroom. I emptied the contents of my old suitcase — full dress: suit, collar, shirt, shoes, socks and a bottle of whiskey wrapped in an old newspaper — not a new newspaper, but an old one. I put it in a drawer of the commode. Then, what a shock! Here I was at the White House. I opened the door [to the adjoining bathroom] and this stark naked man is standing there. "That's all right, come right in. I'm Franklin, Jr. I'm going to take a shower. The plumbing's not so good in this old house!" . . . So there I was at the White House, and within a few minutes I was in the bosom of the family.
>
> Then Eleanor was at the bedroom door, "Yoo-hooh, Yoo-hooh, Oh, Mr. Horst. Dinner at seven, so if you'll dress right away, I'll come and call for you." They didn't let people wander around the White House alone. She took me down stairs and said, "You haven't met the President, have you?" "No, I haven't," I answered. The President entered separately. There were ramps all around [for his wheelchair]. He said, "Haven't I met you before? No? Well, it is so wonderful for you people to come down." (He always spoke as though he were singing. You could waltz to his speaking.) Dinner was plain. We had soup, rack of lamb, dessert and coffee. An ice cream roll for dessert.

*It was to her that Louis confided his life story, assisted by his scrapbooks, in interviews taped during 1960 and 1961.

The President's birthday gift was a gold toothbrush. "It was amusing, as he showed her how to use it." Other guests at the dinner table — sixteen in all — included a Lady Allington and Judge Lehman, a diplomat's daughter who had been a student of Louis's at Sarah Lawrence, and Fanny Hurst. Seated next to Miss Hurst, Louis asked where she lived in New York. "One West 67th Street," she replied. "Well, so do I," he responded. "Oh, you're the one whose mail I get so often!" she said. "Hurst, Horst, you see. (I never saw her after that!) After the dinner, when I went back up [to prepare for the performance] the footman had set out my suit and placed the newspaper and the bottle of whiskey out on the bureau top!"[4]

Louis played as Martha danced *Frontier* on a wobbly platform. Afterward, he gave a glowing report to friends: "Why, her leg went so high, her foot almost touched the dining room chandelier! When she came forward she had to go around in order to avoid it."[5] "After the performance Mrs. Roosevelt said, 'This dear girl hasn't had any dinner! Come along into the kitchen.' And she got out the meat and sliced it." Anxious to catch the train back to New York that evening, Louis hastily repacked his valise and waited for Martha in the downstairs hallway. "The first lady said, 'You're not leaving are you? We thought you and Martha would stay and have breakfast with us.' 'We have to return because we have to teach at the Neighborhood Playhouse early tomorrow,'" he apologized. "When Martha finally came, I realized I had lost my cap. At the last minute the secret service had to look around and finally found it. That dirty old cap! . . . We didn't get paid, but a few weeks later we got photos in the mail."[6] Specially framed with wood said to have been discarded during a White House renovation, the photographs became his most prized possessions.

That spring Louis maintained his long-standing position as a lively guide to good eating places when the company made its second transcontinental tour. They traveled from Wisconsin to Illinois, Montana, and on to Vancouver, British Columbia, where Louis was denied entry until he could produce a birth certificate. There the *News-Gazette* pronounced him "at all times the halo to the figure."[7] After a performance in Seattle they headed down the California coast to San Francisco's War Memorial Opera House. While they were there Betty hosted a cast party in her dance studio on Post Street. Dancers who were meeting Louis's wife for the first time were impressed by her independent success. A member of the San Francisco Allied Dance Group, Betty was creating her own dances to music by Bartok, Honegger, Hindemith, and Varèse — for which her "choreographic facility" was praised by critics — on a program directed by then-resident Henry Cowell. Although her own teaching blended Shawn's exercises with St. Denis's

Eastern philosophies, she was enthusiastic about Graham's new technical work, and invited May O'Donnell and Gertrude Shurr to return as guest teachers at her private studio. Such a situation bemused Louis; his only comment was, "Well, why not?" The tour continued to Santa Barbara, Los Angeles, Florida, Virginia, and ended in Pennsylvania.

The Cornish School in Seattle had also held a reception after the company's performance. There, Louis first met Nina Fonaroff. At the time the twenty-three-year-old dancer was studying acting. After a brief introduction he invited her to attend a master class the next day. Like others before her, from that point onward Nina felt worshipful about the couple: they symbolized the future of the art of dance — sophisticated, intelligent, and vigorous — and upheld a way of life totally dedicated to their art. Nina arranged for a quick departure to New York to take their June course: "Then Martha offered me a scholarship, and I said, 'Yes.' It was as simple as that. I had no other thoughts. . . . After that, all I ever wanted to do was dance with Martha."[8] She would continue her adoration for Graham as a member of the company, and for Louis on more intimate terms. Their liaison would endure in some form for the rest of his life.

In making West Coast arrangements for this transcontinental tour, Frances Hawkins had relied on Merle Armitage. An ardent admirer of Martha, he planned to publish a book dedicated to her work. Enlisting the services of an editor, Ramiel McGehee (earlier the English tutor for Hirohito, the young Emperor of Japan), and an artist, Carlus Dyer, he asked Martha to return to California's Redondo Beach so that they might spend the summer on the manuscript. Exhausted at the end of her California performances, she was in desperate need of a change, he observed. After the last performance in Pittsburgh, Armitage telegraphed: "Tickets on the Chief will be delivered to you day after tomorrow. No answer required."[9] Graham was on the train. Once settled, Armitage forbade any discussion of dance at the dinner table. She swam, read, wrote, and was sketched by Dyer, with whom she had a passionate if brief romance. Two months later, revitalized, she told her host, "This is a rebirth."[10]

During the stay, Martha was able to distance herself emotionally from her devoted colleagues, particularly Louis. He on the other hand preferred to believe that as a couple they had "just drifted apart" at this juncture in their romantic involvement. Both of them had long pondered in relation to themselves Freud's and Schopenhauer's concepts of sexuality, complete with its "mechanisms of repression." Martha had often expressed exasperation that these notions should govern her life and fretted openly over her lack of

Louis Horst at the "age of seven" (penciled on back of photo).

Louis Horst, Mazatlan, Mexico, 1901.

Carolina and Conrad Horst, Calistoga,
California, July 1913.

Betty and Louis Horst at Maplewood
Hotel, New Hampshire, 1912.

Louis Horst, San Francisco, circa 1914.

Julnar of the Sea, Los Angeles, 1919.
Marian Williams, Nancy Jackson, and
Betty Horst as the three odalisques.
Photograph: Witzel.

Ruth St. Denis and Ted Shawn: Duet
from Cuadro Flamenco, California, 1919.
Photograph: White Studio.

Billboard advertising Ted Shawn and Dancers, Metropolitan Theatre, New York City, 2 October 1921.

**Martha Graham and Louis Horst in the
Denishawn studio, circa 1923.**

Isthar of the Seven Gates, the Denishawn Company,
1923. Center: Dancers Doris Humphrey and Lenore
Schaffer. Photograph: White Studio.

**Louis Horst, Martha Graham, and
Socrates at Perry-Mansfield Dance Camp,
Steamboat Springs, Colorado, 1929.**

Denishawn group in music visualization of Psalm 151 by Ruth St. Denis: "Praise Ye the Lord with Trimbrel and Dance." Photographed at Carnegie Hall, 1924: White Studio.

Adolph Bolm and Louis Horst, Little Theatre,
New York City, circa 1931.

Martha Graham and Louis Horst, early 1930s.

Martha Graham and the Dance Group, Louis Horst, and Max at rehearsal of <u>Primitive Mysteries</u>, 1935. Photograph: Barbara Morgan.

Martha Graham in <u>Frontier</u>, 1935. Set: Isami Noguchi. Photograph: Barbara Morgan.

Martha Graham and the Dance Group,
Primitive Mysteries, 1935. Photograph:
Barbara Morgan.

Members of the Dance Group, <u>Celebration</u>, 1935. Photo-graph: Barbara Morgan.

Louis Horst with Spud, and Hanya Holm with goat,
Bennington College, 1938. Photograph: Barbara Morgan.

Dance students at Bennington College Commons, 1938. Left
foreground: Maslow and Martha Graham. Background, left to
right: Nina Fonaroff, Louis Horst in profile, Frances Hawkins,
and Houseley Stevens, Jr. Photograph: Barbara Morgan.

Martha Graham and dancers in her studio, circa 1935. Photograph: Barbara Morgan.

Louis Horst and Martha Graham, curtain call, circa 1936. Photograph: Irving Brodsky

Martha Graham mending Erick Hawkins's pants in Barbara Morgan's studio, New York City, 1940. Photograph: Barbara Morgan.

Louis Horst at the keyboard, circa 1940. Photograph: Barbara Morgan.

Martha Graham in <u>El Penitente</u>, 1940. Photograph: Barbara Morgan.

Martha Hill and Louis Horst at Juilliard, circa 1952.

Louis Horst and dance students at the Fine Arts Forum, Woman's College, University of North Carolina, Greensboro, after a Horst master class in dance composition.

Louis Horst sitting beside
his portrait painted by
Moses Soyer, 1961.

Louis Horst and assistant, Janet Mansfield Soares, teaching a group forms class at Juilliard, March 1962. Students: Larry Berger, Mary Barnett, Myron Nadel, and William Louther. Photograph: Susan Schiff. Courtesy of Dance Magazine.

domestic stability as she listened intently to the details of her company members' sexual experiences.

After her affair with Dyer, Martha no longer believed in the once-convincing argument that "erotic energies must translate fully into vital forces for art," as the Victorian scholar, Peter Gay, puts it.[11] She began to counter Louis's paraphrases of Nietzsche's assertions that drives were "ringed round with defenses," and that the "sublimation of instincts is the work of culture."[12] From her own delving into Jungian texts, she found ways to reckon with Louis's passive sexuality. One wonders if at this point Martha could have found solace in Nietzsche's words on impotence as the failure "to unite two currents, the tender and the sensual. . . . Where they love they do not desire, and where they desire they cannot love."[13]

Whether or not Louis consulted these texts to explain his own deficiencies, he, too, began to blend philosophies and psychologies such as these to explain a person's behavior. His well-known tenderness toward women did produce a sublimation of instincts that worked for culture. If he understood Martha's need to be with a man who desired her as a physical being as well as an artist, he never acknowledged it, but continued to believe in the artist's need to sublimate, to look past ordinary pleasures toward more cerebral aesthetic values. He regularly listed the words great artistry and sublimation as necessary ingredients for great dances: Put content into an "aesthetic pattern" and sublimate it to avoid just exposing the inner self.[14] One wonders if he was also commenting on the guiding philosophy of his own life. Martha's affair may have severed her physical bond to Louis, but their lives as interdependent colleagues remained intact. Although he continued to preach that artists should not be burdened by commitment to any one person, everything he continued to do was "for Martha's sake." Her ability to provide what he considered to be the highest form of communication remained his ultimate pleasure; it was her gift as a dance artist that his unswerving passion championed.

One of Louis's favorite words, "tenacity," best describes his own means for seeing a project through, for making things happen. *Dance Observer* was a publishing outlet for his outright advocacy of Martha's work, but it also enabled him to support other important developments in dance. The magazine continued full coverage of the concert scene and dance activities in colleges, along with a certain amount of good-humored name-dropping. As a sounding board for opinion, the editorial page proved to be a worthy addition to dance journalism. In the November 1936 issue, for example, *Dance Observer* had decried the failure of government support for a Federal Dance

Theatre. In addition the journal provided strong support for the causes of new organizations, such as the American Dance Association, the New Dance League, and the Dance Guild, and voiced the hope that an amalgamation might be possible. The quality of dance criticism also became a dominant concern. The unsigned April 1937 editorial stated that "five rules of good criticism" were to be followed by future staff writers, who must not be affiliated with any one faction of dance and must remain open-minded and above favoritism—a directive that might have been aimed directly at its own editor-in-chief. The magazine also jointly sponsored events at the 92nd Street Y, where a fifty-cent ticket gained entry to one of Louis's lecture-demonstrations. Thus, by 1937 Louis had emerged as not only an indispensable figure among dancers, but also a critic and editor for the one publication that supported modern dance and a person who could impress educators. His stance as an equitable, uncompetitive, and caring mentor and impartial confidant had spread into every aspect of the field.

This was the period when activity in Nazi Germany was stepping up. The tragic explosion of the airship Hindenburg shocked the nation, which was rapidly losing its isolationist stance as a democratic leader for peaceful coexistence. In the theater some people were roused by Clifford Odets's exploration of life's value in *Waiting for Lefty* and some enjoyed sophisticated comedies by Noël Coward, but larger audiences thrived on slick Roxy productions and Hollywood movies. Depression on stage had become as tiresome as it was in the real world and the offerings at Bennington's Armory in summer 1937 reflected a more positive attitude. Hanya Holm's program note for her premiere of *Trend* expressed this sentiment with "there emerges out of the ordeal itself a recognition of the common purpose of men and the conscious unity of life." In 1934 Louis's score for *American Provincials* had used open chord progressions and simple melodic themes that expressed the sense of optimism for the country's future. In 1935 he wrote a set of variations to "She'll be Comin' Round the Mountain" for Agnes de Mille, and three months later *Frontier,* a simple rendering of an American tune in rondo form. At Bennington in 1937, Louis composed *Variations on a Middle West Theme* for his students' Americana studies.

When Martha arrived at the Bennington campus from the West Coast, Louis suggested a temporary cooling-off period, and she began to work on two solos without him. One became *Opening Dance*. Its piano score by Norman Lloyd was, in his own telling, a failure: "Graham was at a turning point, leaving the period of stripping down to essentials. . . . She was beginning to go into something a little more romantic and lyrical. I didn't realize it and she was inarticulate about it. I wrote as though it were still her stark period. I realized I hadn't caught the thing. It wasn't successful."[15] He admitted his unpreparedness for the sudden challenge of taking Louis's place in the studio. In contrast Martha's other solo, *Immediate Tragedy: Dance of Dedication* was more substantial. Henry Cowell wrote the score in San Quentin prison, where he was serving time on a morals charge. Confined, he came up with a creative solution few others had considered. Martha had sent him notes outlining the mood of the dance, its tempo, and its meter. With no specification of the exact length of any section he devised a method he called "elastic form." Norman Lloyd declared with admiration, "We had never seen anything like it. Cowell had written two basic phrases to be played by oboe and clarinet. Each phrase existed in two-measure, three-measure, eight-measure versions, and so on. All that was necessary was to fit a five-measure musical phrase to a five-measure dance phrase — or make such overlaps as were deemed necessary. The process, as I remember it, took about an hour. The total effect was complete unity — as though dancer and composer had been in the closest communication."[16]

Separated from Martha's newest work, Louis began to find greater pleasure in his role as teacher. Alwin Nikolais, who would develop his own wide reputation as a choreographer, was a new student at Bennington and spoke of Louis's inspired teaching: "Louis was the one that changed my life. It wasn't Martha. It wasn't Hanya. It was Louis. . . . He trained my eye. I place him as one of the greatest enforcers of my career. It was success with Louis that made me decide to give up music to become a dancer. His terseness appealed to me and his exactness. . . . You couldn't get away with anything. After you finished a dance, he'd say, 'You know in the sixth measure on the fourth beat, you did this. Why?' He required precise aesthetic reasoning of you."

Nikolais was quick to add that at the beginning he was cruel: "I remember one woman who showed Louis her dance. She stuck her head in the door the next day, and he said, 'You've got your nerve to come back!' Another horrible time, a dancer named Charles — a very effeminate kind of person — showed his study. The night before class I said to Charles, 'You got your Pavane ready?' and he said, 'Oh, yes. It was very easy.' When he did his dance Louis said, 'Well, I don't know if there were fairies in those days, but if there were they would have certainly moved exactly as you did!' Charles never appeared in class again."[17]

Being "taken over the coals" by Horst had become the imperative first step for every modern dancer. Most of them appreciated that important elements of his work with Graham filtered into their assignments. Nikolais elaborated:

He would often bring to his composition classes the new things that were happening, particularly with Martha. I remember the first year [at Bennington], Martha didn't move. She was standing on one foot. The idea in class was that you did not move unless the movement was functional. We didn't dare make a gesture unless it was a significant one and I learned a lot of my craft from him in that particular sense. For the courante — a running dance — I thought, Oh my God, you're not supposed to move. How am I going to do a courante without leaving the one spot on the floor? (Louis used to tell his students afterward, "Well, I remember Alwin once doing a courante, and he did it on one foot and you'd swear he was running.") The next year, he got awfully tired of us not moving, and he said, "Why aren't you people moving? You've got some technique. Why don't you use it? It's boring standing still all the time!" So things changed that way from year to year.[18]

It was Nina Fonaroff's fresh appreciation of Louis's gift as a teacher that fully renewed his self-confidence. Always drawn to his side, whether in rehearsal or in class, and plainly awestruck, she recalled, "He got wonderful, physical results on stage and in the classroom. That was his talent. He gave life to things. He had this talent to feel and understand what dance is. Louis was one of the most truthful human beings. Nothing fooled him. He never acted or pretended. He never put on a false front. He never tried to be affable socially. He was just who he was. [Louis had] an enormous instinct that [determined] his whole make up — his purity, and his spirit."[19] In turn, Nina pleased the master teacher with her bright choreography and flattered him with her responsive manner. Attracted to her at once, Nina become Louis's next love interest within weeks.

Some believed that Louis's friendship with Nina, as with Martha before her, was nonphysical. Together they brought to mind arm-in-arm figures by Paul Klee or a simple Satie melody, in spite of the more than thirty-years difference in their ages. Quiet and even-tempered, Nina had a certain elusive quality; some considered her "mouselike." She had been raised in New York City, the daughter of violinists. Like her mother she was a fine seamstress and cook. "I was brought up [to believe] that you don't talk to critics. And I was like a child. The whole child thing was part of it," she said candidly.[20]

Totally different in type from Martha, the demure dancer was petite, blond, and blue-eyed. Trained in ballet under Michel Fokine, her inquiring mind made her a knowledgeable observer in the world of the arts at an early age. Able to respond sensitively to Louis's points of view, she scolded him for making generalizations on the various styles he taught in his classes and pressed him to refine his ideas. Nestled close to his stocky figure, whether at the theater or in the studio, Nina "was always around. They were great friends — pals," Otto Luening said. "He was her aesthetic hero."[21]

By fall 1937 Nina, too, was living in the Hotel des Artistes, with her mother. For Louis the proximity had the additional benefit of Mrs. Fonaroff's excellent cooking. Nina said about the working arrangement, "That fall I joined Martha, and he made me his assistant [for a course] at Teacher's College." Louis fully enjoyed her company and expressed amazement at "the clever way she could get people to do whatever she wanted, talking her way into anything, whether with a maître-d' in a restaurant or a dancer in a rehearsal studio."[22] At one point Louis decided that she would be a fine advertising representative for *Dance Observer*. He sent her to Ben Sommers, head of the Capezio dancewear company. Nina reported the incident: " 'Can you tell me why I should buy an ad in this little magazine?' he asked me. 'No,' I replied, embarrassed. 'Well then, I'll run an advertisement for the next five years.' I was flabbergasted!"[23]

Nina's first appearance with Martha in the group work *American Lyric,* to a score by Alex North, at the Guild on 26 December 1937 surprised no one. As in the Denishawn days, when Ruth and Ted made sure that Louis had his "women" around him, outsiders assumed that Nina was, like the others, his "choice." She, in turn, was known to have lovers on occasion. Martha Hill commented, "She was valuable as a dancer. Her technique was outstanding, and she was ideal as an ingenue in the new dances being created. She was imaginative and strong."[24] When asked if Louis's position with the company was the X factor of the whole thing, Nina's answer was an emphatic "Yes." Horst had become the X factor in Nina's own career, as well.

Henry Gilfond, managing editor of what he termed the "new" *Dance Observer,* in a surprising move invited the balletomane Lincoln Kirstein to write for the journal. Gilfond then wrote an editorial claiming that a bias toward the modern dance had developed "editorial myopia": "The modern dance no longer needs the kind of defense we intended. It is no longer a stranger in a hostile country. Both as a mature and a popular art form, the modern dance needs no special nurturing."[25] Conflict on the managing board erupted, with Ralph Taylor, who had long mistrusted Gilfond's politics, resigning "in protest." Perhaps in part to placate ruffled feathers, Kirstein took the opportunity to write that Graham had become the "greatest dancer on this continent," although readers knew of his conviction that the classic traditional idiom must serve as "the basis for future possibility in the American theatrical dance." She stood alone in her "strength and catholicity," he wrote in his *Dance Observer* review of *Immediate Tragedy.*[26] Louis remained silent during the scuffle, burying his thoughts while writing a series of feature articles on pre-classic dance forms.

An additional homage to Graham's genius appeared at the end of that year — Merle Armitage's *Martha Graham: The Early Years*. Produced in the same manner as his books on Picasso and Stravinsky, it was a collection of diverse pieces: Horst's list of every performance given to date, supporting reviews, and an article by Kirstein, who this time said, "where once I thought was all blackness has become in a flash, all light."[27] (Years later he would name Martha "one of the world's great artists."[28]) Illustrated with line drawings by Carlus Dyer, other enthusiastic contributors included close associates and personal friends. One of the first volumes to focus exclusively on one modern dance artist, the little book was dedicated to Horst and included a Soichi Sunami photograph of him — in retrospect a kind of thank-you gesture that might be construed as signaling the end of the Graham-Horst intimacy.

Louis himself was urged into publication mainly by Taylor; *Pre-Classic Dance Forms,* a compilation of his monthly articles, appeared in a limited edition of one thousand, selling at two dollars apiece. Inscribing copies to his closest friends, he wrote in one, "To Ralph Taylor who started the *Dance Observer*."[29] Nina responded to his Christmas gift and inscription to her with, "So touched and thrilled over book and dedication."[30] John Martin's 1933 *The Modern Dance* and 1936 *America Dancing: The Background and Personalities of the Modern Dance* (with Louis's name omitted) had obviously spurred the desire to place doctrine into print. In a sense the publishing of their books established Martha and Louis as confident standard-bearers of the serious nature of modern dance.

As artists their jointly conceived modus operandi continued to flourish, with Martha the benefactor of Louis's insistence on form out of emotion. She wrote in the concluding chapter of *Martha Graham*, "The dance has two sides — one is the science of movement, the technique which is a cold exact science and has to be learned very carefully — and the other is the distortion of those principles, the use of that technique impelled by an emotion."[31] Louis's concern was the scientific aspect of crafting dance materials, as Nikolais observed, "He supplied the 'bones' to Martha's 'muscle' . . . He was the eagle-eye for Martha."[32] In combination they functioned with high-powered efficiency, despite the winding-down of their intimacy.

By the new year of 1938 it was obvious to everyone that the illustrious couple of modern dance were no longer emotionally involved. Louis tried to explain that it was not the romantic situation that gradually eroded his work with Martha: "By that time I had made an attachment with Nina."[33] Nina concurred: "The year 1938 marked the time when Louis and Martha separated artistically."[34] But unprepared emotionally or professionally to change, Louis continued to place himself at Martha's disposal as musical director.

Shared group efforts among choreographers were still being attempted during this period. Graham participated in a modern dance evening that presented on the same bill Ruth St. Denis, Hanya Holm, Doris Humphrey, Tamiris, Charles Weidman and others for the short-lived but ambitious Dance International Series. In this spirit of organization the recently formed American Dance Association, another Tamiris brainchild, also presented a concert. On a more modest scale than the earlier Dance Repertory Theatre, Tamiris assumed the A.D.A. presidency, Humphrey became treasurer, and Louis chaired the Artistic Committee. Martha agreed to take part and also appeared on the bill for Dance for Spain, a benefit presented at the end of January 1938 at the New York Hippodrome in support of the victims of the Spanish Civil War. Martha and Louis gave isolated performances on the East Coast, then in March toured briefly with the group through Ohio, Missouri, and to Chicago, where a reviewer identified Louis as having "played an important role in developing Modern Dance in America."[35]

Martha sought inspiration from the fever-pitch political climate of the time for appropriate material for the New York World's Fair Preview Pageant, scheduled for May. She chose as a resource William Carlos Williams's *In the American Grain,* based on documents from American history. The result was *Militant Hymn,* a short group piece, for which Louis's score again used an American folk melody as its theme. The two creators attended a special dinner at the Ford Pavilion in Flushing Meadow and were photographed by the press among politicians and industrialists.

In 1936 Lincoln Kirstein founded a ballet company to present the finest American dancers and choreographers. Among Ballet Caravan's talented dancers was Erick Hawkins. Martha had seen Erick's *Showpiece* in 1937 at Bennington, presented along with a Kirstein lecture on The Classic Dance. She again saw Erick dance and congratulated him backstage after a Caravan performance in New York City some months later. By June 1938, he was having difficulty developing choreographic ideas. Kirstein gave him a loan to study with Graham, and he promptly enrolled in her school's annual June course. He asked to stay on after classes to watch the rehearsals of her new work, *American Document,* and expressed enthusiasm for her minstrel-show concept.

Her company of loyal women had been at work on the material for months, often until three or four o'clock in the morning. Among them, May O'Donnell and Gertrude Shurr had returned from the West Coast to be in it.

Out of the blue, during one rehearsal, Martha announced, "Erick will come in here," to everyone's shock, including Erick's. Dissent grew among some of Martha's dancers, who were "torn philosophically" when Martha then invited Erick to work in her company. Shurr said, "She was bringing Erick in and I was wanting to go out. Martha was very much in love with Erick. We so believed in what she was doing that we were willing to spend those hours of rehearsal — to take all the conniving, intrigue, and everything else. We had to help Martha."[36]

Louis heard grumblings of discontent, but Martha had gone through these phases before and the Group had survived. He concentrated instead on his new companion and the rather lax training of his new, three-month-old dachshund, Spud. No replacement for the beloved Max, this ill-behaved pup, who loved to chew the corners of Indian rugs, kept Louis on the run between assignments. Completing a series of intensive classes in Washington, D.C., he wound up the season giving a June course at Martha's new 66 Fifth Avenue location. He then packed, handed over the key to his apartment to a deserving student for the summer, as was his habit, and left for Bennington with Spud in tow.

Summer 1938 was an exciting time for the modern dance world, and for Graham. By July Erick was given a "principal" role in *American Document,* although he was still listed on the program as an apprentice appearing through the courtesy of Lincoln Kirstein and Ballet Caravan. Otto Luening said, "We called him 'the torso.' Erick went over big with most of us around Bennington because he was such a handsome figure. He was the young guy coming up."[37] Some fretted that Erick began to assume command of Martha's company in a "cavalier" manner, conducting rehearsals and giving technical corrections to dancers who themselves had helped shape the materials.

Martha's and Erick's intense relationship — which would continue until the early 1950s — affected everything. Martha was forty-six; Erick was thirty. The sensuality of his youthful presence suddenly seemed to please her as much as liaisons with much younger women pleased Louis. Friends found her in an exuberant mood, but the romance complicated Martha's position with her dancers. Shurr said, "It was the first time in years that she had a male around for all those love duets. In rehearsals a whole new thing took place that opened up Martha's life. I knew that I couldn't even talk with Martha and say, 'Look Martha, the company's going to change. It's not for me.' I wrote to her, and left."[38] Sokolow and O'Donnell left along with Shurr. Others followed. If Martha was saddened by the loss of those who had been so important to her past successes, she had few qualms about shifting the emphasis of her choreography.

More than one critic has proposed that Erick was placed in Graham's circle as Kirstein's "serpent." Erick suggested ways of partnering and helped define scenes and episodes, standard choreographic procedures in the ballet world. Quick to accept the spirit of modern dance and proud of Martha's shift from "square, frontal" materials to more "spiral," circular patterns, he, too, began to change. But his invaluable experience in ballet had given him some idea of how a dance company operated, and he gradually assumed managerial duties on Martha's behalf.[39]

Luening did not think "Erick was much of a rival to Louis in his professional relationship to Martha at that point. . . . Louis was too valuable to Martha. He was the professional crop."[40] Once on stage Louis played his role as musician, framing the dancer before him. No amount of personal aggravation interfered. Shurr offered another perspective: "As a human being you could never get very close to Martha. I think that Louis had the same feeling. But no matter what emotional things he went through, he would stick it out with Martha."[41] Everyone understood that Martha's personal well-being took precedence over her professional choices during this richly productive period.

The bold experimentation of previous seasons at Bennington had given way by 1938 to a strong emphasis on the fusion of music, design, lighting, and costuming. This was in part to satisfy an administration that sought greater visibility for their other art programs. Martha's troublesome *American Document,* with its ensemble of twenty-three dancers, was fraught with problems. A press release announced, "For the first time in her career, Miss Graham will use a male dancer in one of her own works, and also for the first time, will utilize speech."[42] Martha later justified the inclusion of an actor and text by rationalizing that "our own country — our democracy — has words, too, with power to hearten men and move them to action."[43] Nevertheless, Edwin Denby called the piece a transitional dance and a "complete failure."[44]

Although Louis took his usual position at the keyboard during rehearsals and performances of Ray Green's score for the work, his crowded schedule also included running a composers' forum, designed to air the question of whether music written expressly for dance "could stand alone." In a reverse trend at Bennington, some dance artists were going back to older methods of choreographing to music. Humphrey surprised Louis with her use of Bach's Passacaglia in C Minor for an ensemble work, and although Holm's *Dance of Work and Play* had a specially composed score, *Dance Sonata* was choreographed to existing music by Harrison Kerr. This retrogression caused concern among composers. Although Horst himself used baroque composers

exclusively in his course to teach formal principles, he fully expected returning students to advance to modern and finally to commissioned scores.

Bennington's *Banner* caught the polemical mood of the session:

> Mr. Horst traced the relationship of music to the dance through the
> period when the dancer was impelled to create a work by the inspiration
> of a piece of music. . . . A next step was the complete subservience of
> music to the dance, followed by many dancers trying to do without
> music to accompany their work but this proved to be a nervous strain on
> the audience. . . . [He called] the medium of the body, "a dangerous
> instrument." . . . The dance today is one in which the dance is empha-
> sized, deepened, by the use of music, like a frame around a painting.[45]

To emphasize his position he referred to Graham's achievements. Unfortunately, the other choreographers did not have as opinionated a musical
adviser featured in the local newspaper.

This development annoyed Louis and he struggled to hold his ground on
the issue. The situation with Erick angered him still more, but through it all
Louis maintained a calm exterior. Always a gentleman — he wore his suit
jacket, tie, and suspendered trousers above his rotund belly no matter how
hot it was — no one suspected an ounce of jealousy on his part. Inwardly
seething, he harbored resentment and growing irritation over Erick and
could barely stand his presence at the Commons dining table each evening.
At the session's end Graham's mother was another visitor on campus to meet
Erick as well as attend the festival. Martha Hill recalled that "She stayed at
the Cricket Hill house, where Martha and I always lived. Erick was around a
lot. I'd hear noises in the kitchen at 3:00 A.M., go down to check, and find
Erick and Martha having a cup of tea. This was a period of 'free love,' of
course. You didn't get married."[46] In an odd counterpoint Betty arrived from
California to join her husband for the final performances.

The future for this group of artists was filled with uncertainty. Accustomed to creating several pieces a season, *American Document* marked
Martha's last major attempt before the longest hiatus in her prolific career. It
would be a year and four months before Louis or Erick could prod her into
another collaboration. Uneasy about the future of dance at the Vermont
college, the West Coast contingent of dance educators suggested that the
school of dance might consider joining forces at Mills College for the next
session. Bennington's "five-year plan" between the dance faculty and the
administration was fulfilled. Louis stayed in the Vermont hills with other
members of the faculty for a few more precious days at this place they had
grown to love.

He returned to teaching for the fall semester, with Nina at his side, at Teachers College, Martha's studio, and the independent "Studio 404." They organized lecture-demonstrations throughout the year, while continuing to rehearse with Martha's company on a regular basis. After a month-long "third transcontinental tour" of eleven states with her company of seventeen, Martha and Louis had resolved their personal conflict to some degree. Again a team, they participated in a variety of activities, including several for political causes. They then joined the cast of André Obey's play, *Noah,* for a short run in North Carolina. When the New York World's Fair officially opened on 30 April 1939, the press credited Louis's score for Graham's *Tribute to Peace* as giving the choreography a "singleness of focus."[47] From then on Martha acknowledged Louis's uncompromising work ethic as the source of much that she had accomplished and often referred to this singleness of purpose in statements to the press: "He was rigid in his discipline as any performer must be. He felt of dance as the East Indians do — a celebration of life, but he also saw it as a complete discipline of body and spirit, and such a discipline he demanded from himself and from others."[48] This disciplined state between them would hold steady for another nine years.

Most of the prominent modern dancers created work in their separate ways when in Manhattan, but their summer stays in Vermont continued to link their mission and give a sense of continuity for the field under Martha Hill's wing as artistic director. Now, Hill had received a much-deserved sabbatical and a strained situation had developed as Bennington's administrators hoped to develop a more diversified arts program. In view of these circumstances the School of Dance board voted to hold the 1939 session at Mills College in Oakland, California. Hanya Holm had been guest artist there from 1934 to 1936, and Bonnie Bird, Tina Flade, and Lester Horton had taught the previous summer. Hill explained that "Rosalind Cassidy [chair of the Mills College Department of Physical Education and director of the school's summer session] formally invited Bennington to Mills, and offered us a $20,000 budget";[49] a good portion of that figure would have to go for the faculty's travel across the country.

Dance students who attended the 1939 summer session at Mills studied with an "associate" in a single technique for the first three weeks, then daily classes taught by Graham, Holm, or Humphrey and Weidman for the final three weeks. (Martha arrived for her residency noticeably radiant and in an unusually romantic frame of mind.) The students also participated in an experimental production workshop directed by Martha Hill, with Arch Lauterer, Ben Belitt, and Norman Lloyd assisting. The scaled-down version of Bennington's program did not include the usual final festival performances. Only the ambitious José Limón, with Ethel Butler, Louise Kloepper, and Katherine Manning, managed to produce a concert at season's end. Limón's solo, *Danzas Mexicanas,* to music by Lionel Nowak and produced under modest circumstances, was one of the highlights of the session.[50]

If the dance curriculum at Mills was somewhat modified, the music component was impressive. The Major Course in Music for the Dance staff worked as a team with student musicians and collaborated with dancers for the full six weeks. Lloyd taught keyboard improvisation and a course called Rhythmic Basis of Dance, and Franziska Boas presided over sessions in percussion accompaniment. Horst taught his usual principles of compositional form and style. One of his most talented students was Mercier [Merce] Cunningham: "He took Pre-classic Forms. Martha and I took one look at him and said, 'Wouldn't you like to come to New York?' "[51]

While in residence Louis prepared *Musical Settings,* a collection of short pieces to accompany dance, for publication by Fischer and Brothers. At the session's end he joined Nina in Santa Fe. His good friends Ruth and Norman Lloyd traveled to New Mexico with him. Ruth described the trip: "We had a wonderful time. We stayed about two weeks. At Santa Fe Louis helped us buy rugs. We took a trip looking for Marie [a well-known Indian potter]. We got stuck [in the sand] on our way and discovered the value of piñon boughs. We later found out that Marie was in San Francisco, and when they pointed out that-a-way as Indians do, they were pointing to San Francisco!"[52] Louis expressed to her his disdain at the modernization taking place at one of the pueblos they visited. "The Indians had glass in their windows instead of mica and they owned sewing machines. He had a particular fondness for keeping things the way they were."[53] The group attended the Intertribal Ceremonials in Gallup, where Louis received a great compliment: "I was asked to be judge. They had asked another dancer who was there. He said, 'No, but ask that man with the white hair over there. He knows more about dance than anybody.' There were seven judges — one for costumes, best women's group, etc. I tried to make little comments about who was best so everyone got a prize!"[54]

Back in New York Louis resumed his usual round of teaching, attending two or three concerts a week, and writing for *Dance Observer.* He roamed the galleries between assignments and with Nina selected a Klee watercolor, *Drüber und Drunter,* for his collection. He entered its purchase in his journal next to mention of a social meeting with the composer Ernst Křenek.

Erick had moved into Martha's West 12th Street apartment when they returned from a camping trip in Colorado. If not unduly upset from an emotional standpoint by this latest development, Louis nevertheless now openly expressed his mistrust of Erick, whose Harvard background in philosophy galled him. "He felt that she would be led astray by Erick, who was just another dancer who would never get over his ballet days in terms of movement."[55] But if he considered Erick's manner arrogant, he had to acknowledge the fact that wonderful new duet materials and interesting roles for men were being introduced into Martha's choreography. Erick's point of view, of course, was dramatically different. He was inspired with the "whole new vision of what dance could become. . . . Being around Martha, learning from her; that was a terrific privilege," but thinking back on their eventual schism as partners, he reflected, "If I didn't learn anything else from her, I learned courage. Martha believes that one's life is for art, and I believe art is for one's life, and that's where we differ."[56]

Seeming to have lost her enthusiasm for working alone, Martha presented an unsuccessful new solo, *Columbiad*, at the St. James Theater on 27 December 1939, to Louis's score: "*Columbiad* wasn't very good. It was rather a nice score but it was kind of a dull piece. People liked it but it was not a worthy dance of [Martha's]."[57] Walter Terry wrote a scathing review for the next day's *Herald Tribune:* "The less said about *Columbiad* . . . the better. To state that it is obscure in meaning, unhitched in construction, and accompanied by ear-torturing music is putting it politely."[58] *Every Soul Is a Circus,* also on the program, had taken most of Martha's choreographic energy and fortunately saved the season by showing her comic side, to everyone's delight.

With fifteen dancers and Louis as musical director, the Martha Graham Dance Company gave its "fourth transcontinental tour" from 12 February to 5 April 1940 touring the South, through Texas, California, up the coast to Oregon, Washington, then back through Ohio to New York. As is often the case, incidental experiences stuck in the pianist's mind: "In Eugene [Oregon] on tour we gave a performance in a gymnasium. . . . There was a window open, and during the performance a large bird got in and was flying around. After the show was over, I heard a shot, and then the bird dropped on the floor. Flop! It was kind of exciting in a strange way."[59] The incident may have reflected his own speculation about his fate with the company.

As the Bennington School prepared for its sixth season faced with a severely limited budget, only Graham was invited to be the producing artist-in-residence. (Louis himself had a nest egg of $4,221.08 in 1940.) The United States Federal Service Agency had featured Martha as an independent artist in an unusual radio broadcast, "On with the Dance," about "gallant American women." Although her past image as a matriarch had been Louis's invention and her earlier works created from suppressed desires, her dances now expressed the pleasures she felt as a woman. Her position as a leading authority was in place. Louis believed that greatness is a gift of life — and Martha had that gift. Now, a broadening audience that included the administrators at Bennington agreed. They understood that Louis, Erick (who was asked to teach ballet), and her dancers were essential to her work. The ensemble happily returned to the newly structured School of the Arts devised by the college's president, Robert Leigh. Dance, drama, music, and theater design were placed side by side with various subjects taught by members of the regular college faculty. In the new configuration students could specialize in one of four areas, crossing over to other art disciplines if they chose.

Less auspicious spontaneous events that summer included the occasional soccer game on the Commons, inevitably ended when Louis's dachshund dashed in to wrestle with the ball. Then a great hulking figure ran to the rescue, chasing the dog all over the field. Chaos followed. Everyone dissolved in laughter. Louis and Spud wrecked any hope of completing the game. The Hoosick Tunnel card-playing crowd, to which Louis "belonged" (along with Otto Luening and his crowd), playfully harassed the somber dancers whenever they got a chance. The progressive nature of the place attracted other artists, including Carl Sandburg and Buckminster Fuller. "Bucky" suggested a kind of world umbrella that would keep the bad weather out. Luening remembered the experimental model home that Horst had lived in for several summers: "[Fuller] gave Bennington . . . Dymaxion House, which was very circular and very compact. . . . But when [Louis] gained weight, and could no longer back into the bathroom, he moved. After that the house became a playground for faculty children."[60] Community spirit always ran high; with little else to do, everyone participated in everything. Good times among these artists were an important part of the school's ambiance, but when it came to teaching, Luening and Louis "agreed that we should not let people knock the music all out of shape just because they had a great gleam in their eye about movement."[61]

The topics of discussion in classes were always varied, for Louis continually brought in new music, spoke of recent exhibitions, and discussed concerts he had attended. As issues and themes changed the format of his courses remained the same, to the chagrin of an occasional dissenting voice. To round out his usual twelve-week semester he added assignments in "jazz" and "cerebral" styles. (During six-week sessions, he gave two assignments a week.) Although he did collect copious notes about surrealism and naturalism, these categories never worked their way into his courses. Gertrude Lippincott, an eager student, filled her notebook with lists of his half-sentences that give a sense of his classroom dialogue: "Form. Discipline helps. Manipulation: 1. Put emotion in later. Form first. 2. Construct choice of a thing in a pattern with aesthetic principles. 3. Use material frankly. 4. Be clear. Simple themes can be developed into sequences of movement. Theme must be able to stand repetition. If movement clear then no words necessary." She added some "be carefuls" about interpreting music and keeping to music's structure rather than its sound.[62]

Louis's pedagogy was not without criticism. Some students questioned the strict lifting of musical structure for dance purposes — a view that even Nina would come to share. Cunningham appreciated the discipline needed to adhere to these principles, but said, "My experience with Cage led me to the idea that musical structure per se was not necessarily what was involved, but that time was involved, so that you could use a time structure between the dance and the music. Louis's ideas didn't seem to me to be necessary. I didn't find them pertinent, although I admired him. . . . The Horst ideas I found simply to be nineteenth-century. I could see why he did it. . . . As for me, I thought there should be something else."[63] Although Cunningham eventually came to this conclusion, he like most novices was eager to please. It was Louis who introduced him to formal concepts of structure and insisted on the abstraction of dance materials at the outset.

From 1939 through the early forties, Louis's life centered on teaching and running *Dance Observer,* with Bennington his established home-away-from-home. Articles by contemporary composers had become a regular feature of the magazine, which gave Louis an opportunity to write about his own concepts of time, force, and space as the essential components of all movement — a tenet that had become an important introduction to his modern forms course. Starting in the December 1939 issue with "Understanding by contrast" and over the next few years, he put each specific area of classroom study into print. The documentation of his ideas was invaluable to former students now teaching these materials on their own.

During the 1940 summer session at Bennington the anxiety level in Louis's classes doubled as Betty Lynd Thompson planned her film of selected modern forms studies. The result shows thirteen minutes of dancing, with Graham dancers Ethel Butler, Nelle Fisher, Jane Dudley, Sophie Maslow, Nina, and others clad in jersey skirts, performing their archaic, primitive, medieval, and impressionist dances. Glimpses of Louis at the piano appear as the viewer imagines hearing Satie's *Gymnopédies,* a Bartok bagatelle, or Mompou's *Cants Magics,* selected from the familiar envelopes full of worn music, played so often that everyone could hum their melodies. If filmed to preserve his concepts as a composition teacher, one is left instead with an impression of wonderfully articulate movers showing their studies in a variety of unexplained styles. What is captured for posterity is the depth of commitment these dancers felt toward the notions of their mentor. Graham was to be the sole innovator, having learned from this search of "isms"; clearly these dancers had no chance of finding their own voice within this context. Their work exhibits the exclusive single-mindedness of their mentors that made them exemplary followers and interpreters.[64]

Graham presented two works at the 1940 Bennington festival. In the newly designed College Theatre, with bleacher seating, *Letter to the World* and *El Penitente* were performed on the same evening. Both fine works, the less troublesome *El Penitente* proved to be one of Martha's and Louis's most worthy collaborations. Created in a deluge of last-minute decisions, the score would be the last of eleven Louis composed for Martha and the only one composed before the dance was made. Luening described the process: "Louis got ahead of Martha's planning. [He] got going on it ahead of time." The arrangement for piano, flute, and clarinet evoked a village band. "Bob [McBride], Louis and myself played it. The performance went very well and when the thing was over, Martha called us over for a bow. I thought it was pretty grand of her to do it because we were sweaty and literally in our shorts backstage. . . . She knew that we . . . had a big job . . . Louis was very good on that. He didn't have much time to get it done, but he did it."[65]

Erick felt that the most beautiful performance of *El Penitente* happened in the dining room the night before its premiere: "That was the first pure crystallization of it after Martha had composed it."[66] Erick and Merce Cunningham, both charismatic dancers, were given a substantial share of solo dancing. Casting herself in a sensuous central role flanked by these two men, Martha labeled the sections "virginity, penance, the death cart as a symbol for sin, seduction, the fall of man, the condemnation, the bared cross, atonement and absolution." Her lofty telling of the Penitente's culture concluded with a festival dance.

Both *El Penitente* and *Letter to the World* dealt with relationships between two men and a woman and involved rapidly changing images and narrative structures. *Letter* integrated Emily Dickinson's poetry with a large cast and many sections. As in *El Penitente* dancers played characters, with several duets for Erick and Martha, and scenes of past and present dissolved from one to the other. Martha split her role into two parts—observer and protagonist. The pure ideal of the Poetic Beloved and the forcefulness of the Dark Beloved paralleled the two men in her own life.

If Martha's images were poetic, Louis's were not in his dealings with Hunter Johnson and his score for *Letter:* "I said, 'Cut, cut, cut,' and Kirkpatrick, a friend of Hunter's, said, 'Louis, you're ruining the score.' I said,

'It's too long. One hour and fifteen or twenty minutes. The dance wasn't good — the music wasn't good. So I did cut. We just ended it earlier and it's been cut ever since.' "[67] Luening was a little more sympathetic toward Johnson: "Hunter had a difficult time getting that score done. He was a good composer, but as a musical personality his music might have been a little too developed — too independent for Louis, who would see that the music was not too prominent and detract from Martha's concept of the dance. It must be an accompanying score. Hunter's score was a little thick, a little heavy, which I don't think Louis went for too much. He liked open sound — that was his notion."[68] Once accustomed to this process of composing, musicians like Johnson were soon caught up by the exciting atmosphere of Bennington, where dancers appreciated their music-making talents.

Although Louis was involved in composing *El Penitente* and playing for the grueling rehearsals of *Letter,* when faced with a class of budding composer-musicians he was mercilessly demanding. Hazel Johnson, Evelyn Lohoefer, and George McGeary, who were students in his Composition for Dancers course, were converted to the cause. Each remembered the terror-filled training. For Hazel Johnson, "It was a freeing experience. Everyone loving music and dance. As a woman composer, I fit right in," although little in her background prepared her for the course. Later she agreed that pre-classic forms were perfect models for dance and for composing, but her first battle was to keep a steady tempo and become familiar with the dancer's visual cues. Louis harshly criticized her first study: "The first climax is too strong. It destroys the second," and complained about her thick chords as well. Hazel reasoned that she might just soften the chords in a section he wanted changed for the next playing, after which he bellowed, "Why hadn't you done as I said?" For her next piece, she tried another tack. She needed more contrast between sections, he told her. "The second attempt was not enough. But for my third attempt, I changed register and contrasted size." To this, Horst pronounced, "I didn't say you had to put sign posts up along the way!"[69]

It was an "incredible time" for Lohoefer: "In class Louis sat by the keyboard with his cigar and his dog, and we composers were seated in a row. He called you and you got up and did your thing."[70] McGeary explained the system: "Basically, the assignment was given on Monday. On Wednesday we'd bring it in and then we would have these awful sessions on Friday night and Saturday morning where we kept switching dances and compositions. Everybody cried all the time. The dancers would rehearse, and the composer would sit and gulp at the pieces with all the changes that Louis had made."[71] Lohoefer added:

There's one time I'm not likely to forget. I played my piece while the dancer did her dance — I don't know how many times — (he was not very kind to his dancers). It had a four-note figure. And then he said to me, "Alright, now, don't do bill-i-am (upward) . . . do bill-i-am (downward)." I didn't know what that translation was. I was frustrated. (He could have walked to the piano and said, "Play B natural instead of B flat, reverse it, or start with the last note." But he just roasted me, or tried to.) After more than half an hour of trying to find out what combination of those four notes he wanted, Louis got really angry: "God damn it, when I tell you to do something, don't sit there and refuse to do it!" When he said that, I really got angry. I stood up and slammed both elbows down on the keyboard, and I said, "Jesus Christ didn't have a thing to do with it!" I got up and walked out. I thought, What do I do now? I was pulling the leaves off the tree when he came out. He walked over to me and kind of pushed me on the shoulder and said, "Humph! You have got guts." We became friends. He never gave me a bad time again. What he really wanted was a simple reversal. The only thing that saved me was that I got mad. For him, it meant, "O.K. You can stand up to me, and maybe you'll make it." Anyway, I survived. I went back to class. My music was chosen. I lived through those workshops, barely. He was testing me. I was a rebel in those days, but Louis was never surprised after that. He taught me discipline.[72]

The trial by fire for dancers — to whom he would scream, "Not that foot! The other foot!," never mentioning left or right — and musicians alike culminated in the lively workshop performances at the end of each week. Students presented their musical compositions as accompaniment for selected dance studies. McGeary said, "Louis would rant and then stomp out in the tenth row of the auditorium and say, 'No, no, no. That is not the way you played it on Wednesday night! You played it differently then. Why can't you remember?' He had a memory like nobody since Mozart. Louis tracked each beat and action kinetically, in active participation with the dance, retaining an image in sight as well as sound. Louis could see as well as hear, almost forecasting the next move, and this gave him unusual insight in processing and evaluating."[73] As the latest converts to Louis's ideas about the interdependency of musicians and dancers, Johnson, Lohoefer, and McGeary joined the ranks of professional dance accompanists. Once befriended by the dancers, those who returned to Manhattan often found employment — they had become part of the dance community.

Martha gave only two concerts during fall 1940, again presenting *Letter to the World.* A reviewer wrote that she had renounced her "long woolens" period. This information found its way into print alongside alarming reports of American involvement in Europe. The country was close to a state of national emergency. Shortages increased, although the rationing of food hardly changed the sporadic eating habits of dancers. Other factors made their work difficult. With only two performances in the fall, Graham's brief spring season was followed by the usual June course at the studio. Frustrated by a lack of performing opportunities, Martha relied on a worry-free Vermont summer to create new work. When the 1941 summer session was on the verge of cancellation because of limited enrollment, the dance faculty agreed to teach for room and board and the opportunity to present their work in festival conditions.

Louis may have hoped for a score by Aaron Copland for Martha's new *Punch and the Judy,* the project slated for the August festival, but it went to Robert McBride. He was handed carefully scripted notes containing her ideas on the problems of "the other woman," "the home," and "the political bandwagon" for the thirty-minute piece. The completed score gave the "effect of haste," according to Henry Cowell, and for good reason considering the time constraint placed on the composer. The large cast in her "tragicomedy" included Nina, typecast as the Child, and Erick, delighted with his leading figure of Punch to Martha's Judy. Merce, playing Pegasus, was fast tiring of the role-playing that dominated his dancing parts. Throughout rehearsals, Louis sat calmly at the keyboard, trying to merge the score with Martha's sequence of actions.

Doris Humphrey's project that summer was equally grand in scale, if more formidable in subject matter. "The world situation continually urges me to make some sort of comment — yet the whole thing is so vast that any statement seems silly," she wrote to her mother that spring.[74] Instead, she created *Decade: A Biography of Modern Dance from 1930 to 1940,* made up chiefly of excerpts from her previous works, which became a two-hour, full-evening concert. The surprisingly good turnout of students and audiences meant that the faculty could be paid after all.

A *Dance Observer* article summed up the various activities on the Bennington campus as moving "in the direction of the community and the state, with programs by the drama division at the local movie house, and a Green Mountain Festival of the Arts organized to celebrate Vermont's Sesquicentennial." Under Luening's direction the music division "had itself a busy summer. . . . Here as nowhere else young composers have the opportunity to compose, have their work orchestrated, played, and criticized immediately." Robert McBride was rehearsing with "five of the best woodwind players in the country" for a South American tour sponsored by the League of Composers, a string quartet was in residence, the harpsichordist Ralph Kirkpatrick gave a recital, and there was a concert of Cowell's music. John Martin did a "lecture-review of dance today," and there was square dancing: "All the gatherings, planned and spontaneous, that go to make up the word, 'Bennington.' "[75]

Throughout the six weeks of heavy rehearsing and teaching, the highly charged union between Martha and Erick often exploded. After the session in Vermont, they returned to the Southwest to relax at Cady Wells's ranch. Erick reveled in nights of camping and Martha braved the difficulties of outdoor living, yet their attraction to one another was ample compensation. Louis, Spud, and Nina returned to Manhattan.

chapter eight

1941–1948

"And two men ride a horse,

one must ride in front."

— Louis Horst quoting

Shakespeare

With World War II ravaging Europe, Americans were horrified by President Roosevelt's radio address describing Japan's attack on Pearl Harbor. Members of the Graham company (including Louis's most recent Neighborhood Playhouse assistant, Welland Lathrop, who was filling in for a dancer called into service), on their way to Cuba to give performances at the end of 1941, feared a submarine attack as they left Florida's shore. Surviving from hand to mouth, these artists grimly assessed the limited benefits to be derived from such stage appearances. On a visit with George Grosz in his Long Island studio that fall, Louis and the painter had talked about the world at war. As they stood before the watercolor Louis had selected for purchase, the two shared their feelings of helplessness during this dark period.

One cause for celebration in the dance field, however, was the release of Barbara Morgan's photographic essay, *Martha Graham: Sixteen Dances in Photographs.* Her work was an expression of faith, she wrote: "The war makes me more than ever determined and anxious to preserve and create what beauty I can while I can, and while the dancers can. . . . For the sake of living so fully that it turns into dancing — the human heart — regardless of country."[1] Morgan had been photographing Martha's work since 1938 as Bennington's "official photographer," producing a significant archival record of this vital time of modern dance. Fascinated with light and shape, she looked for the dramatic intent in rehearsal as well as performance before attempting to capture the pitch of each action. She assembled an exhibit of her dance photographs that traveled to forty colleges, and to her surprise sixty others wanted to book it. Then, with Leica camera in hand, she concentrated on photographing more of Martha's work, arranging sessions in the studio on Fifth Avenue, at her own, and at the Henry Street Playhouse in lower Manhattan. She asked Louis to write a choreographic chronology and a compilation of company members with dates of their tenure for the edition's index.

To honor the publication Frances Steloff gave a reception at her book shop that Baird Hastings attended. Spying Hastings in the crowd of well-wishers, Louis introduced him to Martha: "Even though he writes about ballet, he's one of us!"[2] With that, Hastings joined the ever-faithful, if eclectic, family of artists, writers, musicians, composers, and dancers who believed in Graham's genius.

Performances for 1941–1942 were limited to the usual Washington Irving High School recitals, the Academy of Music in Philadelphia, and the culminating, all-important Guild Theatre on Broadway. Erick, who now acted as business representative, began to consider ways to enlarge the company's horizons. In January 1942 he wrote to Elizabeth Sprague Coolidge, who had established a foundation to commission music for premieres in the newly dedicated Coolidge Auditorium at the Library of Congress. By writing to the potential dance patron without first consulting Martha or Louis, Erick evidently hoped to nab commissioned scores from Copland and Hindemith for Martha's choreography, and possibly his own. Receiving no reply, he sent a copy of Morgan's book to Coolidge. In a note of thanks she said she would keep his suggestion in mind. A second letter on June 16 opened an extended correspondence. Mrs. Coolidge mentioned the possibility of commissioning scores by Vittorio Rieti and Bernard Wagenaar. Although respected composers, neither now had any particular interest in writing for dance and their names were soon dropped. The Library of Congress music division head, Harold Spivacke, entered the discussion, communicating directly with Martha as well as with Coolidge, Aaron Copland, Carlos Chavez, and Gian-Carlo Menotti. A continuous flow of letters described delays, gave apologies, and asked questions. Erick's idea for a commission for himself was squelched when Coolidge and Graham began a chatty exchange of letters on their own. Negotiations continued throughout the summer at Bennington and into the following year.

It was apparent to newcomers that Bennington's unofficial master of ceremonies was Louis; his approval seemed to trigger success within the system. Students were quick to note that he was not without adversaries, who begrudged his impatient tirades and unchallenged rule, although few doubted his unfaltering advocacy for modern dance. Nikolais explained that "Bennington's influence flew out all over the country then and afterward. Louis's influence in particular was startling. Everyone who took a course with him went back, and soon pavanes, galliards, gigues, and medieval things were everywhere. In a way, that was devastating. But on the other hand it was the gymnasium circuit that supported the whole touring thing."[3]

The school confronted a variety of mounting problems. Martha Hill recalled, "We were all taking part in the war effort, farming and rolling bandages," although as dancers they had little experience at this sort of thing. "The load of chickens we raised were packed too tightly in their crates. Before we could get them to market, they all suffocated. Bill Bales and I aired, dipped, and plucked the hundreds that ended up in the deep freeze. I think that farm cost more than it made, but it kept all of us busy during the war years."[4] The gas shortage, which made the drive to Bennington prohibitive for potential audiences, threatened the school's economic stability. There were philosophical rifts as well. According to Otto Luening, the school's theater director, Francis Fergusson, had concepts that "didn't go over too well with Martha [Graham] and Arch Lauterer. They had two aesthetic opposing points of view."[5]

Although summer 1942 was independently productive, it was to be the last session of the School of the Dance at the Bennington School of the Arts. Nevertheless Martha, Louis, and others continued as visiting artists for four- to six-week residencies added to the regular college academic year from 1943 to 1945. Despite hardships and curriculum changes, students who came to the campus did learn. "For me," Nikolais said, "the beauty of Bennington was that I came out greatly fired by the art. Because of its time and the merging of these tremendous powers of creativity, there was a force which penetrated the dance, and you became saturated with it, so that you came out devoted toward an art, not toward yourself."[6]

In the months following the 1942 session, while Martha fretted over the inconclusive Coolidge negotiations and created nothing new, Louis turned his energies toward the younger generation of choreographers, giving special attention to those in her company. In a sense they were the couple's artistic children. Fiercely enthusiastic about creating their own work, these performing artists, armed with Horst's compositional disciplines and approval, began the difficult process of finding dance vocabularies of their own. During the summer Louis had written scores for Nina's *Little Theodolina* and Jean Erdman's *The Transformations of Medusa*. Meanwhile, Merce Cunningham worked on his first collaboration with John Cage, *Credo in Us,* "a dramatic playlet for two characters." The acorns had not yet fallen far from the oak, but this supportive, exemplary atmosphere produced a remarkable second generation of dancer-choreographers.

If Louis's self-confidence was beginning to erode, he seldom mentioned it to the maverick mix of dancers, musicians, journalists, actors, and directors who were his friends. Surrounded by lively artists in every discipline he allowed himself little time for bouts of self-pity. If an evening in his schedule opened up he simply placed an ad in *Dance Observer* offering "12 lessons for $12," to which a new round of students responded: "I was getting busier at teaching. I had classes every night. Everyone was taking my composition courses."[7]

Thriving in his role as a teacher, he happily boarded the Long Island train each week of the 1942–1943 academic year bound for Adelphi University. Facing his classroom of frightened students, in typical fashion he would open his roll book and call out to the first name on his alphabetized list, "Let's see your dance." As a reviewer he loyally supported colleagues and former students, along with the stray deserving outsider like Jerome Robbins, whom he met while accompanying a 1939 performance for Dance Cabaret Theatre and declared "a genius." And, inevitably, his protégés (by now, there were many) were accused of coming from the same mold as Graham.

Louis saw this as a stage in their development that they would soon outgrow, but Walter Terry felt differently: a definite trend toward "characterization, humor and colorful staging" was led by Graham and copied outright by new choreographers. This comment referred to Louis's assistants, Nina and Welland Lathrop. While Lathrop went on interminably in his *Harlequin,* "posturing with props and not dancing a step," Nina had her own problems with *Four Dances in Five.* There was more to her group work, *Yankee Doodle Greets Columbus, 1492,* Terry concluded, but he added the discouraging words, "One felt that Miss Fonaroff had forced her ideas into a tight mold rather than allowing those ideas to suggest their own design."[8]

Criticism such as this began to haunt Louis's sensitive and introverted companion. Nina continued to choreograph as meticulously as she did her needlework, usually working alone for many months before showing anything to Louis. When he did write an occasional score for her it was produced almost as an afterthought. Even if his music lacked compassion and his enthusiasm for the collaborative process was on the wane, Nina was delighted. Her choreographic career was not going smoothly, but she could look forward to her role in Graham's new *Deaths and Entrances.*

Previewed during the early part of summer 1943 at Bennington, Martha's latest work was episodic in shape, with a complex interweaving of characters. Her dancers, wearing shoes with their ruffled and petticoated period costumes, assumed a balletic appearance that would have been out of the question a few years earlier.

A film was also made of Martha performing her 1930 signature piece, *Lamentation.*[9] In it, various scenes with Louis, although staged, give an unusually vivid view of the way their professional lives meshed. The movie begins with Kodaly's Piano Piece heard in the background as John Martin reads before the camera from his notes: "Random movement is not dancing." [The new modern dance demands] "sensational skills." [It is a] "simple, eloquent medium."[10] The film then cuts to a view of Martha in a bright red dress posed on the Bennington lawn, Mädl beside her. She strokes the long back of the dachshund, gently curls her into a sleeping ball, and then glances through a musical score. The next scene shows Louis at the piano (now weighing a hefty 220 pounds, according to his War Ration book) glancing toward the unseen performer for sight cues. The camera focuses briefly on his facile hands before a close-up of Graham's foot, then of a stretch of fabric, her twisted torso, and then her face, each frame demonstrating the strength of her dancing.

This film offers a rare view of Graham's early work at a time when film-makers had yet to discover the potential of dance as subject matter. Composers, on the other hand, who had worked with dance, were now being sought for commercial ventures for which "functional" music was needed. Hollywood did not beckon Louis, but Julien Bryan, an independent producer, did hire him to write scores for two documentary films: *Housing in Chile* (for violin, bass, and piano) and *Atacama Desert (North Chile),* based on South American folk themes. Scoring films plainly delighted him, and he was good at it. "Why not come up and hear my music for bad housing in Chile!"[11]

Louis had begun the 1943–1944 season by accepting a position as "resident artist and lecturer" at the Y, adding thirty more sessions of teaching the choreographic process to his already crowded schedule. His concert work with Graham that season included December performances at the 46th Street Theatre (featuring a new work, *Salem Shore,* to a score by Paul Nordoff), followed by several less auspicious events at the New York Central Needle Trades Auditorium and at the Y. The highlight of the spring season was a full week at the National Theatre on Broadway. Louis's work drew praise as "flowing, beautifully shaped, and reticently expressive." Denby wrote, "Of all Miss Graham's scores his are by far the most musical and apt."[12] Conducting the increasingly demanding orchestral arrangements was a time-consuming, tension-provoking job. An accurate as well as inspired reading of untried works was essential, Louis felt, and it was as difficult a task as any he had done during his Denishawn days.

As lead dancer and sole fundraiser, Erick dedicated his full energy to the success of Graham's company. With a program of large-scaled works that were expensive to produce, he now had to concentrate on finding funding sources for longer series in larger houses. Because of his persistence, Martha's ardent supporter, Katharine Cornell, graciously hosted a party in her home that raised $26,000 — an amount the company was able to draw on for the next several years — and she prepared a publicity statement: "As a creative artist . . . produced by America and expressing America, she is without peer."[13] Although thankful for this support, Martha did not always appreciate such tactics to keep the company afloat.

Louis, too, felt increasingly uncomfortable with the situation and was tired of touring. "For the last three or four years I was always thinking about quitting. I was flirting with the idea, but I got to feeling, what will I do without Martha? You know, I was a little thing. I was going to be left all alone. I didn't want to go and play for another dancer like Doris. I felt I'd given my all to her."[14] Nina, wanting an independent life, had moved from her mother's West 67th Street apartment to a studio of her own. Louis signed a lease for a small efficiency apartment only ten days before Betty arrived from California for a three-week visit. This sequence of events resembled those that Martha had experienced: Louis had no intention of divorcing Betty. Her arrival once again confirmed, this time to Nina, his uncompromising position on the matter of commitment.

In the Greenwich Village he loved, Louis settled into his own quarters at 55 West 11th Street, just over a block from the Seventh Avenue IRT subway. Signing a lease for more than one year gave him a newfound sense of permanence — a concession for this aging bohemian, but one he adapted to with ease. His tiny two-room apartment contained his piano, a bed, and a comfortable chair. There was work space for *Dance Observer,* a pullman kitchen where he sometimes scrambled eggs, and booklined walls randomly blessed by icons. Shelves held volumes of music, his favorite kachina dolls, and ashtrays on top of mail to be answered. He hastily placed his collection of watercolors, which now included a John Marin, on available hooks and scattered his Indian rugs underfoot. He was plainly delighted with his bachelor's quarters: "I lived there for eighteen years. [By the time I left] I was paying $71. It had an elevator and a phone booth downstairs. I never lived as long in any place!"[15]

With the 1944 liberation of Paris modern artists began to rekindle a neoclassic approach that thematically combined an upbeat mood with a romantic love of country. On 30 October 1944 Martha caught that spirit, joining America's cultural mainstream with three outstanding works, all with sets by Noguchi. She had waited impatiently for a firm commitment from Elizabeth Sprague Coolidge, writing to Mrs. Coolidge that the commissioning plan was a "first for me and modern dance,"[16] and to Harold Spivacke that "It makes me feel that the American dance has turned a corner, it has come of age."[17] This early optimism had paled as time passed and no scores were forthcoming. Carlos Chavez had been set to work on the "bone structure" of "a legend of American living" script that Martha had prepared for him,[18] but he had not followed through. Aaron Copland, at work on a film score, had promised compliance as had Paul Hindemith and Darius Milhaud. It was these three whose scores received their premiere at the Library of Congress, conducted by Louis and featuring Copland as the piano soloist in the Hindemith.

The circumstances surrounding these creations had been so elaborate and stretched over long periods of waiting that the "dance must come first" theory was soon dismissed. Copland may have admired Louis's abilities as a dancer conductor, but he had his own ideas about music for dance. Whatever his collaborative formula (if there was one), *Appalachian Spring*, a powerful group work in praise of America's pioneering spirit, was an instant success. Copland's music contained joyous phrases easily danced to, in contrast to Hindemith's more difficult, but equally provocative assemblage of sound. Some dancers felt that Hindemith's *Herodiade* (first called *Mirror Before Me*) was not a very good score for dance. The composer David Diamond had a different opinion: "It was a great work," he stated unequivocally.[19] He was the one who had encouraged Graham to use Hindemith by taking her to a concert to hear his music. Martha choreographed what she called a "doom-eager . . . dance of choice" with May O'Donnell as the consoling attendant to Martha's role as one who looks into "the mirror of one's being." Although the third score, Milhaud's *Imagined Wing*, received fair notices, it was *Appalachian Spring* that won cheers all around. Graham and Copland had produced an American classic — without Louis.

By 1945 Martha's and Louis's fragile relationship was held together only by ties of the past. Except for the December and June courses when he taught "the elements of modern choreography" (the two-week course was advertised for $20) he spent as little time at the Graham studio as possible: "It was such a great place — our studio — and after that I felt it wasn't our studio anymore. It was hers. I just couldn't stand the atmosphere. I did so much for her. Then I didn't feel at home."[20] A dreary situation had developed between them, but work kept the couple in proximity. *The Lonely,* a play by

Horton Foote and a Neighborhood Playhouse project that year, contained Louis's incidental accompaniment to Graham's staging. And after completing several isolated dates on the East Coast, the company presented a spring season in Manhattan's National Theatre. Featuring *Appalachian Spring, Herodiade,* and *Deaths and Entrances,* the performances confirmed Graham's strength in the dance world. In an unusual move she shared the bill, with new choreography by Cunningham and Hawkins, a gesture called "more kind than wise" by the *New York Times.*[21] Other critics preferred to concentrate on the earlier commissions, with the orchestra of seventeen instruments under Louis's baton receiving unreserved praise.

After the season Martha and Erick again went camping in the Southwest, hoping that a relaxed summer of vacationing would mend their differences. It had become more and more difficult to combine their professional and personal lives and they had spent a good portion of that year apart. Erick felt increasingly burdened with her artistic ventures; she, in turn, felt her independence thwarted. The more he assumed responsibility, the angrier Martha would become. The relationship was a polar opposite to hers with Louis. At Mills and then Perry-Mansfield that summer Louis mulled inconclusively over his future with Graham's company. Although indignant over Erick's dominance, it was Martha's attitude that upset him most: "There was the little loss of sincerity on her part, [now that] she was getting to have success. The silken strings of success were beginning to grab her, and I was the one who knew her when."[22]

Others felt the need to separate from the company. Even if he appreciated the shared Broadway bill, Cunningham, after years of playing roles from the Christ figure to Pegasus, had grown restless. With his own ideas about dancing he knew he must resign: "I didn't particularly like the choreographic things that I was involved with. . . . I stayed on for several years, but I was beginning to work by myself. . . . the ideas I have been involved with since — have been — very different."[23]

Dancers sought themes to reflect America's elation when Germany surrendered and the war in Europe was finally over. Tamiris's *Go Down Moses* and Graham's *Lamentation,* once so pertinent in their abstraction of human suffering, seemed tame. These artists sought a more jubilant mood and more heroic proportions. Leonard Bernstein, who had collaborated with Jerome Robbins on *Fancy Free,* conducted the first International Music Festival in Prague, going to Europe armed with scores by Samuel Barber, Roy Harris, Aaron Copland, William Schuman, and George Gershwin to reveal the great strides the United States had made in music. Graham had been a consistent forerunner of "democratic" statements, with *Frontier* in 1935 and *American*

Document and *Appalachian Spring* in 1944. But in a surprising turn her dances began to reflect her enticement with Jungian ideas. (Both Martha and Erick had undergone psychological therapy with a psychoanalyst, Dr. Frances Wickes.) The Coolidge projects had, in effect, spelled the end of the Graham company's need of Louis as musical mentor. Now Martha was searching for loftier, more universal themes and moving away from his preachings for abstraction and specificity. Moreover, the commissioning of established composers whose symphonic compositions rarely acknowledged Louis's concepts of music as dance's handmaiden greatly altered her working methods.

For the company's two-week season in January 1946 at the Plymouth Theatre, the Carlos Chavez–scored *Dark Meadow* was finally presented. Insiders felt that Chavez did not match the standards set by other composers because there had not been much of a collaborative effort, but the work proved to be an enduring one. It completed an already popular bill of *Every Soul Is a Circus, Appalachian Spring,* and *Deaths and Entrances,* able to draw full houses in Manhattan. Performed with a ten-instrument "chamber" orchestra the music was "always part of the dancing . . . always at one . . . sensitive and unobtrusive," according to a critic for *Dance Observer,* who praised Louis for his "empathy."[24]

Louis returned from the 1946 tour to chair the YM-YWHA Teachers Advisory Committee for its eighth annual Demonstration of College Dance Groups and to Luening's music faculty at Barnard College where he was asked to "guide choreographers and composers" for the "Greek Games" competition, an auspicious event on the Upper West Side campus. As a "dance judge" for this annual springfest (Henry Cowell was "music judge") he enjoyed the racing chariots drawn by prancing dancers and rooted for the underdog first-year classes as they rolled hoops and jumped hurdles, followed by the dance and music competitions with the goddess Athena as their selected muse.

But the most significant occasion for him was presented at season's end across the street at the McMillin Theatre: he conducted Samuel Barber's score for Martha's new *Cave of the Heart* (first called *Serpent Heart*) for the Festival of Contemporary Music, with Beveridge Webster as pianist and the NBC Orchestra playing under his direction. The event was a special honor for one who had so consistently championed new music for dance. Martha had created the piece with the aid of Columbia University's Alice M. Ditson fund, choosing the legend of Jason and Medea as a subject. Her central role embodied a venomous jealousy, which many people felt revealed the unhappy state of her seven-year relationship with Erick. Shrouded in black in contrast to Erick's scant costume of taped torso and briefs, her stillness opposed his wildly tortured scissor jumps.

In September victory over Japan was declared. The country was light-hearted and its dancers full of hope for the future. But the war's impact had changed America's audiences and a new configuration of artists began to contribute their views. New York City's position as the world center for the arts strengthened as war-torn European capitals struggled to rebuild and art-ists fled to the States. Exponents of the expressionist movement found posi-tions at American universities that embraced their concepts of modernism.

Bennington's armory building, which housed the theater space, became a hospital for returning soldiers. The school's winter session was severely hampered by lack of fuel to heat its classrooms and the summer school of dance was forced to disband, ending the most productive era modern dance had known. Disappointed, its illustrious faculty found other teaching jobs where they could. It would be two more years before the group gathered again under Martha Hill's wing at a new location.

Louis returned to Mills College, where Marian Van Tuyl assigned a favorite student, Beth Osgood, as his assistant: "I was one of the young dancers chosen to entertain him. We were socially active, having supper together every night and taking trips into San Francisco to hear the Budapest Quartet. Louis particularly liked Boris Kroyt, the violist who championed modern compositions. We would hear the Beethoven or Handel and Mozart before the modern piece, usually played after intermission — and then before the final Brahms, Louis would whisper to me, 'Let's go! We've heard enough.' And we'd go somewhere for dinner." Back in his old milieu he mulled over the tedium his father must have experienced as a musician in an orchestra and talked to Beth about his mother and the circumstances of her death. They also visited his sister May: "She was a proper San Francisco matron, it seemed to me. [May perhaps had her own opinion about the charming dancer at her brother's side.] And we visited Betty, who had something to do with running 'Lovers Lodge' in Carmel at the time."[25]

Louis next traveled to Perry-Mansfield, where he lectured and composed scores for Harriette Ann Gray's *The Prophet Said Three* and *In Memoriam*. He also appeared briefly in a short film at the dance camp and went to the Little League baseball games in Steamboat Springs every Sunday. Although Gray did not remember much about their collaboration, she did enjoy the process and his company: "Louis was a genius — great to work with."[26]

Others agreed. Back in New York that fall he produced scores for Edith Wiener's *Humiliation* and for Nina's *Born to Weep*. Reviewing Nina's Y concert, John Martin praised his score-writing as "completely right — gay, tender, without a trace of sentimentality."[27] Louis also began to compose for Gertrude Lippincott, whose tours generally originated in Minnesota and traveled countrywide.[28] "She was a good person doing good things for the profession," and he happily paid his "jolly gentleman debt" to this "civic-minded dancer."[29] Other assignments produced a variety of scores and incidental pieces, including one for a memorial service for Irene Lewisohn. As a composer of "musical settings," throughout the next decade Louis was persuaded into collaborations especially with women choreographers, which allowed him the kind of working relationship he enjoyed undertaking if time permitted. Echoing the manner in which he had worked with Martha in their heyday, he created short scores for piano, sympathetic if slight, focused almost entirely in supporting the action. This necessitated going to the keyboard to work out harmonies or sightread a new section, but he still rarely practiced anything.

As for Martha's newest collaborative efforts, he rarely interceded as he had with earlier composers. By the 1947 *Night Journey,* Louis was present only at orchestra rehearsals in his role as conductor. Even though he had introduced the field to the music-dance connection, he was clearly outclassed by the professionals who now collaborated with Graham. Beginning with the Chavez script, Martha created scenarios for each collaborator, who then entered the studio with a partial score in hand; Martha would show several phases of movement and a great deal of talking took place. Louis's painstaking method of working measure by measure to make the musical ideas serve the dance did not suit these composers. Oscar Wilde had earlier deduced that it is personalities, not principles that move the age. This age was no different from the rest. If Louis was humbled by his exclusion from the studio he still believed it was a privilege to be associated with these artists in any capacity, and continued to express pride in the stunning results Martha achieved with each successive collaboration.

Veterans of the war now came to the studio to study. Advertisements noted, "You may study any type of dancing under the G.I. Bill of Rights." Men who wandered into Martha's studio out of curiosity were grabbed up into a new discipline and eventual employment, the most talented joining her company. With the availability of more men on whom to choreograph, Martha's dance materials changed radically to embrace complex rhythms, broad sweeps of action, and use of contrapuntal techniques, so different from Louis's compositional preferences.

Although less and less inclined to look back, Martha had agreed that the 1947 New York season would include a revival of *Primitive Mysteries.* Rehearsing with the all-woman cast took away precious time from creating something new, so Louis took responsibility for remounting the piece after the first flurry of rehearsals: "So they look like Coxey's Army, but they'll do it."[30] For Martha it was a painful experience and she refused thereafter to reconstruct any work once it had left the company's muscle memory.[31]

When the Coolidge Foundation commissioned a score from William Schuman that would become *Night Journey,* Martha chose the Oedipus legend as her theme. The lore of ancient Greece as a basis for new creations had been cropping up more and more. For example, Jean Erdman's 1942 solo, *Transformations of Medusa,* to Louis's score, was a first notable response to the research of her husband Joseph Campbell, who had produced impressive writing on mythology and the Greeks. In 1947 an unusually intense project at the Neighborhood Playhouse focused on *The Eumenides.* Graham, Sanford Meisner, and Horst spent many hours staging the production with a superlative cast. And the Playhouse School of the Theatre's final demonstration included *Archaic Movement Study based on the Agamemnon Tragedy* to Louis's incidental music. This new direction was emerging in Martha's dances independent of Louis's eye. Nonetheless he tried to express enthusiasm about it, even if he reserved opinion of her heavier use of narrative and plot. He later confessed to preferring *Night Journey* on film — a more appropriate medium for storytelling.

The shift from heros of the American plains to those of ancient Greece demanded more curve and deeper muscular intensity from Graham's dancers. Erick had the statuesque look of a Greek god, but his torso needed contour and his actions greater dimension. Martha sought ways to move the masculine figure through space, replacing the stiff angularity of earlier works with more physicality. Erick's array of lifts, turns, and jumps, drawn from his strong ballet technique, augmented her vocabulary. But Erick had influenced a deeper, more significant level of her work.

According to Agnes de Mille, Martha was at the "apex of her creative powers" when Erick attempted to claim parity with her, "threaten[ing] her very essence. It mattered not that he was not her equal, that he was not even comparable. She loved him."[32] The writer Elizabeth Kendall opined that until Erick entered Martha's life, it had been Horst "who urged her on to a greater iconoclasm. One wonders whether she would have been gentler without Horst, whether it was he who made her so severe about cleansing the sweetness of her Denishawn past from her dances."[33] For Nina, everything changed with Graham when her love affair with Hawkins began: "Erick was the catalyst. A Greek and Latin scholar — pompous and egocentric, he turned Martha's head toward the Greeks. Louis split ideologically with Graham at this point."[34]

Although the Graham contingent was acclaimed in New York City and the recent series of performances had proved that concessions need not be made, audiences in America's regional theaters were less convinced. The years of self-producing were over when the Hurok organization finally agreed to represent the company. Beginning with a Chicago-to-Los Angeles tour in 1946 booked into large theaters, Hurok bet on the theory that modern dance could draw audiences, if not as well as musical comedy, then at least comparable to an American ballet company. He was wrong. He agreed nevertheless to back a second tour in 1947 for "Martha Graham and Dance Company with Orchestra, Louis Horst — Musical Director," again claiming her as "America's Great Dancer," with more success.

The program covers boasted of a "Repertory of Hits" during the February tour to the Midwest and up the East Coast. Participation in the Harvard Music Critics Symposium, which was interested primarily in William Schuman's score for *Night Journey,* was a particularly satisfying experience for Harvard-alumnus Erick. As with modern dance generally, it was still easiest for Graham to find audiences in academic surroundings. She captured Yale's hearts and minds by impressing upon them the many years it took to develop her artistry, reminding her admirers, "I do not make a vision of creativity . . . I never use the word. I live and work out of Necessity . . . as deeply and committally as an animal. There is no choice."[35] Graham symbolized the sensual, intuitive dancer whose artistry could not be trivialized. She also was the most skilled, highly polished dance artist in the field, which Louis never failed to report in *Dance Observer.* When her season of twelve concerts at the Ziegfeld Theatre followed the February tour, superlative comments came from every front. The year-old *Dark Meadow* was called "beyond criticism," with one reviewer labeling it a personal "emanation" and adding, "The quality of the season as a whole was richer than any of them."[36]

If *The New Yorker* assumed that Louis was "Graham's Svengali," neither Graham nor Hawkins felt any particular need to consult him about their artistic plans. Phased out of the art-making environment of the studio and Graham's mind, the public nonetheless regarded him as Martha's mentor. His description in the *New Yorker* feature as "white haired, corpulent, and calm . . . sipping a glass of elderberry wine,"[37] gave the impression of a contented man, but that was only external. It was Erick who now suffered Martha's day-to-day trials; each of his well-intentioned attempts to make Martha's artistry fiscally sound was rebuffed and suspect. The two, however, had reconciled after a period of separation and now shared a place at 257 West 11th Street.

With a contract for $600 to teach at Mills College and glad to get out of town for the summer, Louis boarded a train for California. Edith Wiener, who had performed her *Relent to Tears* to his music that spring, was on the platform to greet him. After his perfunctory weekend visit with Betty, he enjoyed a week's stay with his sister before going to Mills, where he resumed "his munching pattern" with Beth Osgood. If the Mills session did not have the same dynamic quality of the Bennington years, he at least enjoyed a relatively light schedule on his native turf and in good company.

Seldom mentioning Nina (Beth understood they were "good friends"), Louis was consumed in promoting Beth's career: "We would return to the studio where I would work on my studies for his classes, and he would sit doing a crossword puzzle, or practicing Ravel's waltzes. Although devilishly difficult, getting each small configuration of notes correct was good discipline, he explained. Then, for my first choreographic effort, I had a notion that I wanted to use Irish poetry. As I worked in the studio on movement phrases, he began to write a score for me."[38] It was at this point that Louis considered adding a study in impressionism to his modern dance forms course.

Louis saw to it that those under his tutelage benefited from his finely tuned system of nurturing. Back in New York in the fall he advertised his thrice-weekly Music for Dancers classes, in which "the needs and problems of the dancer and the composer are analyzed." In October he joined the writers Doris Hering and Walter Terry to organize a Choreographer's Workshop, to be held the first Sunday of each month at the Humphrey-Weidman Studio Theatre. Within months promising dancer-choreographers from his classes showed their work on the series and were reviewed in *Dance Observer,* and occasionally in the *New York Times* or *Herald Tribune.* Lucas Hoving, a participant, explained the progress:

> For several of us there was an inevitable pattern: Graham student, Louis Horst student, Louis Horst assistant, Teach beginners' classes, etc. And at first you didn't know why you did it or how you should do it, but then, eventually you saw. The main reason for teaching composition: Dance needs choreographers, probably more than the theatre needs playwrights, and we can't afford to miss one single potential. . . . Louis Horst was the most contemporary and somehow unconventional person I knew. Still, when I entered a theatre or some place like that, he stood up to shake hands with me."[39]

Louis's frugal existence did not change. The occasional purchase of an art book or a beef stroganoff dinner satisfied him most. His teaching paid the rent and his living expenses. The sixty-three-year-old musician, now referred to as the "grandpapa of modern dance," had settled into a comfortable pattern of modest living. The previous year the Neighborhood Playhouse staff had gathered with Rita Morgenthau to present him a $3,500 "fellowship" for his "contribution to the creative Arts" as a "distinguished and valuable musician." Pleased, he squirreled away several thousand dollars after purchasing a much needed new suit and a couple of white shirts, items that soon looked as rumbled as the rest of his limited wardrobe. He had also received a painting by his Bennington friend Karl Knaths, to add to the Käthe Kollwitz and George Grosz he had recently purchased, from the National Section on Dance of the American Association for Health, Physical Education, and Recreation in recognition of his services to dance education. He received a second fellowship from the Neighborhood Playhouse in 1947 — this time for $1,000 — in memory of Irene Lewisohn. An occasional commission, such as the Walker Art Center's for an orchestrated version of his score for Gertrude Lippincott's *Invitacion,* was a welcome boost to his savings account. But it was Martha, not Louis, who garnered an award in 1947 from the National Association of American Composers and Conductors, presented at the Waldorf Astoria.

Having reached an age when most people faced retirement, Louis vowed to stay active and did remain a figure of prominence in the dance world for another sixteen years. In a paraphrase of Shakespeare, "Two on a horse and one shall ride," he conceded Graham's leadership.[40] He had known this would happen and had wanted it all along. Unexpectedly, Graham's name became a household word, thanks to a radio program. Craig Barton, a network publicist who later became Graham's manager, suggested the dancer as a mystery guest, "Miss Hush." A jingle recited weekly contained clues to be deciphered by a nation of contestants. The prizes mounted up, as did one wrong guess after the other. Months later and the game solved, her name had become known. More than any other American dancer, Martha claimed Middle America's attention as well as that of a sophisticated generation of conservatory-trained American composers. Louis worried about the consequences of her new-found fame. He had not changed his opinion that the modern dance must not become a popular art; now Martha's head was being turned from the straight and narrow path he envisioned.

The dance scene had reached a moment of relative calm, a *Dance Observer* reviewer observed as he surveyed the field late in 1947. Ruth St. Denis headed her "church of the divine dance" in Hollywood. José Limón had emerged as a major dancer-choreographer and was receiving unprecedented notices from John Martin and Walter Terry. Doris Humphrey produced her masterwork *Day of Earth*. Harald Kreutzberg was almost forgotten. "The truth of the matter is that . . . Kreutzberg is not very important, one way or the other."[41] Mary Wigman's comment, "Don't forget me,"[42] was a distant reminder of the German dancer's influence two decades earlier.

At the end of 1947, Louis entered the following notes in his personal journal: "Nov. 16. Played Nina Fonaroff concert YMHA (aft.) Dec. 26. Heaviest snowfall in NYC. history. 25.8 inches."

During the February 1948 season on Broadway, Erick's presence dominated the Martha Graham Dance Company as lead dancer in *Errand into the Maze, Letter to the World, Night Journey,* and *Appalachian Spring.* The billing order listed the new hierarchy, with Hawkins in slightly smaller print below Graham's own name, followed by O'Donnell, Lang, and Yuriko in diminishing size. "Louis Horst — Musical Director and 'special' orchestra" were hardly visible at the bottom. In charge of a combination of near-impossible tasks, with great seriousness Hawkins managed the company finances and bookings as well as the school, even teaching the Saturday children's classes himself.

Louis had been able to toss a consoling word or zany pun to his "mirthless Martha," but the equally mirthless Erick had no such skill. As he bravely endured one crisis after another his efforts were often demeaned by the willful Graham. Martha soothed Erick's obvious frustration by announcing that his choreography as well as her own would be produced during the thirteen performances at the Maxine Elliott Theatre.

But it was Louis's grumbling in Martha's ear that thwarted any hope of Hawkins achieving parallel status in the company — if his choreography was to be presented in the Graham season, then work by other company members should also be included. Louis would write a score for the talented Yuriko, he told her. When Hawkins had announced plans for a tour of his own four years earlier, to feature his choreography with Pearl Lang as his partner, Louis had used the same tactic, suggesting that he might compose a score for "something happy" to counteract the mood of a country devastated by war. For Lang he created *Graduation Day: The Hills are Ready for Climbing.*

As Louis suspected the response to the shared-program scheme was not enthusiastic. Graham's followers had limited sympathy for the inclusion of other choreographic voices on her programs. Robert Sabin praised Yuriko's study of hysterical fear as "a vehicle for some of the most amazing dancing which New York has seen,"[43] and John Martin liked its "characteristically excellent score,"[44] but Erick's work fared less well. His two solos, *John Brown, A Passion Play* and *Stephen Acrobat* (set to poetry), were dismissed by critics who took issue with the assumption that the Graham company might be his choreographic domain. "It looked more like Hawkins' Wake,"

Musical America snarled.[45] In contrast, Martha was producing some of the finest work of her career.

The fact that the relationship between Martha and Louis was increasingly strained was not revealed in her expressions to the public. Appearing at a fund-raising event for *Dance Observer* to celebrate its fifteenth year of publication, she voiced her unreserved appreciation. The magazine described the event:

> The curtain rose on a tableaux of six attractively embarrassed mahatmas seated in civilian clothes about an old refectory table. Louis Horst, at the end, retained a pose of dignity while Agnes de Mille twinkled her eyes at him from her end of the table: and Martha Hill, Doris Humphrey, Martha Graham, and Hanya Holm, each in her own charming way, solved the problem of gazing out at the audience for four full minutes while an ovation of the first magnitude filled the house.[46]

Never particularly comfortable in the limelight Louis accepted congratulations for past achievements graciously, but typically shifted any conversation about himself to one about dancers and dancing. As each speaker spoke of his importance to the field, Louis "writhed with ambivalent emotion. . . . The mortified master of the evening disclaimed, in the end, the praise heaped upon him, drew out his watch, and announced, to a new burst of delighted applause, that the program was about to begin."[47] *Musical America* concurred, "With pioneers . . . and younger dancers demonstrating — one could not but feel the force of the young and ample art. There were . . . many high moments in the dancing, but the program was memorable principally for its recognition of Mr. Horst without whose influence the history of the Modern Dance would have run a less assured course."[48]

chapter nine

1948—1954

"A veritable one-man

university of the arts."

— *Norman Lloyd*

I n summer 1948 the American Dance Festival found a new home at Connecticut College on the banks of the Thames River in New London. Louis was asked to serve as Martha's conductor and to teach his usual pre-classic and modern forms courses, along with Music for Dancers with Norman Lloyd. Once moved into a roomy suite in Knowlton Hall, which was to become his summer residence for the rest of his life, the usual entourage of women freely visited his first-floor quarters with little regard for the troubles others were having elsewhere in the dormitories. To the chagrin of the administration couples were "living together" and house mothers were assigned to keep close watch on the situation, which contributed to Erick's discomfort with campus regulations.

Louis's closeness with the dancers provided him one of his few comforts at a time when his future seemed particularly bleak — his latest score, *Ominous Horizon*, had a prophetic title. Beth, having graduated from Mills College and now serving as Louis's assistant, was well aware of his shaky emotional state. Coupled with his sense of rejection was his feeling that "Graham's inventive period had become a wooden one. He rattled on about Martha. She didn't need him anymore, he said. Martha could be abusive in front of others. He felt useless. She wasn't showing him things anymore. She was throwing away what she had been. He realized the ruthless way she was. It was part of her makeup. Yet he felt he started the whole thing and in a fuddy-duddy way he rattled on about that a lot."[1]

Others sensed the mounting discord. Ruth Lloyd said, "He was miserable [over Martha and Erick] and he resolved to quit."[2] Recalling loud noises on the staircase followed by dead silence during a company rehearsal, one of the dancers said, "Everyone froze. Someone said, half joking, 'Sounds like Louis just did Erick in!' "[3]

The festival's August concerts, boasting a "full" orchestra, marked his final assignment with Martha. Newly commissioned scores demanded accomplished players. Ruth Lloyd said, "We felt that the quality of the performances by the musicians, now that fuller instrumentation was used, was not very good. Inviting Juilliard students seemed worth a try. As they say, the rest is history. [Louis was] his meanest, whiniest self. Norman had put both the Connecticut situation and his faith in the students on the line for this and we were disheartened. There was no way we could explain Louis and the Juilliard kids to each other or Louis to himself. Fortunately, they did play for him and were otherwise well treated, but this was a very bad time for Louis."[4] By the end of the summer he had impressed almost everyone as an impossible ogre. "Even the Lloyds wouldn't talk to me!"[5]

The usual tensions of a dress rehearsal developed into catastrophic proportions during the first "music with dance" run-through of *Wilderness Stair* (later *Diversion of Angels*). The Norman Dello Joio score, giving the illusion of lyricism with shifting tempi and meters, was full of complexities. Aware that the composer was not particularly enthusiastic about having his music used for dance in the first place, Louis attacked the problems of an unfamiliar score in agitated confrontation with the inexperienced orchestra members. Martha and Erick stood by as Louis, in a cantankerous tirade, pressed the musicians to get difficult passages right, continually interrupting the dancers' run-through. Frustrated, Martha conferred with Erick and then turned to the pit and said, "Look Louis, this has got to stop!" When he refused to acknowledge her command, she stormed up the aisle. Having just arrived on the scene, Nina entered the lobby of Palmer Auditorium as Graham brushed by. " 'I could kill him,' Martha seethed. And I could see in her eyes that she would."[6]

Louis finished the rehearsal and in a huff retreated to his room to write a formal letter of resignation to the Martha Graham Foundation. Beth was with him as he struggled to compose it at his battered typewriter. "He needed tender loving care. . . . He felt humiliated publicly," she said.[7] Nina added, "Louis didn't speak for two weeks. He didn't communicate. He was shattered — totally despondent. 'Why go on living?' he would say to his friends."[8] "We tried to cheer him up. 'You have your teaching,' " Hazel Johnson told him, knowing he was very depressed. "He was tired of being yelled at and told what to do."[9]

He described the final scene of his career with Graham as a dramatic parting on a par with his last performance with St. Denis:

> At the end of that season, I resigned — couldn't take it anymore. . . . Suddenly in New London she acted so badly that I got disgusted with her. After the last performance I went into her dressing room. And I said, "This is my last. I'm resigning. You can take two weeks notice. . . . I just have to leave." I still had to conduct one number. After the concert there was the usual yells and all. And then, she finally dragged me out, grabbing my hand, saying, "Now you don't need to think that this is our last bow and concert together." I said, "Well, I'm afraid it is," bowing to the audience, and the curtain going up and the curtain coming down, giving our bows. "No, it won't be," she answered. We [were] talking together during all the applause. She said to me before she left (I stayed a day or two longer), "I can't talk to you now, but I want to talk to you when we get back." And she did. We had dinner. She said, "Why do you feel you have to go?" I said, "I can't explain it. I just have to go." She said, "Well, I wish you wouldn't." I said, "I know, but I've turned over a page, and I'm not going to turn it back." Those words were kind of cheesy and corny but I just had to say it. She said, "Won't you even teach at the studio anymore?" And I said, "No." And she said, "Well, there won't be any choreography taught then, because if you won't do it, then I won't have any." And that was that.[10]

Within the month, Martha and Erick were married — a spur of the moment decision made on vacation in Santa Fe. On 7 September 1948, at the First Presbyterian Church, Cady Wells and the church organist witnessed their marriage. Erick was thirty-nine; Martha was fifty-four. Erick wanted to "clarify the ambiguity of their relationship."[11] Louis was outraged. "I told her not to marry him!" he said over and over to anyone who would listen. "She just slipped a note under my door, telling me she and Erick were married. Can you imagine? After all those years? A note under the door."[12]

Others considered the decision just as foolhardy. "Marrying Erick was a great mistake on Martha's part," the outspoken composer David Diamond agreed, sensing that Erick was unsure of his own sexuality. "His stage presence was muscular and superficial . . . like a man more suited for a Greek chorus. Erick as a performer was not in keeping with the sensuous contours of the movement that now dominated Graham's technique." Out of place in the work, Erick was also out of place as Martha's husband. Diamond was not surprised that personal difficulties between the married couple were "beyond control" in a matter of months.[13]

Ten years had passed since Martha and Louis had separated romantically. Now she rejected everything they had built together and her sudden
marriage to Erick was the final blow. With his letter of resignation Louis may
have believed that the most important aspect of life's work was finished, but
he came to understand his own influential power. However, it would be a full
seven years before a letter from Martha resolved the emotional schism
between them.

Gertrude Shurr tried to rationalize Martha's behavior: "You had to
divide Martha, the artist, the genius, the great creative person. What she did
was sufficient, but as a human being, all of us understood that she was very
bad in some respects, particularly the way she would handle people."[14] Other
Graham dancers learned to guard themselves against her manipulative ma-
neuvers. They knew that without Louis as a buffer they would be caught in
the escalating crossfire between the choreographer, Erick, and the management.

Distraught upon his return to Manhattan, Nina "didn't dare leave him.
He needed me."[15] Marian Van Tuyl's husband, Dr. Douglas Campbell, suggested that he might benefit from professional help. With self-effacing humor, Louis recounted his single session on a therapist's couch: " 'What do
you do for a living, Mr. Horst?' 'I work with dancers — young women
mostly.' 'What do you do in your free time, Mr. Horst?' 'Go out to eat and to
concerts, with young women mostly,' was the reply. 'Do you have any
hobbies?' 'No.' The psychiatrist responded, 'Mr. Horst, I suggest that you
take up an activity with your hands. May I suggest soap carving?' That was
the last time I went to him!"[16]

Severing his ties with Martha after an intense twenty-two years did not
change his life as drastically as he feared it might, and his deep depression
eventually lifted. "The minute I left [Martha's company], I got more things to
do. More honors came to me than I ever had before, although I got a lot of
them in association with her. I began writing movie scores around that time
too." When he thought about the prospect of a return to the fold, he
rationalized, "I was getting older and they were touring with a bus after
this."[17] His lifelong involvement in a field in which the dominant forces were
youth and experimentation had begun to wear on him.

Yuriko was on stage during that fateful event in Connecticut. Although
her own experiences with Martha had taken various turns, she maintained a
strong allegiance to the choreographer, later becoming a prime mover in
preserving the repertory. Speaking philosophically of the emotional ties
Martha had made and broken with many of her associates, including Louis,
she said, "Martha loves that person [so intensely] that when that attachment

is too long, she has to get away. With Martha, partings are always difficult. It was the same with Erick. She never stands still. She is a changing person. Whether a manager, a dancer, an artistic adviser, or a lover, few survived those harsh partings. Few managed to escape Martha's rejection without feeling 'used.' "[18]

Louis's new commitments differed little from the early Denishawn days, when "there was a thing to be done, and I was there to do it."[19] Attention to detail continued to fill spare hours of his day — *Dance Observer* to paste up, scrapbooks to maintain, and reviews to write between teaching assignments. With his piano now in use more as a sorting and arranging space for music and printer's galleys than as a musical instrument, he enjoyed listening to all-important Yankee games or symphony-on-the-air broadcasts on the radio. When his doctor preached the virtues of a healthier diet at his annual check-up, he reproached himself and sighed over the ham sandwich special on his plate, but it tasted even more delicious. His refrigerator nearly empty most of the time, he continued to live on luncheonette fare.

Louis had no intention of changing his ways. At sixty-four he seemed to relax with the mood of postwar prosperity. Though separated from Martha's work, he enjoyed an ever-widening reputation as a teacher and a critic. Living somewhat in the shadow of his past glories, he focused his attention on others who felt a more compelling need to create.

By the late forties, the best of his students taught his course verbatim, giving identical assignments and using the same musical accompaniment. They did so with his approval, unlike Shawn's frustrated protégés, who had been forced to buy certificates. When a gifted dancer worked diligently for Louis, he became an ardent supporter of that talent. Others sought his counsel when creating new departments, invited him to their campuses for master classes and short residencies as guest critic, and sent their most talented graduates to study with him. An increasing number of college academicians appreciated the scholarly way he related dance to social and cultural contexts, and valued his recommendations in defense of promotion and tenure for their dance faculties. More than one historian may have recognized his ideas as those used by the Viennese school of art history at the end of the nineteenth century, but Louis's reassuring words on behalf of physical educators were able to soothe anxious deans. Deemed an accurate judge of people, his letters of recommendation for jobs were to the point and given considerable weight.

His social attributes made Louis an agreeable addition in wide circles, but as a teacher he was as merciless as ever. For this second generation of dancing zealots, surviving each assignment was a significant occasion. If a result pleased him, the reward was high regard and the possibility of participating in a workshop performance. It was still behind the closed doors of the classroom that he was most influential. One student remarked that she was "compelled to work against the hair shirt of an imposed structure," with Horst presiding over the creative process "like a ferocious midwife willing the birth of even the most stubborn imaginative offspring."[20] Another feigned a debilitating ankle injury for the full six-week session after making the mistake of calling her first assignment a lullaby. "You came eight hundred miles to perform a lullaby?" he asked incredulously.[21]

In a sense his selection process during class time was a microcosm of the larger dance arena, where his nod signaled acceptance at auditions for choreographers. Louis's gauge for measuring competency began with a student's willingness to compete against his rigorous demands and ended with the student's power to "reinvent" a model that did not change over time. Specific assignments had even become standard criteria on which choreographic ability could be weighed; "She did a beautiful earth primitive" or "His allemande was one of the best in years" denoted considerable choreographic talent.

Each year Louis watched a number of gifted dancers and actors move into other creative arenas, take jobs in other cities, or leave the field altogether. Only the toughest survived in Manhattan. Those who endured hardships in order to stay in the profession won his deepest regard: "To be a modern dancer you have to have a philosophy of poverty."[22] He recognized the growing professional demands placed on would-be choreographers for technical mastery in ballet as well as modern technique. He knew that when dancers left his classroom, prepared to create their own dance visions, they were quickly frustrated by the lack of opportunity to show their work. He had become the lone, worn voice demanding personal vision, creativity, and the need for invention. At the same time he retained a sense of responsibility for sustaining the careers of established choreographers. Denishawn's children — Humphrey, Graham, and Weidman — monitored the concert scene as closely as had Shawn and St. Denis years earlier, but they were looking for talented dancers who might join their own companies rather than at choreographic competition.

Louis joined John Martin and Walter Terry as they endeavored "through criticism to foster the best in our theater of dance."[23] Certain ground rules held for tenacious dancers with choreographic ambition. A dancer joined the professional ranks after mastering one of the established modern dance techniques, assimilating its implied compositional style, then studying with Horst. The next step was winning a place on a "young choreographers" concert — usually judged by the ever-present Humphrey and Horst — or renting the Upper East Side citadel for modern dance, the 92nd Street Y, to produce a concert on one's own. After months of preparation the culmination was a one-evening performance. The policy worked along the lines of other presenting spaces, such as Carnegie Hall and Town Hall, which rented to musicians for their debut concert, thus guaranteeing a small audience of loyal followers and a review or two. If superficially this system provided opportunity, it was increasingly difficult for new talent to break into the small circle of established leadership dominated by artists in their prime.

In theory, choreography remained very much a part of the curricular plan at the Graham school. Although Louis attended Martha's concerts without fail and continued to review her work, he kept a certain distance from her studio. But she did ask him to teach composition one spring and he consented. After that, "I was so upset. I couldn't do it again. I said, 'No, It won't work.' "[24] Nevertheless, Martha's dancers continued to seek his advice. Confiding about difficulties with the company and between Martha and Erick, he told them, "She wouldn't listen to me! Now look at the mess she's in!"[25] Even though removed from the scene, he knew she had a serious drinking problem, but accepted her condition: "Martha likes Irish whiskey, and she got me to drink it!" In an aside, he advised, "Jamieson's is good — or Bushmill. Don't buy the rest!"[26] If Martha's work was deemed "beyond criticism" in the United States, Europe was not receptive to her company. Irreconcilable differences would soon separate Martha and Erick once and for all. Company morale was at a low ebb.

During the next years, Louis completed a score for a Bryan short documentary film, *Rural Women,* and then wrote accompaniment for another film, *Flowers of Williamsburg,* that paid $1,500. But it was scores such as *Frontier, Heretic, Primitive Mysteries,* and *El Penitente* that revealed his particular style. (A former student, pianist, and advocate, Daniel Jahn, eventually published *Primitive Mysteries, El Penitente,* and *Three South American Dances* in a limited printing, along with a volume of his own original scores written as accompaniment for Horst's courses.) The stark, repetitive themes of his musical voice were reflected in his critical writing, pedagogy, and philosophy. Diatonic, tonal, mostly consonant, his music, like his life, was unable to sustain introspection. Martha's new search into the dark resources of the mind clearly disinterested him, although he appreciated her ability to state it. He still preferred the stoic sounds and images of the Southwest and Spanish American cultures.

Louis continued to compose for Graham's dancers and monitored their progress in rehearsal. He had orchestrated the piano piece written earlier for Yuriko's *Tale of Seizure* and created new music for Helen McGehee for an Audition Winners' Concert at the Y. She said, "I choreographed *Man with a Load of Mischief* first to counts. . . . We rehearsed at his apartment at 55 West 11th Street. (Tiny!)" Reviewers of the work mentioned Louis's "admirable music" and called her duet with Robert Cohan "a pert commentary on the 'never underestimate the power of a woman' theme." McGehee commended Louis for playing at the performance: "Such generosity! The fee for composing was so minimal — just enough to save face for a very young and impecunious dancer. . . . He always got at what was wrong and what worked. All those lofts he climbed to, at all those terrible hours, to lend his objective eye and his gift of friendship."[27]

Having resigned from the Graham company to work independently, Nina gave concerts at the Y rather than the more formidable midtown Broadway houses. Her new company included McGehee as well as Jack Moore and Doris Rudko — dancers who became assistants to Louis in ensuing years.[28] Louis assisted her occasionally as pianist and composer as he had McGehee, but these collaborative efforts, though well wrought and interesting, created little impact. Invited to prepare a piece for a series sponsored by Bethsabee de Rothschild at City Center, Nina rehearsed arduously in collaboration with a young composer with whom she had fallen in love. Yet she returned to Louis for guidance.

His blend of intuitive and analytical qualities held her, as it had Martha, but by 1951 she admitted, "I couldn't stand the repetition anymore. Being with Louis didn't open up any choreographic thing [for me]." She was no longer able to find the creative leap by using formal principles of music harmony and counterpoint to solve problems of movement invention. Understanding styles through social and art contexts did not develop one's personal style. Although she still assisted Louis at the Neighborhood Playhouse, mentally she rejected his teaching philosophy outright. Some people complained that Nina would just sit there next to him without saying a word. She later confessed, "I realized that I didn't really believe that the musical forms translated themselves into dance, or released the imagination."[29]

With the same impetuousness that had driven her to study with Graham thirteen years earlier, "She went head over heels into studying the theater," Martha Hill recalled, "going to see Laurence Olivier every night when the Royal Shakespeare Company first came to New York, even selling her collection of art books in order to buy tickets."[30] She became enamored of the teaching of the Playhouse's acting mentor, Sanford Meisner, who professed to train actors "viscerally." Leaving the modern dance field altogether, she began to teach ballet to actors. If Louis and Nina met only occasionally thereafter, it was clear that he never stopped loving her.

A scene filmed at the Connecticut College Summer School of the Dance in 1951, *Creative Leisure,*[31] shows the heavyset man in his usual suit and tie at the keyboard accompanying his students. The episode is not unlike the one captured years earlier at Bennington, but the outstanding difference is that Graham's image is nowhere in evidence. His own man at last, his professional separation from her was clearly visible to friends and colleagues. Nowadays when a student asked him if Graham technique would best complement the rigors of his composition classes, he responded, "Why Graham?" But whenever the opportunity arose to praise his oldest colleagues in print, he was their strongest ally. Doris Humphrey, who also taught choreography at the American Dance Festival, was one who received his deepening respect. "Miss Humphrey has again demonstrated what a great choreographer she truly is," he wrote in a review of *Night Spell,* praising it as "a glowing work which builds with a wealth of emotionally lyric and fantastic phrases to a shining climax achieved on the very last note."[32]

If Louis had given modern dance a share of "morality," as Lincoln Kirstein suggested, he nevertheless continued to live as he pleased, closely tied to the bohemian values of his youth. Unperturbed by the inconvenient aging process, he found companionship when he wanted it from a bevy of women who studied with him, assisted his classes, or worked with him on *Dance Observer.* He had grown fond of blonds, although raven-haired beauties still caught his attention. A few women considered his behavior questionable, but most felt privileged in his company. The actress Marian Seldes recalled, "I would sit on his piano bench like a puppy dog, and dote on his every word."[33] He occasionally lunched with men — other pianists or writers on his staff, and Norman Lloyd engendered his strongest paternal feelings. But clearly he preferred the company of women: "I live in a feminine world."[34]

Ruth Lloyd defused any notion of impropriety: "Louis might give a romantic impression in the way of Brahms or Liszt. He did not seem like a Lochinvar to me, but he flirted always and we all loved it. There was always the awareness that one was a female and he liked us."[35] Never one to suffer from the occupational hazard of being too close to his students, Louis was confident of his ability to charm. He dealt with a colleague who had "lecherous tendencies" by gingerly reorganizing *Dance Observer* schedules to avoid further disturbances. He excused the man's poor behavior by saying to the women, "He tries to imitate me. The trouble is, he does it so badly!"[36]

One student for whom Louis took a special liking was Shirley Ririe, whose subsequent career combined teaching at the University of Utah and co-directing the enduring Ririe-Woodbury Dance Company. His notice of her was again evidence of his uncanny ability to identify talent. Her poignant reminiscences reveal the way he became involved with women toward the end of his life:

I came from a very conservative Mormon background. Louis loved the ladies, and he took a personal interest in me. [He recommended the Connecticut College summer dance session: "That will give her a good introduction," he wrote to her father.] Since Louis had written this nice letter, I think he felt a little responsible. [Arriving on campus four weeks into the session,] Louis asked, "Are you alright? Is the dorm O.K.? You must take my class." Then he said, "When you come into the city you must take this course again, because you've only had half of it." I really loved studying with him. He didn't put me into tears. I found him kind, benevolent and interesting. I saw him in a real different light. I was twenty. He asked, "Do you have a job? You come type for me on Saturday mornings." I'd type until lunchtime, and then he took me out to different restaurants. We'd go to galleries after lunch.

Sometimes we'd hold hands walking down the street. That was very hard for me at first and then I thought, "Oh, hell, why not? People can think he's my grandfather, or my father, or they can think he's my lover. I don't care." . . . It was such big stuff for me, a little country girl from Utah — me and Louis Horst. I was a virgin. I was very clear with him that I didn't do things and he respected that. I never went to bed with him, but we did kiss and neck some. I would say, "No, I can't do this," and he never pressed that, ever. He knew of my terrible fear of this relationship. I didn't know how to deal with it, so he respected that. He'd kid me and chastise me for my naiveté, but he respected it. It was hard to handle on one side, but on the other, it wasn't at all.

I loved him in a way that I've never loved anyone else. It wasn't sexual. It was because he was, in my mind, so great, so kind and loving and charming. I felt he was really helping me, and he respected my wishes. When I was with him it was the most natural thing in the world. He made me feel as if I was the only person who was important . . . that I must pursue dance. I must choreograph. He had a way of making me want to do my best. He pushed in a loving way, not a negative way. There was an expectation and this gave me a sustainment that I could produce. He would guide me. He made music live for me, gave me a sense of the period, and the style and form that the musician was working on—the whole historical and aesthetic kind of understanding and I'm eternally grateful for that.

He was sick when I left [after the first year to get married]. "You're going to Utah to teach and bury yourself!" I came back to New York for a second year. He said, "O.K., now you're married. Things should be different." And I said, "No, I still feel the same!" I was back doing the same things on Saturdays.[37]

If this scenario was virtually the same for many women, the underlying truth was that these relationships were essentially platonic. His all-too-quick respect for propriety, doting idolatry, and unending desire to be with inexperienced women he could nurture was replicated again and again. Ririe's story perhaps sheds light on the nature of his intimacies with Graham and later Fonaroff—both women consider this subject unspeakable—and reopens the unanswered question of his sexual impotence.

More significantly, Ririe remarked that she "felt he identified me as talented. I felt that was real. . . . I'm a pretty good reader of people and their motivations, and I sensed that it wasn't because he liked the girls. That was secondary and I felt they weren't crossed in any way. I think he handled that well. He was honest."[38] This frank disclosure describes a pattern of familiarity others experienced—some less intimate, but as intense in his offer of intellectual support. With or without sexual innuendo, his selection process always began with dancers he considered most talented.

In fall 1951 the Juilliard School of Music opened a dance division headed by Martha Hill. The new faculty at 120 Claremont Avenue in uptown Manhattan included Antony Tudor, Margaret Craske, Doris Humphrey, José Limón, and Martha Graham, with several company members to teach on their behalf, Anne Hutchinson (Guest) for Labanotation, and Louis. The changing world of artists and new ideas about art-making had the faculty's sympathy, but its students had to be solidly trained and maintain the highest respect for dance as a disciplined art form. Aligned with this major conservatory, the division would take a significant lead in establishing an educational model for professional dancers. Hill's vision of the "American dance" began as a five-year degree program that included high technical skill in ballet as well as modern dance, three years of compositional study (including a course in ballet arrangement), three years of Labanotation, and four years of literature and materials of music.

One afternoon a week Louis reigned in the sixth floor's "607" orchestra-room-turned-studio, one of three spaces to be shared for dance. The location may have been different, but his message and manners were the same. "Looking wise and solemn with his deadpan humor — Louis Horst — probably the most loved character in modern dance," began Margaret Lloyd's description of him for the *Christian Science Monitor,* with "massive head, now heavily crowned with white, his ice blue eyes and bland face devoid of emotion." She recorded his encouraging words to students: "You're young. You can do anything. Use your imagination. If you can move your leg in one direction, you can move it in others."[39] (Louis never offered dance terms, such as shift, alternate sides, or lunge; he was always the musical observer in his figures of speech.)

Still cantankerous and even more short-tempered — which was not out of line with the school's rigorous handling of its performers — Louis had no sympathy for what he perceived as undisciplined behavior. "You don't have your B section finished? Why not?" The student was not allowed to sit down until a B section was invented on the spot, only to have him bark, "O.K. Now do the whole dance." His assistants — Natanya Newman and Jack Moore — humored the aging doyen and dealt with any rebellious antics during practice sessions. Thus prepared (and subdued) the dancers showed the usual pavanes, galliards, and allemandes for two semesters of study, a full year of modern forms assignments, then trios, quartets, and quintets, if two years later they reached his "group forms" course.

Being on the Juilliard School of Music faculty pleased him. Twice a year he made an introductory speech before an audience of musicians in the Juilliard concert hall (as he had done at Bennington and Connecticut College), explaining the dances they were about to witness in programs that also included pieces from Humphrey's and Tudor's composition classes. He regularly attended music events at the school, reveling in works played by the Juilliard String Quartet or a guest appearance by Emil Gilels and taking in the occasional Wednesday "One O'clock Concert" after downing his lunch of honey bun and soup in the school's cafeteria. But his greatest energy was reserved for the classroom. His observations and cryptic comments plagued everyone; once students were deemed talented by Louis they were doubly pressed to choreograph.

Even superlative dancers like Dudley Williams were not exempt. Not always prepared but wanting to succeed, Williams knew how to fulfill an assignment — he improvised. Louis would be silent for many seconds and then marvel, "That's it! Let's put that on the workshop." The many hours of labor Williams needed to reconstitute what had happened in the instant took place when Louis was elsewhere. The following week, Louis would ask to see the dance again, demanding the return of any missing important component.

Louis would task struggling students with "Let's see it again," before suggesting more logical progressions. At the same time he pointed out positive elements—the clever varieties of patterning or the handling of spatial relationships. This mixture of praise with great expectation of something more profound pressed the most resistant students into motion. If a concert presented by a former student was not up to his standards, he would shake his head in disbelief and say, "But she was a student of mine" or "She took my course, she should know better!"[40]

But it was clear that another level of meaning was being taught, as his longtime assistant Doris Rudko explained:

> Louis gave a sense of form and structure. That's what he developed in dancers. The basis of all composition is the relation of form and concept—the outward observable form and the inner concept. A work of art must have a combination of personal language and uniqueness, which is all wrapped up in one's being, supported by that other element called craft which formalizes it, puts it in rightness and order, and makes it a crafted work of art. He taught that craft is discipline with the outward observable form at one with the inner content. The movement had to communicate to him kinetically. If they knew their theme in its outward observable form, which means in its absolute articulateness— if they then perceived what it is, then they could intuitively use it. The tools are only there to serve that.[41]

The world of music composition was changing as rapidly as that of dance. Utility music—music written for a definite purpose—had now become a lucrative occupation for many composers working in the growing entertainment industries of film and radio as well as theater. The highly profitable streamlined incidental music composed for film changed the economy of those composers who had once created scores for dance simply for the opportunity to be heard. Electronically produced sound and the wide availability of recordings and—by the mid-fifties—of the portable tape recorder changed the choreographer's relation to music. Unlike the neighboring Columbia-Princeton Electronic Music Center and other universities Juilliard staunchly refused to incorporate an electronic composing studio, which indirectly affected the dance department, since public concerts were required to use the school orchestra. Completely comfortable in this conservative environment, Louis had grown as sedate as his old Viennese professor, whose remark "Satie, who?" had once sent him into furious rebellion. Now he willingly presented his lecture-demonstrations on the pre-classic forms for Juilliard's piano majors and joined his old friend Norman Lloyd in the school's Literature and Materials of Music course to encourage the liaison between dance and music. Even if Louis's passing interest in new musical trends mildly acknowledged the work of John Cage, Gunther Schuller, and Lucas Foss, his own musical reputation rested firmly in the world of dance.

The Korean War of 1950 to 1953 left an uneasy generation of youths in its wake. Louis pondered over the erosion of trust toward authority in dance and fretted over unruly "village" types. Avant-gardists such as Anna Halprin, who later claimed Louis as mentor, perceived his assignments as empty exercises in formality. Wigman's Gestalt methods for drawing dance movement from the inside out, now taught at the Nikolais school, offered an alternative as did Humphrey's methods. Still, no one was able to develop a more viable format than Louis's for the training of choreographers.

Using as a measure the demands made in his pre-classic course during the 1930s and 1940s — twelve studies, one to three minutes long, completed in twelve sessions — Louis unhappily pointed to the diminishing number of assignments actually completed by students in the 1950s. He complained vociferously when it took weeks for students to show their beginning assignments. His stubborn refusal to continue until an entire class had completed each stage of the process brought each class to a near standstill. Working at this snail's pace until everyone understood the material viscerally and intellectually contributed to the classroom's look of seeming complacency.

At the American Dance Festival in summer 1952 Paul Taylor was one who suffered through pre-classic forms: "He taught me very early that the limitations you set up for yourself are a very important part of choreography. . . . Louis taught how to limit your palette."[42] A majority of student-dancers still valued Louis's teaching in the 1950s, but some considered his A-B-A forms "baby talk." They began to find other means of shaping movement, in some cases totally rejecting the concept of "theatricality" in favor of systems that used improvisation and chance.

Reaching into his jacket pocket periodically for either his pencil and roll book or to draw a cigarette from the pack (his doctor had banned cigars), Louis continued to observe each dancer's attempts as he had for the last twenty-five years, waiting for surprise. His eyes, now more watery than old friends remembered, gazed through the curls of smoke at each anxious student with calm good humor — until the first "wrong" move called for a command to stop. Once the dance acquired his basic requirements of form, it was a prize possession to be rehearsed, polished, and performed.

As a pianist Louis found his declining control at the keyboard more and more frustrating. Only those works he had played continually for his classes since the late twenties stayed in his fingers. Now provided with excellent accompanists — all experienced and loyal musicians who knew what he wanted — Louis no longer accompanied assignments, preferring instead to sit at the long end of the studio in a hard-backed Windsor chair. He had been warned of a bad heart condition after an attack. "No, no, no!" he bellowed at his pianists, with the same impatience as when he interrupted bewildered dancers midaction, but he relied heavily on their abilities.

His classes continued to host a steady stream of note-taking "out of the gymnasium" educators, whose company he enjoyed. One of them, Esther Pease from the University of Michigan, asked him to be her subject for a doctoral dissertation. Drawing from her notes, two interview sessions taped in spring 1952, and articles he had written, her 1954 dissertation *Louis Horst — His Theories on Modern Dance Composition* also contained a brief biographical sketch and described his teaching methods and course content. In these interviews Louis spewed out succinctly worded definitions that illuminated his penchant for calculated abstraction. Pease captured his ideas about the correlation of modernism among the arts:

> As art becomes more asymmetrical, rhythms should also take their place with more freedom, using fives and sevens, and mixing rhythms. Writers Virginia Woolf and Gertrude Stein managed the same break-up of rigid patterns. Poets refused to be tyrannized by symmetrical and traditional meters, so now we have *vers libre* — in fact, it doesn't look like poetry when you see it, sometimes. We don't feel that we have to be bound by pedestrian symmetrical rhythms of two, four, eight, and three, six, nine. Just because we begin a composition in 4/4 time doesn't mean we have to stay with it throughout — we have much more flexibility in our rhythm. . . . Uneven rhythms are part of our "bag of tools" for now. These things move in cycles. Symmetry arises because of balance. In a five, the three and the two are not balanced. I can show you a drawing of Matisse where one eyebrow relates to the other almost like a three to a two, and you'll find when he draws vases that one side will compare spatially with the other side in a similar ratio. This automatically creates distortion. . . . Making a count of five into a unit of two and a unit of three . . . creates unevenness, what I call dissonant rhythm.[43]

In his earlier search for the unusual, Louis had analyzed musical asymmetry. The use of syncopation, single beat per bar, crossing the bar line, changing accents, and mixing meters had become common devices. "One must try the impossible to achieve the improbable," he preached. The same components were being cultivated by visual artists, who began to fracture the image with new "pop" and "op" art styles. But dancers were going back to the ordinary, using "rock" beats and pedestrian, everyday movement, much to Louis's chagrin. For him, "pedestrian" meant the evenness of classical rhythm: "If you are a pedestrian sort of person, you go along in the same rhythm — you never get out of it. Pedestrianism is uninteresting — it means to walk. We speak of pedestrian art, implying that it is common and uninteresting. We want to be strange enough to get away from the pedestrian rhythms of the classes — away from four centuries of everything being set. . . . Learn form, assimilate it, and it will be used intuitively. You can forget it. Learn to look for styles and subtleties, and figure out their mathematical components so that they can be assimilated as technique if desired . . . then forget it."[44] For the professional choreographer these "learned" experiences were what produced facility.

Few people questioned his statements or came close to finding alternative methods for teaching composition during the fifties, but Louis's methodical system had become stale through repetition. Although the wizened figure of authority was still adored, even his most ardent admirers sometimes had to admit that "everything seemed to look alike" in his protégés concerts. Composers under his tutelage concurred. Returning to composing for dance in 1954, Evelyn Lohoefer described the similarities she found in Louis's teaching: "From 1942 to 1954 his course for musicians was exactly the same. He just taught a formula. No change. He must have been bored to death! Back in '42 I knew nothing. He was tough on me, but in '54, although he was not wondrous, we had a mutual respect for each other. Once in a while I'd give him something of mine to listen to. He criticized the piece 'straight out.'" Later, to her surprise, she found him open to her composing style for Jack Moore's *Target* and Paul Taylor's *Post Meridian*: "No one understood it, but Louis liked it."[45]

Louis's acumen kept others serving with him on virtually every dance panel and committee in Manhattan alert. As chairman of the Choreographers Workshop and on the board of advisers for Theatre Dance at the Y, he served with customary good will as their organizers publicly praised his gentlemanly qualities, privately thankful for his sanctioning presence. One such panel fidgeted after viewing a work one member demolished as "lacking in meaning" in angry response to its minimal "emptiness." Then, after a barrage of like comments — "Terrible," "I don't understand it," and "What's happening to the field?" — Louis said simply, "It's a fine work," and reversed the onslaught of criticism.[46]

A banner year, 1953 was the start of a decade filled with events celebrating Louis's various achievements for dance. Receiving these accolades graciously, he noted each award with cryptic comments in his journal along with the most recent detective novel he had finished reading. "To hundreds of dancers throughout the length and breadth of the land, he is 'Louis,' the stern teacher, the kindly advisor, the patient critic, the indomitable encourager, the firm friend," Robert Sabin waxed.[47] His reputation as "judge" or choreographer's critic on university campuses continued to flourish. A photograph of him, broadly smiling, seated in the middle of 100 undergraduate women in black leotards on a gymnasium bleacher, was taken at the tenth annual Arts Forum at the University of North Carolina. Such picture-posing was standard fare for the illustrious Louis — "the grand importentate," as he would live to call himself on his eightieth birthday. The forum also hosted Saul Bellow, Henry Cowell, and Franz Kline. Arlene Croce, then a student, wrote about the occasion that the guru of modern dance asked his followers to "experience life." On a similar panel for the Modern Dance Council of Washington, D.C., Louis continued to preach his well-known views on music and its relation to dance. The council's journal quoted him as saying, "The dancer and the musician have a responsibility to present an integrated form determined by the dancer whose purpose is to evolve a heightened awareness of life, not merely a presentation of the surface."[48]

Ralph Taylor, now in his nineties and still a fond supporter of the Graham Company, knew that Louis loved what he did: "That was a man who was dedicated to the work ethic in every way, which I admired greatly because I never had that talent! I knew he had a heart problem, but he never showed it. He had developed difficulty with his nose, and had a characteristic scraping noise before he'd talk, but outside of that, he was fine. He wasn't really out of condition. He often carried a bag full of printed material that must have weighed thirty-five pounds."[49]

For Louis Manhattan was "where it all happened. You must come to New York if you want to dance." But his summers in Connecticut were the highlight of his teaching. Virginia Freeman, who later co-founded, danced, and choreographed for the Washington, D.C.-based company Dance Quartet, was his assistant. "Those summers were at the foot of Louis Horst and it was just wonderful! I drove him to an Indian area, Quaker Hill, or else Watch Hill where we'd walk across the sand. We'd listen to the ocean. Then we'd go to his favorite restaurants. The lobsters and the butter never stopped, nor did his Manhattans or his references to, 'I'm not supposed to be doing this!' " But at the time, she sensed his diminishing influence on her peers. "I think people were scurried away after pre-classic. This was the era with a lot of Nikolais and Merce people saying you don't have to do it that way. We weren't getting any postmoderns yet, but there was a rub. If Louis felt it, he was generous."[50]

Each summer, when no one else offered to review the school's concerts,

Louis took on the task, writing with his usual precision about each dance event for the *New London Evening Day.* Freeman said, "I had heard these snide remarks that he always fell asleep. 'Louis doesn't see my dances.' It was true, the breathing would become more regular and the head would hang. But somehow he saw through the eyelashes. He was sharp as a tack. He would write a few notes during intermission, and then go back and smoke and type with three or four spaces between lines, so that he could insert. . . . Then he would speak and I would type until he would go nuts with the rhythm of my typing because he would compose while he talked. Sometimes I would do a better copy for him. I would go to the scrapbooks at the college and I would say to him, 'Two years ago you said . . .' "[51]

When he left to get back to Manhattan in time for the rousing 1953 World Series, with the Yankees playing the Brooklyn Dodgers, he found waiting a personal note from the president of Connecticut College, Rosemary Park: "We regret that New London does not have a professional baseball team . . . so that we could offer you everything your heart desires, but perhaps absence from the ball park makes the heart grow fonder and therefore we contribute in a negative way."[52] He also returned to a possible eviction from his West 11th Street apartment. "The landlord was trying to get tenants out with a rent increase. They were trying to evict him by claiming that he was conducting a business there," Freeman recalled. "Doris and I tied up anything that had to do with *Dance Observer.* We drove over to Taylor's perfume factory with everything that had to do with the business end so that he could stay."[53]

Other changes had taken place. Ruth Draper, John Gielgud, and Helen Hayes were among the Neighborhood Playhouse's sponsors when it moved to a new location at 340 East 54th Street. The new Board of Directors gave a citation for twenty-five years of service to Louis and Martha — their names once again linked. By now Martha had severed her professional as well as personal connection to Erick, who had already begun a fulfilling relationship with Lucia Dlugoszewski. Bertram Ross, learning his role in *Night Journey,* recalled, "The first thing Martha wanted to get was the physical image [of Oedipus] before we started. I think one of her reasons for doing that, especially since she was doing Jocasta, was to wipe out any memory she had of Erick. [She spoke of] accepting, facing whatever one was and living it through."[54]

Depressed and alone, Martha continued her slow decline into alcoholism. Desperately searching for ways to help, Rita Morgenthau and Bethsabee de Rothschild hoped to reestablish her friendship with Louis, suggesting an occasion in honor of his seventieth birthday. Taking their advice, Martha invited hundreds to celebrate, including St. Denis, Shawn, de Mille, Holm, and Weidman. The party, held at her studio at 316 East 63rd Street, was an elegant affair to which the press was invited. One more year of leadership had passed for the "acidulous man whose iron discipline had fallen heavily on virtually every famous American dancer since Ruth Saint Denis," pronounced a *New York Times* article after the event. "The revolution in the dance has become evolution," Louis was quoted as saying as he "unbent" to celebrate, "allowing birthday cakes and bottles of liquor to clutter his piano." His enthusiasm had not flagged throughout his years around dance, he told the reporter, "because I still like the painting painted yesterday or the piece of music composed yesterday instead of going around saying, 'Beethoven is good enough for me.' "55 Walter Sorell paid homage to the septuagenarian as "the synthesis of a conservative and revolutionary who knows that you should only knock down walls when you know how to build. . . . This iconoclast, this breaker of rules has endowed many American dancers with knowledge, discipline, law and order."56

The celebrations over, Louis continued his round of appearances as guest critic. In January he delivered a lecture, "Form in Movement," at an Adelphi University symposium in which Henry Cowell spoke on "Rhythm and Percussion" and Hanya Holm taught technique, and in March addressed the Women's Faculty Club in Williamstown, Massachusetts, prompting a local writer to caption his review, "Modern Dance is not longhaired."57

chapter ten

1954–1964

"A curious intimacy —

A distant closeness."

— Martha Graham

ouis explained his reconciliation with Martha in the following way: "For a long time she never would say anything about what I'd done for her, but then she sent me a letter. It came from Belgium, out of the clear sky."[1] She wrote from the Century Hotel in Antwerp on 23 April 1954:

I just want to write and thank you a little bit — for all you've done to make me — to help me. All has not been easy for my heart or for my body but it has been wonderful. I think of you many times here in Europe and speak of you all the time. . . . Every press conference carries your name some place in it. Praise be the A B A form to say nothing of the others. I have had a curious time here . . . a time of reevaluation. . . . They say they have no choreographers. I say they have no Louis Horst. The utter amazement they have when I say that choreographers are trained in America is naive. Then I say it is a musician who trains them, and they are dumbfounded. . . . It seems that the thing most amazing is that we as Americans have a culture other than the movies or Russian ballet transplanted. Curious so dead a thing as "modern dance" should have importance. . . . I can only write a short note now. Principally to thank you in a little way for all you have helped me become . . . to transmit. I am on my way to Vienna. I shall see you on the streets there. I only wanted this to tell you that you are doing a great and valuable work in training the creative instinct to express and make manifest what it feels as urgent. . . . All love, Martha."[2]

For Louis the letter reaffirmed Graham's affection, and it had a settling effect. Virginia Freeman recalled seeing the letter and hearing references to it from Louis during the 1954 summer at Connecticut, "as if all was now resolved, like his now famous A-B-As."[3] He said to another of Martha's past worshippers, "You know, Yuriko, I really am grateful for what Martha did to me. It was hard at first. She forced me to find my own way in the world — become my own person. I am happier now."[4] He commented on his renewed friendship with Graham to Jeanette Roosevelt in 1961: "We're very good friends. After a show we go and eat something. I gave her discipline because she was a wild one. I was the tail to her kite." Closing a scrapbook, he commented, "At least it's a history of Graham at the beginning." "And a history of you too," Roosevelt reminded him. He replied, "Well, I'm not so important."[5]

As his age advanced, so did his need to summarize the vision of the field he had spent a lifetime developing. With a desire akin to a composer's final chords of a symphony, Louis had begun to take every opportunity to express his philosophical leanings in dance. The second season of Monday-night lectures at the American Dance Festival opened appropriately with Martha on 13 July 1953. Louis reported in the *New London Day*, "It is always inspiring and exciting to hear Miss Graham proclaim her gospel of the dance, but difficult for a reporter to do full justice to the occasion."[6] Doris Humphrey's lecture was equally illuminating. A "genuinely exciting experience," she explained her theories of choreography, stating that the basic principles of modern dance are "personal and human rather than impersonal and abstract."[7] Wedged between these two leaders, his own lecture-demonstration focused on the modern dance and "its search for new forms of communication," and he concluded that "the modern dance is concerned with the discovery of new movement, new ways to use the body, new ways to communicate and a new vocabulary . . . punctuating exposition of a theme with beguiling examples of wit."[8]

Walter Terry introduced Ted Shawn as the "great gentleman of modern dance," for his lecture in this Series. Shawn, who had rarely visited the campus since creating his own summer school and festival at Jacob's Pillow, spoke eloquently, not about himself but François Delsarte. The lecture brought forth Louis's own evaluation of the theorist's ideas, for he, too, had adapted the essence of Delsarte's philosophy on meaning and gesture.

Louis himself opened the lecture series in summer 1954 by presenting the usual short dances to illustrate the various points that gave "a panoramic view of the various forces which have influenced the contemporary dance," Norman Lloyd wrote. "Horst is a veritable one-man university of the arts.

He had been a dominant figure in establishing the modern American dance as a serious art form. His answers to the basic question of what makes art modern are authoritative and clear. The arts of today are the result of rebellion against our immediate past and a more conscious knowledge of ourselves as people."[9]

The highlight of the series was an appearance by the college's resident aesthetician and philosopher, Susanne K. Langer, who had recently published *Philosophy in a New Key* and *Feeling and Form*. Both books were favorite references for Louis, and he relished invitations to her little salt-box house on the Connecticut River in Lyme. He called her speech a true "revelation," and praised her "keen and searching intelligence," especially since her writing placed dance so significantly among the other fine arts. He quoted her as saying, "Dance, autonomous and possessing its own primary illusions, abstracts the interplay and interaction of powers by making a living rhythm for perception. . . . A dance is an apparition of eternal powers in conflict and resolution; a rhythmic balance of powers created for perception."[10] The philosopher's ideas fully reinforced his own; he could not have said it better.

Reviewing Carleton Sprague Smith's lecture, "Music for the Dance," Louis took an opportunity to draw swords once again on the subject of music in relation to dance. He struck the old theme of Germany's Gebrauchsmusik: "If a dance performance holds the stage, the music, of necessity, must play the lesser supporting role, whether it be back-stage or in the pit," he wrote, dismissing Smith's opinion to the contrary.[11]

Besides the lectures and editorials, Louis opened himself to interviews and any other outlets that would give his ideas permanency. But when public recognition came his way, he tended to be deprecatory. In 1955 he received the Capezio Award. "One doesn't react at my age. I mean I didn't jump up or down shouting hooray. Of course I was happy to hear I'd gotten it, but I've developed a policy of indifference. It prevents disappointment."[12] But undoubtedly the award was the greatest public recognition he had received to date. With Nina at his side, he accepted the award that read, "For his unique contribution to the modern dance as composer, accompanist, teacher, critic and general force for progress."[13] Louis preferred to think that he was chosen instead "for endurance and defence [sic] of modern dance for the past forty years."[14] Graham, Humphrey, and de Mille were there to celebrate, as were the critics Anatole Chujoy, John Martin, and Walter Terry. Eli Wallach paid tribute to Louis as his favorite teacher, "who happens also to be composer, accompanist, guide, sage, and critic to the world of dance," and presented the award "for making dance a vital element in the contemporary theatre in

America."[15] Martin called him "a dominant figure in the development of the American modern dance."[16]

In his acceptance speech Louis outlined the high points of his forty years in dance and alluded benignly to the illustrious succession of "matriarchs" for whom he had toiled. Then, thanking the "disinterested generosity of Capezio," he confessed, "I have never spent a nickel in their shop!"[17] De Mille wrote that Louis spoke of "all the dedicated and devoted artists with whom he had had the privilege of achievement; and he also wished to thank those who had tried and failed, because without them, the great could not have gone so far."[18] According to Robert Sabin, the occasion was "one of the happiest of its kind . . . for the conviction that the award was well made was overwhelming and unanimous."[19] Louis was most pleased that the new president of Juilliard, the composer William Schuman, had attended the luncheon and sent a congratulatory letter saying, "In choosing you this year there was a unanimity of approval that is even rarer in the art world than the political one. In accepting the honor you were wise and witty and exactly what I have come to expect from you."[20]

Louis received acknowledgments of a more tangible sort in 1961. A new dance studio at Perry-Mansfield (funded by an anonymous alumna) was dedicated in his name. The sculptor Peter Lipman-Wulf was commissioned to create a bust to be completed in bronze and Moses Soyer was asked to paint a portrait. If immortality was not assured, Louis was pleased that his colleagues and friends felt him worthy of these honors.

Dance Observer was Louis's most expressive outlet. As editor and writer he had used the power of words in support of dance, and the small publication had become a stabilizing force in the ephemeral world of dance. A confident writer, he continued to be responsible for the entries on dance in the *Encyclopedia Britannica,* he agreed to write articles on "The Story of Ballet" and "Modern Dance" for *Keyboard Jr.,* a journal about music for children, and there were still his summer reviews for the *New London Evening Day.* Always the dance advocate, he penned each assignment with the same sense of duty he gave to his scrapbooks.

Throughout, Louis's voice spoke for dance as a high art, the goal of which, for both dancer and audience, should be communication. As the uncontested leader for modernism in dance he spoke about subtle differences between the modern and ballet styles: "There is much more physical consciousness of the body and use of the torso for expressive purposes [in modern dance] than was ever found in the ballet. . . . The philosophy is different; the ballet doing a modern dance is always a modernized ballet, and the modern dancer doing something that might be balletic is always, in a sense, balletic modern." Even though the battle between ballet and modern dance had dissipated, Louis was growing disenchanted: "People come to see Graham as they own a Cezanne, not because they like it but because it's the thing to do. It is the highest form of commercial art, but modern dance is too creative, too misunderstood. It has to have time. . . . In the '30's, dance was in a state of revolution; now it's in a state of evolution. . . . Modern dance [is] getting too lyrical. I am hoping that someone will come along with a new purity and a goal. It needs a shot in the arm. . . . A dance should have a style and it should not be too mixed."[21]

With his health in obvious decline, Louis worried about the dismal prospect of a nursing home. "Doris still taught even when her hip was so bad she could hardly get to the classroom. If the mind is still lucid then I can still teach."[22] He continued to accept invitations to previews, fund-raisers, and dinner parties, and prepared short speeches or special lectures at request — events he found pleasurable if tiring. He now took cabs for short as well as long distances and paused for his companion to take his arm if a staircase seemed precarious. As his pace slowed and he stopped more and more often to catch his breath, those who accompanied him accepted his condition with calm.

After he suffered another mild heart attack in 1955, friends worried about his loss of stamina. His doctor again advised him to cut down on smoking, watch his diet, and take a shot of brandy before going to bed. "He tried but still loved to eat," Hazel Johnson said. She was aware of his frailty during the months of recovery: "He was unsteady — cautious at curbings, unsure of his footing."[23] And his handwriting had deteriorated rapidly. The once sure strokes now took a slight quivering path. Louis signed his Christmas cards in red crayon, knowing that his friends would appreciate the primitive quality of his increasingly childlike penmanship. More often now he would say to a potential student, "You had better come to study with me soon. I won't be around forever!"

The writer Don McDonagh later charged that Horst was "a symbol of the fixity. . . . His once fervid enthusiasm for modern dance had turned into a series of cavils against the creative efforts of the younger generation. His creative composition course, which was the product of his understanding of the ideological currents of the 1930's, had fallen upon sterile days."[24] To substantiate this view McDonagh had only to point to the now famous blank review Horst penned in response to Paul Taylor's equally empty choreography in his first independent concert. A leading performer in Martha's company, Taylor was anxious to develop his own choreographic voice, and so in *Epic* he walked, using a complicated system of counts to a taped voice that repeated, "At the tone, the time will be . . . ." "The program begins and I'm standing there . . . in a freshly ironed suit that I haven't worn since coming to New York. The phone lady is making her announcements and I'm remembering the tricky counts and executing interesting street gleanings, but, sooner than I would've guessed, a few of the audience rise from their front seats and head up the aisle. . . . The solo over, I go offstage and tell the girls not to expect a large house. . . . A few weeks later Louis Horst's review comes out in *Dance Observer*. . . . John Martin, one of the first to go up the aisle, predicts in a Sunday column that the Horst review is to become a collector's item. . . . Martha shakes her gnarled finger and accuses me of being a 'naughty boy.'"[25]

Louis's blank review, Doris Rudko recalled, was born over two martinis: "After Paul's concert at the Y, we went to the tavern across the street. After his first cocktail, Louis shook his head. 'How am I going to write about it?' Then after the second martini, he said, 'I've got it! I won't say anything! Just leave a blank column, and sign my name!'"[26] The four column inches of blank space was signed at the bottom "L H". Horst had made his point. From Taylor's perspective the review represented Horst's severest criticism, especially since this advocate journal of modern dance was established to reflect the creative importance of the art: "I realized that no matter how scientific or abstract you get, you can't escape meaning."[27]

Everyone credited Louis with *Dance Observer*'s longevity. In January 1958, Lois Balcom attributed its zeal to the "fidelity of a managing editor whose interest has never flagged and who has expressed a phenomenal devotion to the modern American dance and American dancers through 238 successive *Dance Observer* issues." (Ralph Taylor, Louis's silent partner and loyal friend for those twenty-four years, was not mentioned.) She noted that of the forty-nine literary periodicals that began in the same year, only the *Dance Observer* was still being published. Comparing Volumes 1 and 24, she concluded that the journal's "goal toward which it strives today is certainly the same goal which the founding editors established," even if the early editorials dealt with the "tortured subject of modern dance versus . . . and of course the other side of the versus was inevitably the ballet." Most significantly, *Dance Observer* had remained "uncompromisingly non-commercial," bolstered only by an impromptu benefit whenever funds were low.[28]

Actors and directors were reminded of his influence on their careers when, earlier that season, Louis appeared as part of the Neighborhood Playhouse teaching staff in a television special produced by NBC-TV for its "Wide Wide World" series. Featuring the career of the actress Joanne Woodward, the film showed a "typical" rehearsal, with Louis droning counts "1, 2,

2, 2, 3, 2" to a group of performing men while Ted Dalbotten at the piano pounded away at a gigue. "Now boys, let's see the war dance," Louis instructed from the sidelines. "And now let's see a romantic allemande called *Parting*."[29] If the program's airing was meant to show the kind of training that had developed the star, it also gave the Neighborhood Playhouse prestigious exposure and a well-deserved tribute to its faculty and director, Rita Morgenthau.

Adding to the already formidable number of articles written about Louis, Marian Van Tuyl pigeonholed him between classes for an interview that became a major article in *Impulse 1954*. Then the June 1958 issue of *Dance Magazine* contained a feature article that praised the long reach of his influence as a teacher. After thirty years, Louis's philosophy for teaching remained constant: "Technique frees the body for general action — composition, using dramatic problems, frees it for specific action. Composition helps students to direct, to understand form and dynamics."[30] Some months later *Dance Magazine*'s little column, "The Name Dropper," recalled an ever-popular tale from the Denishawn days about Horst:

> Once an errant *coryphee* was called on the carpet by Miss St. Denis for behavior which seemed to fall short of perfection. The novice grew a bit rebellious and dared to point out that the house rules were not applied impartially to one and all. Why, for instance, was there never any censure for their dashing musical director, Louis Horst? "Darling," replied Miss Ruth loftily, "We need Louis!" At 75 . . . it's still difficult to imagine him as one to be bound by curfews.[31]

Indeed, Louis continued to enjoy daily encounters with attractive companions. In March 1959 Akiko Kanda, a Japanese dancer studying at the Graham school, presented two dances with scores composed by Horst on the Contemporary Dance Productions series at the Y. Louis offered to pay her tuition at Juilliard so that she could study with him. A *Dance News* article explained, "Throughout his life, Louis had sponsored talented dancers he considered special who needed his help, and few could ignore Akiko's extraordinary presence." The writer innocently added that Horst "even volunteered to produce new scores for her dances, although he had not written a note for the last five years."[32] This last burst of enthusiasm on his part took place at the same time that he no longer bothered to keep programs and clippings in orderly fashion.

His best stories rarely appeared in print, but were shared with his closest friends over drinks and during a good meal in one of his favorite haunts. Solemn advice was always forthcoming about love: "A woman in dance should not marry. She will spend her energy in the kitchen and get pregnant. Her career will be over." One of his talented students gave up her career and worked to put her husband through law school. "Then he left her for another woman! What a shame. Her life was ruined." "Must you marry?" he asked the unsuspecting companion of one of his favorites. After two hours of constant harassment about the woes of wedlock, he gave up: "Well, I guess you'll be alright."[33] As a peace offering the prospective groom presented Louis with little sketches of archaic figures stretching their limbs. Pleased, he used them as *Dance Observer* fillers.

To another he insisted, "Artists have to live in cold-water flats — and you have to watch out for *agriculture!*" He talked of Martha breaking away from Denishawn and making her first solos when she was twenty-nine: "You are at that age," he told Virginia Freeman. "Don't end this to become somebody's wife and mother of children."[34] Even Joanne Woodward's personal life did not escape his criticism. Meeting the actress (then very pregnant) at a street corner on Madison Avenue, he bellowed, "Oh, Blondie, Blondie, you can't dance now, can you!"[35]

Don McDonagh wrote that Horst's "string of assistants became the cushion" at the end of his career.[36] In fact, Louis had always had the luxury of a team of assistants and pianists surrounding him. Even his sister May, who never quite understood what her brother did for a living, expressed amazement during a visit to his Juilliard classroom at the admiring students who sat at his feet. She whispered a thank you to his assistant: "I know he needs you. He couldn't possibly dance a step on his own!"[37] The aging guru of the modern dance world certainly selected his companions with an eye for variety, choosing those he felt were destined for the call, and he also protected them. After Nina's departure in 1952 Virginia Freeman became his assistant at the Neighborhood Playhouse. In 1956 Doris Rudko took over for Freeman at Connecticut College and remembered, "I'd eke out the reviews for the *Day* with him the way I'd eke out student's compositions. I'd sit at the typewriter and he dictated. It was always a task. He always had someone, I think, to put him to the task."[38]

His pattern of working had not changed over the years, with the exception of his declining agility, which meant that his assistants felt more comfortable meeting him in front of his apartment. Rudko "would pick him up by cab . . . calling him before I left my apartment on Riverside. Always punctual, he would be waiting in the lobby. [After his class] we generally went round the corner to the greasy spoon for lunch and then back to his apartment to work on some portion of the *Observer*."[39] Each year he depended on her more.

Louis's years were marked by annual teaching contracts, holidays with his extended dance family, Thanksgiving hosted by Nina's mother, Christmas day at Martha Hill's, birthday celebrations every January. The break before second semester gave him a few weeks to catch up with out-of-town dancers, then came performance workshops, lecture-demonstrations, and spring projects such as the annual Y young choreographers event, Graham's Broadway season, and students' final assignments. There were the usual brief visits West in June to see Betty, and then the train ride with other staff members to the American Dance Festival for six weeks of teaching. In the city his weeks predictably were Tuesdays and Thursdays at the Neighborhood Playhouse, Wednesdays at Juilliard, and Tuesday and Thursday evenings free to teach on his own or for courses on nearby campuses, where "He edited, he pared, he pruned with the faith that the healthy plants would survive."[40]

Graham, who now lived in a high-rise on 62nd Street and York Avenue, had become increasingly anxious about Louis living alone. A new apartment complex was under construction at 440 West 62nd Street, right across the street, that overlooked the East Side rooftops. She inquired about an apartment for him, then invited him to spend a few days with her and Geordie in a house she had rented on Shelter Island to talk over his possible move. She scolded him for eating the wrong foods and not taking care of himself. At her urging he signed a lease for a one-bedroom apartment — a decision he soundly regretted for what would be the last three years of his life. Under Graham's protective wing he was both pleased and dismayed. "The relationship between Martha and Louis at the end was warm and caring. She kept him in view," Ruth Lloyd commented.[41] Once again he was charmed by Martha's possessiveness and recognized the advantages of their shared "European" doctor at nearby Doctors Hospital and of a twenty-four-hour doorman.

His sleek apartment faced rooftops to the west and to the east, from his kitchen window, barges, two bridges, and the East River Drive. And the giant closet served as a fine location for a new *Dance Observer* office. Louis placed his typewriter on his desk, got the necessary *Dance Observer* papers organized, stacked his reams of music on top of his piano, and placed one or two Indian rugs on the floor. Never bothering to unwrap his art collection, once he resumed his schedule, he knew almost immediately that the move was a mistake. Cabs seldom ventured into the area unless called, meaning long waits in the lobby. The angled glimpse of Martha's living room was not an equal exchange for the freedom he had enjoyed in his Greenwich Village milieu. He wished out loud that he could have his old apartment back. Louis had given up the vitality of the Village, with its array of restaurants and easy access to the subway, for a posh East Side residential neighborhood of relative isolation. No longer able just to walk down the block to the variety or newspaper store, the change was dramatic and depressing. He spent more time napping in his easy chair — sometimes throughout the night or until he received a call from Martha reminding him to turn off the lights and go to bed.

Friends sensed his loneliness. Virginia and Beth solemnly agreed to take a cold supper to him whenever they were in New York, hating the sadness they felt as he waved goodbye down the long, impersonal corridor of his new high-rise. Virginia saw that "Louis was fragile then, away from the bustle of the Village where he felt most at home."[42]

One weekend, Martha observed that Louis's living room lights did not go on. Frantic, she called Martha Hill at Juilliard on Monday morning to find out his whereabouts. An alert was sounded among the assistants: "Have you seen Louis? Do you know where he would have gone?" Hill asked. By afternoon Louis showed up, having taken a leisurely train ride back to the city from the home of friends in Connecticut. Tired of being watched over he huffed, "Missing? Of course not. I just went away for a few days."[43]

Graham's *Clytemnestra* had been received as an epic work of genius. *Night Journey* had become an elegant film. Another film was being shot in lecture-demonstration format at the studio that focused on the breadth of Martha's technique. The project was called *A Dancer's World*. Louis invited his Juilliard favorites along for a preview of the dance segments. Seated in the center of the proceedings, his stocky, white-haired presence dominated the scene. Deeply moved as he watched the shifting groups of exquisite dancers, the world he had helped create swirled around him.

With his first book, *Pre-Classic Dance Forms,* now well established and even translated into Spanish, Carroll Russell prompted him to release the long-awaited volume on modern dance forms. Russell was an admirer of Horst and one of Martha's earliest backers in the thirties. She started to attend his classes, tape recorder in hand, to capture anecdotal remarks. After watching jazz studies he complained, "I didn't feel the aura of city life," or "You need a little more characterization — a gangster's moll or anything you want to do," or "You got there a count too soon. Frankly, you supposedly jazz babies will never get to it. I'm trying to get you to be a little more jazzy."[44] She caught his words, and once they were transcribed, she asked Graham to write a preface. Louis supplied copies of his articles published in *Dance Observer,* assorted photographs, prints, and music collections to accompany the proposed text. Russell then negotiated with Marian Van Tuyl, who took the slight volume to press. When *Modern Dance Forms in*

Relation to the Other Arts was finally released, he gave each of his assistants a copy, and that was that.

Students occasionally asked him to sign an edition, but never one to assign readings or texts he did not bother to mention that the book was in print at the beginning of each semester. Instead, he brought original prints, cut-outs from the *New York Times,* illustrations, postcard reproductions, and mimeographs of music to accompany each assignment, as he had for years. A review of the book praised Louis's ingenuity in showing the relationship of the arts as "succinct and pungent evidence of his standards. [Horst's ability to relate all the arts to] central aesthetic canons [make him a] "bold adventurer in space and time [where] everything is grist to the choreographer's mill."[45] Although the publication of the book signified the worth of his teaching and Louis was honored that Russell had given her time to the project, he knew that his most valuable teaching could happen only in the classroom. To the question, "Why not a book on Group Forms?" Louis replied halfheartedly, "Well, maybe some day."[46]

His last journal entry in 1962 mentioned the death of Nina's mother, and noted, "One o'clock concert at Juilliard: Janet Mansfield Soares" — the first to present a full concert of original choreography on this Juilliard series. Although his enthusiasm for record-keeping had faltered, Louis was invariably the one to remind a colleague of a board meeting, and arrived ten minutes before the designated hour as usual. Once settled in a meeting he remained the most aggressive advocate for new directions for the field. Freeman remembered that he was the lone voter at each season's summer festival planning session for the inclusion of Nikolais or Cunningham on the faculty — a vote cast in the interest of new energy and the inclusion of more avant-garde creators of the dance community. Throughout his life Louis understood talent — its multiplicity and changeability.

But dance artists were beginning to rebel against a tired sameness that seemed to prevail within the entire arts scene during the fifties, and for many of them Horst was the epitome of the establishment. Louis's writing seemed protective of his favorites, making the freer spirits who preferred not to study with him uncomfortable. Louis's intolerance of sloppy and undisciplined behavior of any kind grew more evident. He championed individualism as long as students had learned the traditional rules they intended to break. He had come to hate qualities that were self-expressive, sentimental, undisciplined, childish, and rude — precisely those that often charmed young choreographers. Some believed that his teaching was monopolized by the kind of choreography the establishment would find acceptable.

Louis reported pedantically, "I've had thousands and thousands of students — at least 2,000 just at the Neighborhood Playhouse. When you add up the years at Connecticut, the Neighborhood Playhouse, at Juilliard, my own private classes, not counting spring terms at Sarah Lawrence or those three winters once a week at Teacher's College, and at Bennington . . . with twenty-five in each class, and even if people didn't study with me, know me through reading *Dance Observer,* there have been thousands."[47] Of all of his students Louis considered upstart Paul Taylor one of the most extraordinary, and was amused and not unduly surprised to witness Taylor's return to formality in his new *Aureole.* (Years later Taylor admitted that the dance was "an attempt to get what I've learned in Louis Horst's classes out of my system. As Louis would've wanted, the dance's steps have been limited to a few basic seed steps — themes to vary in speed, direction, sequential order, and any other way that might make them seem less redundant. . . . Something about simplicity has been on my mind."[48]

But Taylor's choreography was essentially mainstream in relation to the new turn of events beginning to brew in the Judson Church basement. A *Village Voice* dance writer, Jill Johnston (who had first published in *Dance Observer*), turned her dance pages into pervasive essays about the unsettling performances there. Another young critic, George Jackson, began to take on various writing assignments for Louis. In 1960 Louis refused his comments on a Pierre Boulez score, saying "Let's skip the music," but by 1963, when he submitted a review of a Judson Church event, it enraged Louis. "He actually hung up on me!" Jackson recalled. "I was shocked! I didn't know why he was so angry, but he never asked me to write anything again."[49] Louis did not truly understand the experimentation, Doris Rudko knew: "This was a period of enlarging the whole vocabulary of dance. Different concerns with space and time came out of the whole Einstein revolution, taking dance in new directions and disturbing what was considered the ongoing way. . . . Louis didn't really understand the extremes."[50]

If the Judson scene was an irritant to Louis's aesthetic sense, the new plans for Lincoln Center's New York State Theatre for Dance fired his political anger. Articles had begun to appear in *Dance Observer* addressing "the moral challenge" of Lincoln Center's board of directors and fearing that the modern dance would be "left out."[51] His intolerance most often displayed only to close friends, Louis seldom brought these views to the printed page in his reviews, which were known for their particular generosity to younger talents. In fact, his deepest concerns were political as he worried about the future of the arts, with the big organizations taking over, and the state of the world in general.

In the catastrophic year of 1963, when John F. Kennedy was assassinated and Lyndon Johnson became President, Louis was approaching his eighth decade. Sporting his tweed cap and gold pocket watch, Louis's stout figure and distinguished profile with its hooked nose and triple jowls still caught one's eye as he took his seat in a crowded theater. For a celebration of his seventy-ninth birthday at Martha's apartment, a collection of $350 from colleagues and friends paid for the bronzing of Elena Kepalas's newly sculpted portrait bust, to Louis's delight. Kepalas had photographed and sculpted his worn, massive jowls from every angle over a period of many months. Of all his portraits, this was his favorite. The remaining money paid for a deluxe double-bed and headboard to replace the old cot he had slept in for years at West 11th Street.

In December 1963 Martha and Louis each received an honorary Doctor of Humanities degree from Wayne State University in Detroit. Because of Louis's heart condition his doctor did not want him to fly to the Midwest for the award. Knowing how important their joint award was to him, Martha agreed to travel with him by train. Scheduled to travel for two days before the event, they took what would be their last cross-country trip together. One calamity after another made the journey unpleasant and tense. Martha missed a connecting train. They had to wait for hours before the next one.

A full twenty-four bedraggled hours later, the illustrious team arrived on campus, a golf cart taking them to the speaker's platform mid-ceremony, minutes before the awards were to be bestowed. Louis's citation read: "As musician, artistic advisor, teacher, editor, critic, and author, Louis Horst has influenced immeasurably the careers of leading modern dancers who have set out on new paths of creativeness in this age-old art. The breadth and depth of his knowledge of music literature, his skill as a composer for dance, and his insistence on principles of artistic integrity helped Martha Graham during the years of their association to reach her present eminence in her art of dance."[52]

This tribute countered Walter Terry's comment that Graham's entire repertory boasted specially commissioned scores "not only serving her own choreographic need but giving inspiration and outlet to contemporary creators of music. . . . The world of music is indebted to her as one who has fostered, probably more than any other living choreographer, the art of the contemporary composer,"[53] with no mention at all of Louis and placing Graham as the originator of the idea.

Returning to the city a few hours before his Neighborhood Playhouse classes were to begin, Walter Sorell scolded him for pushing himself beyond his limit. "You're exhausted. Go to bed. I'll call the Playhouse and explain."

Louis would not hear of it. "He rested in his overstuffed chair for awhile, gathered his music for the day's teaching, and was out the door."[54]

By his fourth decade of teaching, Louis had affected virtually every dance department in the United States. Students became teachers of more students. Artists such as Pina Bausch, Lucinda Childs, Martha Clarke, Jennifer Muller, and Meredith Monk were some of the dancers just starting to study with him at the beginning of the sixties. His methodology for the teaching of dance composition had become part of the formal mode of compositional practice for modern dance in the concert hall and in the studio. But more and more maverick groups of dancers were rebelling against Graham's and Humphrey's and Horst's dominance. At Judson Church a group of dancers would pass the hat after free-flow performances in which anybody with anything to show, did — without ceremony or audition. A new era of concert supporters emerged from the foreign flicks at Waverly Street and the paperback bookshops and coffee houses to the shelter of Al Carmines' open-church environs. Dance Theater Workshop would soon present groups of choreographers on weekend series in Jeff Duncan's live-in loft. Laura Foreman would begin her Choreo-concerts at the same New School West 12th Street address that had presented Graham and Horst in lecture-demonstrations years before. The YMCA's Clark Center would soon begin to produce a series for new choreographers.

As more experimental notions attracted young artists, the begrudging Horst was more often than not misunderstood. Unquestionably he represented the establishment. Doris Rudko suggested that "possibly the reason for Louis's many years of success was that . . . modern dancers had to create their own dances. With nothing to pass on, no repertory to perform, choreographing was a necessity. They had to compose."[55] Nina described Louis as "an instinctive critic. He was there, insisting upon a foundation that brought the best qualities forward."[56] Another dancer called it "a habit of truth."[57]

During the final years of his teaching, Louis's "surgical" scrutiny of each choreographer's beginnings became more laborious. He had always taught beyond inspiration and his classes in the early 1960s were more confrontation than engagement. By then it was not unusual for a young student to spend a half hour in front of him, going over the movement content of a two-measure theme to rid it of any repetitive materials. In one pre-classic class, Trisha Brown attempted a study based on high energy. Using a simple basic motive, she repeated a violent, half-improvised churning action to a point of exhaustion. If exciting to watch, it was far removed from the assignment Louis expected to see. "No, no, no," he shouted, "that's not it." Frustrated, Brown, like generations of others before her, did not understand why her movement was not "it." Obstinate instances such as this had always been part of his uncompromising teaching; Brown's traumatic experience was nothing new.

In the classroom he raged; in his writing of four or five reviews for *Dance Observer* each month he handled rebellious behavior by simply not mentioning it, directing his most enthusiastic comments toward Graham exponents. To the public eye Horst held staunch allegiance to the community of dancers, whether a big unhappy family or not. In private he might nickname Graham's *Eye of Anguish* "Angst and Hogwash," but he had not missed a single premiere performance during her career. If a casual reference, such as "chocolate baby," seemed racially prejudiced, dancers knew that years before, when traveling by train in the South, he had created a scene by refusing to remove himself from a "blacks only" car. A man of unyielding principles, he might tell with tongue in cheek a female companion "You're going with every Tom, Dick or Louis." "He had an appetite and intensity of spirit, economy of line for succinctness of energy, and these were aspects of his wit as well," a friend remarked.[58]

When Louis returned from Wayne State he was totally exhausted, Rudko recalled. A week later, on 12 January 1964, Martha held an eightieth birthday party for him at her studio and again hundreds of wellwishers were invited to the celebration. Sitting on a whimsically constructed throne among his women, Louis voiced the good fortune of his longevity once again. A second birthday party took place on what would be Louis's last Wednesday at Juilliard. A gray day threatened snow. He wished he'd worn his galoshes, he said. "Snow is forecast," he told me. Between classes Mary Chudick, the dance office secretary, brought the cake with one candle to the studio and an impromptu "Happy Birthday" chorus erupted from the roomful of students. Louis feigned surprise and gave thanks from his proud position as a new "octogenarian." With a weary wave that suggested it was time to get back to the "strange shape" design studies, Louis hastily slipped a digitalis pill under his tongue. A cup of water arrived to go with the pink-frosted cake he balanced on his knee.

The next day, after teaching at the Neighborhood Playhouse, Doris Rudko and Louis walked to their usual retreat for French toast. Later, they hailed a cab at 55th Street. During the nine-block journey Louis again reached for his medicine and seemed to be experiencing some pain. "Are you alright?" Doris asked. "I'm O.K.," he answered. Doris "waited in the cab as he walked up to the door of his building, before driving off. Later I got a call from Nina saying that he had collapsed in his lobby."[59] Geordie, now administrator for the Graham School, was at her desk a block away. "I was taking care of the school. No one else was around. His doctor called to say that Louis had to go to Doctor's Hospital. There was no ambulance available, so we drove Louis in the doctor's own car. I said, 'Can I stay with you?' But he didn't want me there, so Nina came to be with him."[60]

His old friend Ralph "dropped everything and rushed over when I heard the news. He was in pretty bad shape. He couldn't speak clearly. He fought like a tiger. He didn't want to die. It took quite a number of days before the old devil got him. I was there very frequently." Louis asked Ralph to be the executor of his estate. "I didn't want the job particularly. I didn't know what it entailed, but he insisted, so I had my brother-in-law, Louis Himber, draw up a will. Louis wanted to be cremated. We discussed it, and I said, 'Well, what do you want done with the ashes?' He said, 'Just toss them over New York.' "[61]

Refusing to appear distraught to Horst, Graham arrived each day carefully made-up and dressed in bright reds, and each day she called concerned friends to report his condition. "What can we do for him? Do you think he will survive this?" she fretted to Norman Lloyd.[62] According to Rudko, Louis's condition improved over the next week and he seemed in fairly good spirits. When she took the galleys for the February *Dance Observer* to him, they walked down the corridor together. "They were ready to release him. Then, on a Sunday, he suffered another stroke. I went to see him, but Nina would not let me enter his room. I felt as though I had deserted him! Here I had spent practically every day with him for the last eight years, and suddenly Nina enters the picture out of the clear blue after years of being out of his life!"[63] Other friends viewed her return as a godsend.

The second stroke left Horst paralyzed on one side. Nina, determined to keep steady vigil, sat quietly nearby, passing the time with her needlework. "Even during his final illness Louis retained his wry and trenchant sense of humor. On the night of his admission, when he was laying in hospital just following a stroke and looking very limp and white, the private nurse arrived at about midnight and said, 'Good evening Mr. Horst, my name is Ethel Sheehan.' 'Ah, good old Jewish name,' said Louis. 'Oh no, Sir! I'm Irish,' she replied. Louis turned and rolled his blue eyes with a look of utter disgust and hopelessness — she had not got the joke."[64] His "archangels" Martha and Nina took turns being with him. Both were at his bedside when on 23 January 1964 the doctor pronounced him dead.

Ralph Taylor, as executor, had the job of taking care of the cremation.

I tried to arrange to hire a plane to go up and toss the stuff all over New York, but I found out it was illegal to do that, so I arranged a substitute.

I remembered that Katharine Cornell had an estate on the Hudson River . . . and her estate ran to the water, and that she was a friend of Louis's and Martha's. We arranged two cars — very quickly after his death — and rode up there. Martha was supposed to come. That day she developed what somebody said was a terrible headache, and she didn't come. There was always something slightly mysterious about that. I always felt that maybe Martha had imbibed a little too much just to get away from her troubles — because it was a terrible shock to her when Louis died.

We all rode up there to his estate and I had found a poem that seemed to fit the occasion in some book of poetry. And I had somebody take this jar which had Louis's remains in it — just powder — and as he dumped this powder into the river, I recited a poem. Nina was there with her lawyer. She was continually followed around by her lawyer. He was very anxious to talk to me about getting the pictures. He wanted to make sure that I understood that she was going to be the one to distribute them to friends, so that they each got a picture. The wording in the will did mention Nina — that's why he was there at the funeral. He took this opportunity — he knew that I would be there so that he could talk to me. Louis had us set up a bank account so that Himber could continue to remit regular payments to his wife, Betty. That was part of his old German gentility. It always bothered him — the fact that he had been married, and he had abandoned her on the Coast.

He had a bunch of bonds. There were a couple of hundred dollars left in the account, so we turned it over to the library along with the surplus copies of the *Dance Observer*. I presumably had the sole key to his apartment and there was an awful lot of stuff to inventory. And things had disappeared from the first time I entered the apartment. . . . Louis had left specific instructions in his will that his paintings should be divided among his friends. This was never done. He left one of them, I'm sure, to Nina, being one of the friends. But she took all of the paintings and said that she would distribute them. . . .[65]

Louis's curly maple grand piano went to the Graham studio, along with his old traveling satchel containing the Kepalas bronze. According to Taylor, Martha never again entered Louis's apartment: "The only thing she did ask me for was Louis's marvelous new bed. She called and said, 'Would you mind if you gave it to a deserving couple who couldn't afford a decent bed?' I said, 'By no means,' and we arranged to have them remove it."[66] Martha decided that *Dance Observer* should cease publication after Louis's death. He had been the journal's leading force, and it should not continue without his leadership. Ralph agreed.

Nina explained that she supervised the dismantling of the apartment with a young dancer, Jean Leary. Nina gave one each of Louis's Indian rugs to Muriel Stuart and Martha Hill: "I thought they should have something of his."[67] Nina herself kept the icons, books, paintings, and personal effects that remained. Louis had long promised his scrapbooks, musical scores, and papers to Genevieve Oswald, the curator of New York Public Library's Dance Collection at Lincoln Center. Within a few weeks after his death, cartons arrived there to be sorted and cataloged — a job that would take years. After Betty died of alcoholism a few years later, the remaining monies in her trust supported a scholarship fund in Louis's name at the Juilliard School, where formal dance composition courses based on his methods continued to be taught.

Epilogue

A committee was formed in 1984 to plan events in celebration of Horst's centennial. Lectures and concerts in honor of modern dance's "architect" were scheduled across the United States. At Juilliard on 17 January 1984 *El Penitente* and *Medusa* were performed, colleagues spoke in tribute, and a letter from Martha was read for the occasion in which she said, "I feel so deeply that without him I could not have achieved anything I have done."

While the NYPL Dance Collection prepared a Horst exhibition displaying original scores and an array of photographs and personal items, at the Riverside Church theater Martha's ensemble performed *Primitive Mysteries* and musicians played *Celebration.* The program also presented works by former students, after a bevy of slides flashed on a screen with his voice (edited from Jeanette Roosevelt's 1961 interviews) exclaiming, "I only took a simple idea . . . I was just a wall to grow on . . . a tail for Martha's kite . . . a ballast."[1]

At a reception afterward in the church's tower crowds exchanged "Louie" anecdotes and pondered his influence. "In this country, why are we choreographically so far ahead? You don't think it was because of thirty years of Louis?" Doris Rudko asked.[2] Ruth Lloyd said wistfully, "Of all my friends, Louis is the one I miss the most."[3] An honored leader still, the image of Horst as Indian chief, smoking wampum with his tribe, seemed to prevail even at this belated memorial.

"I cannot believe that any of us who are dancers would be what we are or that the dance itself would be what it is today if Louis Horst and the *Dance Observer* had been missing from our lives. We cannot be really objective about either of them — you never can be about the absolutely indispensable," Graham had written.[4] "Louis was there!" His contribution was "nothing short of heroic," Nikolais exclaimed.[5]

Still, it was Graham's genius that inspired Louis to act. "Come along now, Martha! We have the studio in a minute," Martha Hill could hear Louis saying. "His brightest days were in caring for Martha."[6] If she was his motor side, then he was her mental side, observers concurred. Graham confirmed that it was Louis who trained "the creative instinct to express and make manifest what it feels as urgent."[7]

"A curious intimacy exists between artists in a collaboration. A distant closeness,"[8] she later told a reporter — an interesting remark because of its relevance to her unusual relationship with Louis. At age ninety-six Graham once again reminded us of this curious intimacy, when she choreographed her one-hundred-and-eightieth work, *Maple Leaf Rag,* for the sixty-fourth season of her company. The piece begins with a few mournful chords of a dirge. It stops. Martha's voice is heard. "Louis, play me the *Maple Leaf Rag!*" she pleads. Then, up tempo, the syncopated Joplin melody begins, encouraging a vibrant dance that passes "in the instant." At *Maple Leaf Rag*'s finish, once again the musician's sure if ghostly presence has lifted Martha out of her doldrums long enough to complete another work. It would be her last fully realized creative effort before her death on 1 April 1991.

"Dance yields to music. Music yields to dance," Louis had written in 1925, perhaps recognizing that in his own life, he would most often be the yielding one. On his way to Vienna he mulled over the "wedding of music and dance," and worried that "both sacrifice too much at times."[9] Throughout his career his "luft-pauses" helped to suspend the most sensitive moments in the early development of modern dance. His constant support significantly affected the quality and quantity of its artistic achievement. Some people have suggested that his longevity as a teacher who repeated himself over and over again placed generations of dancers who went through this rite of passage under his spell. Louis's aesthetic conditions set an unavoidable standard of excellence.

Throughout his life Louis lived exactly as he pleased: "I've always done everything I wanted to do."[10] He was fortunate enough to be at the right places at the right times. Doris Humphrey's claim that he was a bundle of contradictions held to the end — the most contemporary and somehow most unconventional person his associates knew.

In his own estimation, dance had at least managed in his lifetime "to turn away from two forms: the dry technicalities of the ballet, and the vague formlessness of the 'interpretative' dance."[11] New ways of expression had been found through "deep study and rigorous training" so that future generations of dancers might find paths of their own, as he wished. "Modern dance now has a past it can examine. It can have a future," he remarked with acuity.[12] His role was central to that past. "I do not prophesy where the dance is going next or who the new great dancer will be. The important thing is, it is going!"[13]

Notes

Abbreviations and Collections

MG, Martha Graham. LH, Louis Horst. JR, Jeanette Schlottman Roosevelt. JS, Janet Mansfield Soares.

DH-EA	Dartington Hall, England, Elmhirst Archives, Graham Collection
LC-ESC	Library of Congress, Music Division, Elizabeth Sprague Coolidge Collection
NYPL-DC	New York Public Library for the Performing Arts, Dance Collection
DH	Doris Humphrey Collection
DS	Denishawn Collection
HC	Louis Horst Collection — 500 items in 92 folders including Chronology; Journal; Classroom notes; Interview tapes by Marian Van Tuyl; Personal notebook ca. 1939–1943; Photograph album ca. 1907–1915; Record book; Scrapbooks, Vols. 1–29, 1915–1962.
HT	Helen Tamiris files
HW	Humphrey-Weidman Collection
TS	Ted Shawn Collection
NYPL-MD	New York Public Library for the Performing Arts, Music Division
HC	Louis Horst Collection — includes manuscript music; published music.
UCLA-RSD	University of California at Los Angeles, University Research Library, Ruth St. Denis Collection
YBL-MDL	Yale University, Beinecke Library, Mabel Dodge Luhan Collection

Introduction

Opening quote: Marian Van Tuyl quoting Louis Horst, March 1954, 4.

1 E. Pease quoting LH, 1965, 4.
2 T. Shawn, May 1969. TS NYPL-DC.

3   LH to JR.

4   M. Van Tuyl quoting LH, March 1954, 6.

5   E. Pease quoting LH, 1965, 4.

6   LH to JS, 1962.

7   MG, 1957, 10. From "Little Gidding" of T. S. Eliot's *Four Quartets*. Graham used the phrase in her 1957 film *A Dancer's World*. Full quote: "And when the dancer is at the peak of his power he has two lovely, fragile, perishable things. One is spontaneity, but it is something arrived at over years and years of training. It is not a mere chance. The other is simplicity but that, also, is a different simplicity. It is the state of complete simplicity, costing no less than everything, of which Mr. T. S. Eliot speaks."

8   LH to M. Van Tuyl, 1954, 3.

9   MG, 17 January 1984.

10 M. Van Tuyl to JS, 12 March 1986.

11 Humphrey, 7 June 1927.

Chapter One

Opening quote: Louis Horst, taped interview with Jeanette Roosevelt, 1960–1961.

1   LH to JR.

2   Ibid.

3   Ibid. Martha Graham would later ask her colleagues to watch over the mature musician, whose delicate hands matched a sensitive constitution, by repeating "his mother said she'd never raise him" (M. Hill quoting MG to JS).

4   LH to JR.

5   Ibid.

6   Ibid.

7   Ibid.

8   Ibid.

9   LH to JS, 1959. Class notes.

10 LH to JR.

11 Ibid.

12 Ibid.

13 LH to JS.

14 Ibid.

15 LH to JR.

16 Ibid.

17 Ibid.

18 G. McGeary to JS.

19 LH to JR.

20 Ibid.

21 Ibid.

22 Ibid.

23 Ibid.

24 Ibid.

25 Ibid.

26 Ibid.

27 Ibid.

28 Ibid.

29 Ibid.

30 Ibid. Three days later Taft's rival, Teddy Roosevelt, was shot and wounded while making a campaign speech for reelection.

31 A. Lass, August–September 1985, 101.

Chapter Two

Opening quote: François Delsarte, quoted in Jane Sherman, *The Drama of Denishawn Dance,* 1979.

1 M. Schumach quoting LH, 17 January 1954.

2 Horst never went back to claim his violin. John Paterson, a childhood friend and fellow violinist, wrote to Louis thirty-nine years later, "If you want that violin, I'll send it to you. If you want me to sell it, name a price. You asked to turn it over to Betty, but we lost track of her." He then reminisced about their exploits with $20 worth of fireworks, their teacher Louis Persinger, and the wonderful "floating dumplings" Louis's mother made. Paterson stayed with the San Francisco orchestra throughout his life.

There is another version of how Horst was hired by the Denishawn troupe. According to E. Stodelle, May believed Betty was the first to become associated with the newest happenings in expressive dance, and while dancing with Denishawn, told Louis about the job. In his journal, however, Louis mentions leaving San Francisco with a violinist from the San Francisco Orchestra to join St. Denis at Sacramento. The first performance was in Medford's Gage Theatre. Betty arrived October 21 from San Francisco. Louis's first reference to Betty as a dancer is a journal entry noting her first appearance with the company in January 1916.

3 LH to JR.

4 Ibid.

5 Ibid.

6 M. Schumach quoting LH, 17 January 1954.

7 LH to JR.

8 Ibid.

9 T. Shawn, 1960, 67.

10 LH to JR.

11 Ibid.

12 Ibid.

13 Portland *Oregonian,* 1917. Clipping.

14 4 May 1917. Clipping.

15 San Francisco *Chronicle,* 4 May 1917.

16 Herring, 1917. HC NYPL-DC.

17 San Francisco *Chronicle,* 23 April 1917.

18 R. St. Denis quoting Delsarte in J. Sherman, 1979, 5.

19 J. Sherman, 1983, 16.

20 T. Shawn, 1960, 11, 15.

21 Ibid., 69. Years later Shawn would build the most enduring home for dance in the woods of Jacob's Pillow in Massachusetts.

22 LH to JS.

23 A decade later Graham lay on her studio floor in New York, exhausted after long hours of

rehearsal with Horst, and said, "Louis, play me a ragtime" (MG to R. Sherman, 4 April 1974).

24   T. Shawn, 1960, 92.

25   Cohen, 1972, 33.

26   LH to JR.

27   Hollywood *Citizen,* 27 July 1917. Clipping.

28   R. Schickel, 1984, 244.

29   LH to JR.

30   B. Hastings, 1948, 229.

31   LH to JR.

32   Ibid.

33   P. Rall quoting R. St. Denis, 9 June 1917.

34   LH to JR.

35   J. Sherman quoting A. Douglas to JS, 25 May 1987.

36   G. Sargeant to JS.

37   J. Sherman quoting A. Douglas to JS, 25 May 1987.

38   LH to JR.

39   Ibid. Along the way, Louis noted any out-of-the-ordinary event in his journal. One evening less than a month before, Wilson's famous declaration, "The world must be made safe for democracy," the musician spotted the President in the audience.

40   Ibid.

41   Los Angeles *Record,* 1917. Clipping.

42   LH, 1963, 6.

43   The collections he assembled have since played an important part in the reconstruction of these early works.

44   R. St. Denis, 16 February 1930. UCLA-RSD.

45   M. Van Tuyl quoting LH to JS, 12 March 1986.

46   Ibid.

47   J. Sherman quoting A. Douglas to JS, 25 May 1987.

48   R. St. Denis diary, 12 November 1919. UCLA-RSD.

49   LH to JR.

50   Ibid.

51   J. Sherman quoting A. Douglas to JS, 25 May 1987.

52   T. Shawn, 1960, 93.

53   MG quoted, Santa Barbara *News Press,* 25 October 1920.

54   Omaha *Bee,* 21 October 1921.

55   *New York Mail,* n.d. Clipping.

56   G. Sargeant to JS, 13 March 1987.

57   MG quoted, *New York Mail,* 5 December 1921.

58   J. Sherman quoting A. Douglas to JS, 25 May 1987.

59   LH to JR.

60   R. Lloyd to JS.

61   T. Shawn diary, 1925. TS NYPL-DC.

62   LH to JR.

63   A. Kisselgoff quoting MG, 19 February 1984, 50.

64   Nietzsche, 1886, 81, 87.

65   W. Roberts quoting MG, August 1928. Cited in Armitage, 1937, 97.

66   M. Coleman quoting LH, November 1949, 130.

67   Denishawn's 1920 *Soaring* used ideas initiated by Wigman. It even has the same title as a section of her earlier *Four Dances*.

68   LH, 1963, 6.

69   D. McDonagh, 1973, 33.

70   *New York Dance* Review, 1922. Clipping.

71   J. Sherman, 1979, 102.

72   T. Shawn diary, 1925. TS NYPL-DC.

73   LH to JR.

74   Ibid.

75   According to the tour program Horst "discovered, selected, and arranged" the music of Charles Tomlinson Griffes for *Ishtar*.

76   LH to JR.

77   Before this the only original score "especially composed" by Horst was for Shawn's 1919 solo *Japanese Spear Dance*.

78   G. Sargeant to JS.

79   T. Shawn diary, 1925. TS NYPL-DC.

80   T. Shawn, 1960, 116.

81   LH to JR.

82   T. Shawn, 7 November 1921.

83   T. Shawn diary, 1925. TS NYPL-DC.

84   LH to JR.

85   S. Shelton, 1981, 181.

86   Delsarte's basic law of "three zones" was to become significant in developing her use of "contraction and release." For her, the contraction of the pelvis would provide the impulse of every action, not the breath and heartbeat so basic to St. Denis's and Humphrey's motivation for creating movement.

Chapter Three

Opening quote: Friedrich Nietzsche, *Beyond Good and Evil*.

1   T. Shawn diary, 1925. TS NYPL-DC.

2   LH to JR.

3   Ibid.

4   Nietzsche, 1887, 514; 1886, 90.

5   LH to JR.

6   Ibid.

7   Ibid.

8   Ibid.

9   R. St. Denis, 1938, 215.

10   A. Schoenberg, 1923, 137.

11   R. Sabin, February 1953, 24.

12   J. Lepeschkin, 30 June 1974. HC NYPL-DC. Lepeschkin wrote that according to his daughter, Hedi (who studied with Horst at the American Dance Festival at Connecticut College in the 1950s), Dr. Stöhr earned an M.D. to please his father, but instead became a pianist-composer. He left his native Austria because of the rise of Fascism. In 1939 he taught at the Curtis Institute, where Leonard Bernstein and pianist Walter Hautzig were his

students. He then became resident composer at St. Michaels College, later joining the faculty at Trinity College, Vermont.

13 These conflicts were used much later by one of Horst's last students, Martha Clarke, in her *Vienna: Lusthaus.*

14 LH, Summer 1925, 7.

15 LH, 21 June 1925. DS NYPL-DC.

16 R. St. Denis, 7 July 1925. DS NYPL-DC.

17 LH to JR.

18 Ibid.

19 E. Bugbee quoting MG, 19 April 1926. Cited in M. Armitage, 1937, 96.

20 LH to JR.

21 Ibid.

22 M. Lloyd, 3 March 1936.

23 LH to JR.

24 Ibid.

25 Ibid.

26 D. Rudhyar, 27 August 1925(?). YBL-MDL.

27 O. Luening, 1980, 269.

28 Ibid.

29 N. Fonaroff to JS, 12 July 1984.

30 O. Luening, 1980, 269.

31 O. Luening to JS, 7 July 1989.

32 Ibid.

33 L. Leatherman, 1966, 51.

34 Nietzsche, 1887, 162.

35 M. Lloyd, 3 March 1936.

36 B. Paris, 1989, 41.

37 A. de Mille, 1952, 148.

38 JS, 1958–1964. Class notes.

39 LH to JR.

40 JS, 1958–1964. Class notes.

41 *New York Times,* 19 April 1926.

42 LH to JR.

43 Ibid.

44 H. Tamiris, Fall/Winter 1989/90, 31.

45 E. Bugbee quoting MG, 19 December 193–. Clipping.

Chapter Four

Opening quote: E. Bugbee quoting Martha Graham, 19 April 1926.

1 LH to JS.

2 LH to JR.

3 S. Ririe quoting LH to JS.

4 M. Cole quoting LH to JS.

5 G. Shurr to JS.

6 A. de Mille, 1952, 145.

7 T. Tobias quoting M. O'Donnell, Spring 1981, 75.

8   E. Bugbee quoting MG, 19 April 1926. In an analogous relationship, seventy years earlier the philosopher John Stuart Mill spoke of his wife, Harriet Taylor, as his "touchstone of philosophic worth" (P. Rose, 1984, 136). Louis's own philosophic worth was to be tested through a reverse touchstone. His unswerving belief in women artists, like Mill's, was unusual during this period. Drawing his ideas almost word for word from Nietzsche's glorification of "super-man" (a striving for that superhuman state attainable only by a worthy few), Louis was to make Martha the glorification of the "super-woman." His loyalty to her and to other women in dance came at a time when he might have chosen to advance his own musical career instead.

9   LH to JR.

10   M. Armitage, 1937, 110.

11   MG to R. Sherman, 4 April 1974.

12   LH to JR.

13   A. de Mille, 1952, 145.

14   LH to JR.

15   M. Hill to JS.

16   B. Buchanan quoting MG, 2 February 1930.

17   D. Humphrey, 7 June 1927. DH NYPL-DC.

18   S. J. Cohen, 1972, 73.

19   M. Hill to JS.

20   E. Stodelle quoting LH, 1984, 50.

21   W. Terry, 1975, 49.

22   D. McDonagh quoting G. Shurr, April 1973, 11.

23   M. Hill to JS.

24   F. Kemp quoting MG, March 1927. Also in M. Armitage, 1937, 97.

25   W. Roberts quoting MG, August 1928. Also in M. Armitage, 1937, 97.

26   LH, September 1929, 39.

27   LH to JR.

28   Ibid.

29   G. Shurr to JS.

30   Many years later, when Graham had become a ruling figure of modern dance, she was able to proclaim with certainty, "There is no competition. You are in competition with one person only and that is the individual you know you can become. This is the thing that makes the dancer's life the life of a realist, and gives it some of its hazard and some of its wonder" (MG, 1957. Also in M. Van Tuyl, 1969, 9).

31   C. Wagner, 10 October 1927.

32   L. Marsh, 15 October 1927.

33   H.H., 15 October 1927.

34   H. Tamiris, Fall/Winter 1989/90, 70.

35   Both Tamiris and Horst saw themselves as missionaries for an American dance to the end of their parallel lives; thirty years later Horst featured Tamiris's doctrines in his equally long-lived periodical, *Dance Observer*.

36   Page had studied with Adolph Bolm and occasionally performed with his company. From 1926 to 1928 she was the first American to appear as a guest soloist with the Metropolitan Opera Ballet.

37   R. Page, 1978, 144.

38   LH to JR.

39 Ibid.
40 Ibid.
41 Ibid.
42 M. Hill quoting LH to JS.
43 MG to R. Sherman, 4 April 1974.
44 M. Van Tuyl quoting LH, March 1954, 2.
45 E. Pease quoting LH, 1965, 5.
46 LH to JR.
47 Ibid.
48 Ibid. Horst later dedicated his book *Pre-Classic Dance Forms* "to Irene Lewisohn, whose foresight first made possible new experiments in these old forms" (LH, 1937, iv).
49 LH to JR.
50 Ibid. It was not until 1935 at the Bennington College Summer Program that his course was actually named Pre-Classic Dance Forms. In 1930 he called the course Music Appreciation. In 1933 the catalog for Perry-Mansfield reads, "Survey and Use of Music in relation to the dance." For his first summer of teaching at the Bennington Summer School, his composition course was described as "An analysis of dance composition from the standpoint of the musical forms of many periods," and at Sarah Lawrence College 1934–1935 he taught Composition in Dance Form.
51 A. Sokolow to JS.
52 M. Van Tuyl quoting LH, March 1954, 2.
53 A. Sokolow to JS.
54 S. Anawalt quoting MG, 12 October 1988, 40.
55 R. Taylor to JS.
56 A. de Mille, 1952, 123–24.
57 Ibid.
58 Ibid.
59 Ibid.
60 LH, September 1929, 39.
61 A. de Mille, 14 October 1986.
62 Frances Steloff loved books and writers of them even if she seldom read their contents. Entrenched in the shop from nine to six, six days a week, she reigned until she died at age 101.
63 W. Terry, 1975, 73. In 1927 Horst, Graham, Humphrey, Tamiris, and Elsa Findlay (a friend of John Martin's) had gone to the *New York Times* editor as a group and "got John a job" as the full-time dance critic (LH to JR). Intimates knew that Horst played with the idea of writing about dance himself.
64 LH, September 1929, 39.
65 T. Shawn, November 1930, 3.
66 LH to JR.
67 J. Lewitan, June 1931.
68 Yvonne Georgi was a student of Dalcroze and Wigman. In charge of the ballet company at the Hanover Opera House for many years between 1926 and 1970, her ballets during the twenties were examples, in her own words, of "Gesamtkunstwerk [total art work] . . . giving form and shape to their surroundings (stage-space, costumes, lighting, decor, movement) and their own expression" ("Tanz für das Theater," Berlin *Die Illustrierte Zeitung*, 1928). *Das seltsame Haus* to Hindemith and *Robes Pierre & Co.* to Wilckens were popular successes. She was also one of the first to consider using electronic scores.

69 M. Turbyfill, 1930?.

70 M. Watkins, June 1929, 28.

71 LH, May 1929, 39, 57.

72 M. Wigman, n.d. HC NYPL-DC.

73 J. Anderson quoting MG, 25 May 1986, PH 21.

74 LH, September 1929, 39.

75 M. Watkins, April 1930, 51.

76 J. Martin, 1936, 194.

77 L. Bogue, 1984, 87.

78 LH to JR.

79 LH to JR.

80 G. Shurr to JS.

81 J. Limón, 1965, 71.

82 MG, 1930, 250.

83 LH to JR.

84 G. Shurr to JS.

Chapter Five

Opening quote: Letter from Martha Graham to Dorothy Elmhirst, 7 September 1931.

1   MG, 1930, 249.

2   L. Kirstein, 1970, 194.

3   MG, 1930, 249.

4   A. Sokolow to JS.

5   G. Shurr to JS.

6   A. Schoenberg, 1975, 67.

7   A. Schoenberg, 1967, 214, 215, xiv. Schoenberg taught students at the University of California at Los Angeles and the University of Southern California from 1933 to 1938. After three years of teaching he realized that the greatest difficulty for students was how to compose without inspiration. "The answer is: it is impossible. But as they have to do it, nevertheless, advice has to be given. And it seems to me the only way to help is if one shows that there are many possibilities of solving problems, not only one." Like Schoenberg, Horst believed in teaching strict musical analysis to illustrate a wide variety of departures from the fictitious "norm."

8   LH to JR.

9   Ibid.

10 LH quoting Nietzsche, December 1929, 17.

11 Ibid.

12 J. Martin, 4 March 1929.

13 M. Hill to JS.

14 A. de Mille, August 1991, 137.

15 A. de Mille, 1952, 125.

16 B. Bird to JS.

17 W. Terry quoting MG, 1975, 53.

18 E. Isaac, 19 April 1926. Cited in M. Armitage, 1937, 41.

19 A. Helpern quoting D. Bird Villiard, 1981, 88.

20 M. Hill to JS.

21 Ibid.
22 G. Shurr to JS.
23 LH to JR.
24 D. Jowitt quoting B. Schönberg, Spring 1981, 55.
25 S. J. Cohen, 1972, 90.
26 V. Carleton, 17 November 1929.
27 J. Martin, 10 November 1929, 134.
28 R. Lloyd to JS.
29 MG, 1930, 249.
30 R. Garland, 6 June 1930.
31 B. Morgan, 1941, 12.
32 LH, 1961, 57.
33 B. Morgan, 1941, 12.
34 D. Jowitt quoting B. Schönberg, Spring 1981, 45.
35 E. Kendall, 1979, 205.
36 A. de Mille, 14 October 1986.
37 LH to JR.
38 R. Hughes, 25 June 1990, 30.
39 O. Daniel quoting MG, 1982, 255.
40 A. Helpern, 1981, 48.
41 LH to JR.
42 O. Daniel quoting MG, 1982, 257.
43 LH to JR.
44 Cleveland *Plain Dealer,* n.d. Clipping.
45 LH to JR.
46 "Dance Visions," 7 May 1930, Seattle *Post-Intelligencer.* Clipping.
47 D. Rudhyar, 27 August 1925 or 1926. YBL-MDL. Rudhyar, a popular lecturer on the spiritual effects of sound, had begun to compose for Humphrey after unsuccessful overtures for possible collaboration with Graham dissolved, as they had earlier for Otto Luening.
48 M. D. Luhan, May 1925.
49 M. Armitage, 1937, 96.
50 MG, 1930, 249.
51 W. Sargeant, 1937, 114. Sargeant was a writer and musician who later married Martha's sister Geordie.
52 R. Taylor to JS.
53 Ibid.
54 LH to JR.
55 A. Kisselgoff quoting MG, 19 February 1984.
56 Louis kept a leatherbound record-book of every thriller he ever read, alphabetized by author. Over eighty pages of thousands of books were listed along with recommendations from friends. After finishing a novel he placed an "x" by the title (a system he also used for keeping track of finished assignments with students). Mickey Spillane's *I, the Jury,* and Stewart Sterling's *Too Hot to Kill* and *Five Alarm Funeral* received two "x"s, to indicate a second reading.
57 LH to JR.
58 MG, 193–, 16. Clipping.
59 R. Taylor to JS.

60 LH to JR.
61 H. Koegler quoting J. Martin, Spring 1974, 18.
62 A. Levinson, 1991, 102.
63 LH, 1961, 52.
64 T. Shawn diary, 1925. SC NYPL-DC.
65 LH, 1961, 53, 57, 59.
66 Ibid.
67 Ibid.
68 M. Phelps quoting LH, 51.
69 G. Lisitzsky quoting LH, 5 May 1934, 3.
70 Ibid.
71 W. Terry, 1975, 53.
72 MG, 193–, 16. Clipping.
73 M. Van Tuyl, March 1954, 6.
74 D. Diamond to JS.
75 N. Fonaroff quoting LH to JS, 12 July 1984.
76 W. Riegger, 1937, 36.
77 LH to JR.
78 W. Sorell, 1969, 54.
79 LH, May 1930, 17.
80 LH to JR.
81 M. Blitzstein, March–April 1931, 39–40.
82 Ibid.
83 LH to JR.
84 W. Palmer, 1978, 70.
85 E. Denby, 22 May 193–. Clipping.
86 C. D. Isaacson, August 1931, 58.
87 R. Lloyd to JS.
88 J. Lewitan, June 1931, 23.
89 P. Love quoting M. Austin, 1934, 87.
90 MG, 7 September 1931.
91 L. Engel, 1974, 55, 56.
92 R. Lloyd to JS.
93 L. Engel, 1974, 56, 57.
94 Ibid.
95 LH to JR.
96 T. Tobias quoting M. O'Donnell, Spring 1981, 78.
97 A. Kisselgoff quoting MG, 19 February 1984.
98 A. de Mille, 1952, 155–58.
99 R. Taylor to JS.
100 LH to JR.
101 B. Bird to JS.
102 LH to JR.
103 D. Jowitt quoting B. Schönberg, Spring 1981, 37.
104 R. Taylor to JS.
105 LH to JR.
106 A. Copland, 1984, 183.

Chapter Six

Opening quote: Louis Horst, taped interview with Jeanette Roosevelt, 1960–1961.

1   A. de Mille, 1934.
2   LH to JR.
3   A. Sokolow to JS.
4   R. Sabin, 1964.
5   H. Gilfond quoting LH, February 1936, 15.
6   Ibid.
7   N. Lloyd, 1965, 47.
8   R. Lloyd to JS.
9   A. Schoenberg, 1967, xiv.
10   LH quoting Klee, 1961, 21.
11   G. Lippincott, 1964, 5.
12   R. Taylor to JS.
13   Hunter Johnson. NYPL-DC Oral History.
14   J. Martin, 21 November 1932.
15   T. Tobias quoting M. O'Donnell, Spring 1981.
16   J. Martin, 21 November 1932.
17   Philadelphia *Public Ledger,* 13 November 1932.
18   J. Martin, 4 December 1932.
19   J. Martin, 8 January 1933.
20   R. Taylor to JS.
21   M. Hill to JS.
22   After *Six Miracle Plays* Louis added a third genre, "religious and secular medieval," to his modern dance forms course, following "primitive" and "archaic." The three areas of study shaped the Backgrounds of Modern Art section of his second-year course, with dancers additionally visiting Manhattan's medieval Cloisters museum for inspiration.
23   Typed on stationery with letterhead: "Martha Graham and Dance Group. Louis Horst — pianist." HC NYPL-DC.
24   M. O'Donnell, 1979, L. Small. NYPL-DC Oral History.
25   M. Van Tuyl, 1954.
26   Gallup, New Mexico, 23 August 1933. Clipping.
27   G. Shurr to JS.
28   Ibid.
29   R. Taylor to JS.
30   V. Freeman to JS.
31   B. Hastings to JS, 5 September 1987.
32   M. Hill to JS.
33   N. Lloyd, 1965.
34   T. Tobias quoting M. O'Donnell, Spring 1981.
35   G. Shurr to JS.
36   R. Taylor to JS.
37   Environments similar to the Bennington School had cropped up in the early thirties for actors, such as the Group Theatre, a loosely organized assembly of actors, playwrights, and directors sharing talents in the idyllic setting of Brookfield Center, Connecticut. A variety of musicians and composers also enjoyed productive months in the Berkshire

Mountains of Massachusetts, which by 1937 developed into the Tanglewood workshops and festival.

38 R. Lloyd to JS.
39 D. Jowitt quoting S. Shearer, Fall 1984, 23.
40 G. Shurr to JS.
41 R. Lloyd to JS.
42 H. Holm to JS.
43 S. Kriegsman quoting H. Holm, 1981, 23.
44 LH to JR.
45 MG, 8 January 1989.
46 N. Lloyd, November 1951, 132.
47 R. Lloyd to JS.
48 M. Hill to JS.
49 F. Morton, October 1935.
50 J. Bohm, 18 August 1935.
51 O. Luening to JS.
52 MG, 1936, 255.
53 LH to JR.
54 MG, 1936. Clipping.
55 LH to JR.
56 Ibid.
57 H. T. Parker, 18 May 1932.
58 LH to JR.
59 Ibid.
60 M. Hill to JS.
61 G. Shurr to JS.
62 R. Taylor to JS.
63 W. Terry, 21 July 1936. Cited in *I Was There*, 1978, 1.
64 M. Anthony, Spring 1966, 13.
65 O. Luening to JS.

Chapter Seven

Opening quote: Martha Graham, *The Dance Magazine*, March 1927.
1 Bronxville (New York) *The Campus*, 18 January 1937. Clipping.
2 N. Lloyd, November 1951, 132.
3 E. Roosevelt, 1936.
4 LH to JR.
5 M. Hill quoting LH to JS.
6 LH to JR.
7 R. Grover, 1937. Clipping.
8 N. Fonaroff to JS, 12 July 1984.
9 D. McDonagh, 1973, 123, 124.
10 Ibid.
11 P. Gay, 1986, 90.
12 P. Gay quoting Nietzsche, 1986, 88.
13 Nietzsche, 1887.

14 M. Van Tuyl quoting LH, March 1954, 4.

15 S. Kriegsman quoting N. Lloyd, 1981, 154, 155.

16 Ibid.

17 A. Nikolais to JS.

18 S. Kriegsman quoting A. Nikolais, 1981, 254.

19 N. Fonaroff to JS, 12 July 1984.

20 Ibid.

21 O. Luening to JS.

22 LH to JR.

23 N. Fonaroff to JS, 12 July 1984.

24 M. Hill to JS, 7 January 1986.

25 H. Gilfond, October 1937, 91.

26 L. Kirstein, October 1937, 94.

27 L. Kirstein, in M. Armitage, 1937, 27.

28 L. Kirstein, 1970, 194.

29 R. Taylor, private collection.

30 N. Fonaroff, 1937. HC NYPL-DC.

31 MG, in M. Armitage, 1937, 104.

32 A. Nikolais to JS.

33 LH to JR.

34 N. Fonaroff to JS, 12 July 1984.

35 *Chicago Tribune*. Clipping.

36 G. Shurr to JS.

37 O. Luening to JS.

38 G. Shurr to JS.

39 Although delighted with his new association, Hawkins continued to work with Ballet Caravan for another season, performing in the Eugene Loring/Aaron Copland ballet *Billy the Kid*.

40 O. Luening to JS.

41 G. Shurr to JS.

42 1938 Graham press release.

43 MG, September 1942, 565–74.

44 E. Denby, 12 May 1944, 230. As was the case with many of Graham's pieces, opinions changed when *American Document* was revived. The *Nation* called it "nobly framed" and "flawlessly executed" (L. Kirstein, 3 September 1938, 230, 231).

45 Bennington *Banner,* 8 August 1938.

46 M. Hill to JS.

47 *American Dancer,* May 1939.

48 MG, 1964, 46.

49 M. Hill to JS.

50 A film by Ampix productions, *Young America Dances,* documented the session at Mills. An experienced crew spent four days on campus filming, and the final footage gives a rare glimpse of classes, rehearsals, and social gatherings. Neither Louis nor his classes were filmed.

51 LH to JR.

52 R. Lloyd to JS.

53 Ibid.

54 LH to JR.

55 R. Taylor to JS.

56 S. Kriegsman quoting E. Hawkins, 1981, 261, 260.

57 LH to JR.

58 W. Terry, 28 December 1939. Cited in *I Was There*, 1978, 54.

59 LH to JR.

60 O. Luening, 1980, 354.

61 S. Kriegsman quoting O. Luening, 1981, 273.

62 G. Lippincott notebook. HC NYPL-DC.

63 S. Kriegsman quoting M. Cunningham, 1981, 258. In Cunningham's search for principles for dance composing, his methods of formula and chance would influence new waves of choreographic prowess and, in turn, be questioned.

64 Thompson called her silent movie *Compositions in Modern Forms by Martha Graham Dance Group*. The film can be viewed in the Dance Collection at the New York Public Library for the Performing Arts, New York City.

65 O. Luening to JS.

66 S. Kriegsman quoting E. Hawkins, 1981, 206.

67 LH to JR.

68 O. Luening to JS.

69 Hazel Johnson to JS.

70 E. Lohoefer to JS.

71 G. McGeary to JS.

72 E. Lohoefer to JS.

73 G. McGeary to JS.

74 D. Humphrey, 1941, Good Friday.

75 E. Rosenblatt, August–September 1941.

Chapter Eight

Opening quote: Louis Horst quoting Shakespeare, *New London Evening Day,* 17 August 1954.

1 B. Morgan, 9 December 1939.

2 B. Hastings to JS.

3 S. Kriegsman quoting A. Nikolais, 1981, 255.

4 M. Hill to JS.

5 O. Luening to JS. Francis Fergusson later wrote the influential study *The Idea of Theatre: The Art of Drama in Changing Perspective* (Princeton, N.J.: Princeton University Press, 1949).

6 S. Kriegsman quoting A. Nikolais, 1981, 255.

7 LH to JR.

8 W. Terry, 25 January 1942. Cited in *I Was There*, 1978, 140.

9 The film was produced by the Harmon Foundation jointly with Simon and Herta Moselio. NYPL-DC.

10 J. Martin in the film *Lamentation,* 1943.

11 Hazel Johnson quoting LH to JS.

12 E. Denby, 12 May 1944. Reprinted in *Dance Writings,* 1986, 230.

13 K. Cornell in MG press release. HC NYPL-DC.

14 LH to JR.

15 Ibid.

16 MG, 1943–1945, letter to Coolidge. LC-ESC.

17 MG, 1943–1945, letter to Spivacke. LC-ESC.

18 MG, 1943–1945, script to Chavez. LC-ESC.

19 D. Diamond to JS.

20 LH to JS.

21 J. Martin, 1945, 185.

22 LH to JR.

23 S. Kriegsman quoting M. Cunningham, 1981, 258.

24 R. Lippold, March 1946, 36.

25 B. Osgood to JS.

26 H. A. Gray to JS.

27 J. Martin, 10 November 1946.

28 Lippincott continued to commission scores from Horst as well as from Cowell through 1953 for dances that she kept in her repertory until 1960.

29 B. Osgood to JS.

30 M. Cole quoting LH to JS.

31 The next revival of *Primitive Mysteries* took place at Connecticut College's American Dance Festival in memory of Horst in 1964, and has since reentered the repertory.

32 A. de Mille, August 1991, 151.

33 E. Kendall, 1979, 208.

34 N. Fonaroff to JS, 12 July 1984.

35 E. Stodelle quoting MG, 1984, 180.

36 J. Martin, 16 March 1947.

37 A. Gibbs, 27 December 1947, 35.

38 B. Osgood to JS.

39 L. Hoving, Summer 1969, 11. Hoving taught beginning composition of Juilliard.

40 LH quoting Shakespeare, 17 August 1954, 2.

41 W. Terry, 3 July 1947.

42 J. Martin quoting M. Wigman, 4 August 1946.

43 R. Sabin, April 1948, 42.

44 J. Martin, 27 February 1948.

45 C. Smith, April 1948.

46 J. Campbell, May 1948, 60.

47 Ibid.

48 C. Smith, April 1948.

Chapter Nine

Opening quote: Norman Lloyd, *New London Evening Day,* 20 July 1954.

1 B. Osgood to JS.

2 R. Lloyd to JS.

3 H. McGehee to JS, 29 September 1985.

4 R. Lloyd to JS.

5 LH to JR.

6 N. Fonaroff to JS, 12 July 1984.

7   B. Osgood to JS.

8   N. Fonaroff to JS, 12 July 1984.

9   Hazel Johnson to JS.

10   LH to JR.

11   D. McDonagh, 1973, 210.

12   LH to JR.

13   D. Diamond to JS.

14   G. Shurr to JS.

15   N. Fonaroff to JS, 12 July 1984.

16   LH to JS.

17   LH to JR.

18   Yuriko to JS.

19   LH to JR.

20   N. Smith, January 1974. HC NYPL-DC.

21   K. Ellis to JS.

22   N. Van Tuyl quoting LH, March 1954, 6.

23   W. Terry, 1 September 1946.

24   LH to JR.

25   Ibid.

26   Ibid.

27   H. McGehee to JS, 29 September 1985.

28   Jack Moore later cofounded Manhattan's Dance Theater Workshop and joined the dance faculty at Bennington College. Doris Rudko would make her own significant contribution as a dance composition teacher.

29   N. Fonaroff to JS, 12 July 1984.

30   M. Hill to JS.

31   Produced by the U.S. Department of the Army. NYPL-DC.

32   LH, 17 August 1951. *New London Evening Day.*

33   M. Seldes to JS.

34   Umanya quoting LH to JS.

35   R. Lloyd to JS.

36   LH to JS.

37   S. Ririe to JS.

38   Ibid.

39   M. Lloyd, July 1953, 10.

40   LH to JS.

41   D. Rudko to JS, 22 August 1980.

42   R. Coe quoting P. Taylor, 1985, 198.

43   E. Pease, 1965. Pease went on to develop a dance department at the University of Michigan.

44   Ibid.

45   E. Lohoefer to JS.

46   V. Freeman to JS.

47   R. Sabin, January 1953, 21.

48   Quoting LH, *Modern Dance Council Journal,* Washington, D.C. Clipping.

49   R. Taylor to JS.

50   V. Freeman to JS.

51 Ibid.
52 R. Park, 3 September 1953. HC NYPL-DC.
53 V. Freeman to JS.
54 B. Ross, Winter 1974, 10.
55 M. Schumach, 17 January 1954.
56 W. Sorell, 10 January 1954.
57 Unidentified newspaper, Williamstown, Mass., 1 March 1954. Clipping.

Chapter Ten

Opening quote: Martha Graham, *New York Times,* 8 January 1989.
1 LH to JR.
2 MG to LH. HC NYPL-DC.
3 V. Freeman to JS.
4 Yuriko quoting LH to JS.
5 LH to JR.
6 LH, 14 July 1953.
7 LH, 11 August 1953.
8 T. Ingle, 4 August 1953.
9 N. Lloyd, 20 July 1954.
10 LH, 27 July 1954.
11 LH, 17 August 1954. Carleton Sprague Smith was chief of the New York Public Library
    Music Division at the time.
12 J. Kanner quoting LH, May 1955.
13 Capezio Award, 15 March 1955. HC NYPL-DC.
14 J. Kanner quoting LH, May 1955.
15 E. Wallach, 15 March 1955.
16 J. Martin, 15 March 1955.
17 R. Sabin quoting LH, May 1955.
18 A. de Mille, February 1956, 43.
19 R. Sabin, May 1955.
20 W. Schuman, 16 March 1955. HC NYPL-DC.
21 M. Van Tuyl quoting LH, March 1954, 3.
22 LH to JR.
23 Hazel Johnson to JS.
24 D. McDonagh, 1970, xi.
25 P. Taylor, 1987, 79.
26 D. Rudko quoting LH to JS, 4 April 1988.
27 R. Coe quoting P. Taylor, 1985, 198.
28 L. Balcom, January 1958, 7.
29 LH in NBC's "Wide Wide World." Video. NBC Archives, New York City.
30 LH quoted, *Dance Magazine,* July 1958.
31 D. Duncan, March 1959.
32 *Dance News,* September 1959, 30.
33 LH to JS and A. Soares.
34 V. Freeman quoting LH to JS.
35 J. Woodward, 22 April 1984. Neighborhood Playhouse administrators constantly re-

minded Louis of his significant impact on the theater world. One ex-student, Charles Aidiman, producer, director, and actor in *Spoon River Anthology* had written, "[Louis] taught me everything I know about the meaning of form in art."

36   D. McDonagh, 1970, xi.
37   M. Forbes to JS.
38   D. Rudko to JS, 4 April 1988.
39   Ibid.
40   N. Smith, January 1974. HC NYPL-DC.
41   R. Lloyd to JS.
42   V. Freeman to JS. Old friends continued to correspond. Anne Douglas [Doucet] wrote occasionally from her home in Malibu, sharing news of their Denishawn colleagues. Her last letter tells of Pearl Wheeler's death and Miss Ruth's eighty-sixth birthday celebration, adding that "Miss Ruth's stories are exactly the same."
43   JS, personal recollection.
44   LH, 1961, 120.
45   J. Chamberlain, October 1961, 122.
46   JS and LH, 1963.
47   LH to JR.
48   P. Taylor, 1987, 135.
49   G. Jackson to JS.
50   D. Rudko to JS, 22 August 1980.
51   R. Sabin, February 1959.
52   Wayne State University honorary doctorate citation. HC NYPL-DC.
53   W. Terry, 1959.
54   W. Sorell, March 1964.
55   D. Rudko to JS, 22 August 1980.
56   N. Fonaroff to JS, 12 July 1984.
57   N. Smith, January 1974. HC NYPL-DC.
58   Ibid.
59   D. Rudko to JS, 22 August 1980.
60   G. Sargeant to JS.
61   R. Taylor to JS.
62   R. Lloyd quoting N. Lloyd quoting MG to JS.
63   D. Rudko to JS, 4 April 1988.
64   N. Fonaroff, Summer 1984, 10.
65   R. Taylor to JS. When St. Denis and Shawn celebrated their fiftieth wedding anniversary, it was a social occasion that stirred the dance world. Like the Shawns, Louis and Betty remained legally married until their deaths. Betty's serious alcohol problem, continual requests for cash, and asking for word from Louis (at one point even suggesting that Nina might write in his behalf) were a source of irritation. May's letter of 25 November 1962 to Louis reported, "If only something could be done to stop [Betty's] drinking but I guess that's too much to hope for." May's chatty notes from San Francisco mention trips to Taos and a possible move to a retirement village in Chula Vista with her longtime companion, George. Evidently, Betty continued to worship her husband from afar, even if her only information about him came from the monthly *Dance Observer* he sent her. On 2 November 1963 she wrote, "My love to you Louis darling, always you are my dearest one." The letters were usually about money and her declining health after two disfiguring operations for cancer

that deeply depressed her. In a letter dated 20 November 1963 she wrote to Louis, "My life is over and I long to have it end." HC NYPL-DC.

66 MG to R. Taylor. After her own death on 1 April 1991, Martha Graham's ashes were cast over the Monte Cristo Mountains of New Mexico.

67 N. Fonaroff to JS.

Epilogue

1 LH to JR.

2 D. Rudko to JS.

3 R. Lloyd to JS.

4 MG, December 1958, 151–52.

5 A. Nikolais to JS.

6 M. Hill to JS.

7 MG, December 1958, 151–52.

8 MG, 8 January 1989, 6H.

9 LH, Summer 1925.

10 LH to JR.

11 LH, 1961.

12 E. Pease quoting LH, 1965, 7.

13 P. Mansfield quoting LH, December 1962, 1.

References

Anawalt, S. (1988, October 12). "Turning Point," *New York Times Magazine*.

Anderson, J. (1986, May 25). "Martha Graham Recalls Her Roots," *New York Times*.

Anthony, M. (1966, Spring) "Percussion with Santa Claus," *Dance Scope*, 2:2.

Armitage, M., ed. (1937). *Martha Graham: The Early Years*. San Francisco, Armitage. (Reprint 1978, New York: Da Capo.)

Balcom, L. (1958, January). "Silver Anniversary on a Shoe-String," *Dance Observer*, 25:1.

Bird, B. (1985, June 10). Personal communication. Telephone.

Blitzstein, M. (1931, March–April). "Dancers of the Season," *Modern Music*.

Bogue, L. (1984). *Dancers on Horseback: The Perry-Mansfield Story*. San Francisco: Strawberry Hill Press.

Bohm, J. (1935, August 18). *New York Herald Tribune*.

Buchanan, B. (1930, February 2). "Like the Modern Painters . . . ," *Evening World* (New York). Cited in Armitage (1937), 97.

Bugbee, E. (1926, April 19). *New York Telegram*. Cited in Armitage (1937).

——. (193–, December 19). "Martha Graham Warns Girls of Hardships in Dance Career," *New York Herald Tribune*.

B. W. (1931, February 31). "Martha Graham and Her Group," *New York Telegram*.

Campbell, J. (1948, May). "Editorial: Applause," *Dance Observer*, 15:5.

Capezio Award. (1955, March 15). Program.

Carleton, V. (1929, November 17). "Dance Repertory Theatre Begins," *Evening World* (New York).

Chamberlain, J. (1961, October). "Book Review: Modern Dance," *Dance Observer*, 28:8.

Coe, R. (1985). *Dance in America*. New York: Dutton.

Cohen, S. J. (1972). *Doris Humphrey: An Artist First*. Middletown, Conn.: Wesleyan University Press.

Cole, M. (1984, August 23). Personal interview. Audiotaped and transcribed.

Coleman, M. (November 1949). "On the Teaching of Choreography. Interview with Louis Horst," *Dance Observer*, 16:9.

Copland, A., and Perlis, V. (1984). *Copland 1900–1942.* New York: St. Martin's.

Creative Leisure. (1951). Film. U.S. Department of the Army. Filmed at Connecticut College.

Dancer's World, A. (1957). Film. Martha Graham, choreographer-director. Nathan Kroll, producer. Commissioned by Pittsburgh WQED-TV. New York: Brandon Films.

Daniel, O. (1982). *Stokowski: A Counterpoint of View.* New York: Dodd, Mead.

de Mille, A. (1934). "To Be the Most . . . ," *London Star.*

——. (1952). *Dance to the Piper.* Boston: Little, Brown.

——. (1956, February). "Rhythm in My Blood," *The Atlantic Monthly.*

——. (1986, October 14). Letter to author.

——. (1991, August). "Martha Graham," *Vanity Fair,* 54:8.

Denby, E. (193–, May 22). "Ballet Lovers View . . . ," *New York Herald Tribune,* iv. Clipping.

——. (1944, May 12). "Graham's American Document and Primitive Mysteries," *New York Herald Tribune.* In *Dance Writings,* ed. Robert Cornfield and William Mackay, 1986. New York: Knopf.

Diamond, D. (1988, June 2). Personal conversation.

Douglas [Doucet], A. (1987, May 29). Letter to J. Sherman.

——. (1991, August 31). Letter to author.

Duncan, D. (1959, March). "The Name Dropper," *Dance Magazine,* 33:3.

Ellis, K. (1990, 4 August). Personal conversation.

Engel, L. (1974). *This Bright Day: An Autobiography.* New York: Macmillan.

Fonaroff, N. (1937). Letter to Louis Horst.

——. (1979). Interview by E. Kendall.

——. (1984, Summer). "Louis Horst," *Dance Research: The Journal of the Society for Dance Research,* 2:2.

——. (1984, July 12). Personal interview, London, England. Audiotaped and transcribed.

Forbes, M. (1962, February 10). Conversation with author, New York City.

Freeman, V. (1988, August 19). Personal interview, Alexandria, Va. Audiotaped and transcribed.

Garland, R. (1930, January 6). "New Dance Theatre Scores a Success," *New York Telegram.*

Gay, P. (1986). *The Tender Passion: The Bourgeois Experience, Victoria to Freud.* New York: Oxford University Press.

Gibbs, A. (1947, December 27). "The Absolute Frontier," *The New Yorker,* 23:45.

Gilfond, H. (1936, February). "Louis Horst," *Dance Observer,* 3:2.

——. (1937, October). "Editorial: The New Magazine," *Dance Observer,* 4:8.

Goodman, J. (1978). Interview with José Limón. "Encores for Dance," in *Selected Articles on Dance, 1966–1977,* ed. J. Fallon. American Association for Health, Physical Education, Recreation, and Dance.

Graham, M. (1920, October 25). Quoted in Santa Barbara *News Press.*

——. (1921, December 5). Quoted in *New York Mail.*

——. (1930). "Seeking an American Art of the Dance," in *Revolt in the Arts,* ed. O. Saylor. New York: Brentano's.

——. (1931, May 20). "Interest in America . . . ," *Michigan Daily.*

——. (1931, September 7). Letter to Dorothy Elmhirst.

——. (193–). "Dance: An Interview," *Federal Theatre Magazine.*

——. (1936). "He Really Dances . . . ," *Los Angeles Times.* Clipping.

——. (1937). "Graham 1937," in *Martha Graham: The Early Years,* ed. M. Armitage. San

Francisco: Armitage. (Reprint 1978, New York: Da Capo). Contains reviews originally published in various newspaper articles.

——. (1942, September). "American Document by Martha Graham, with Four Scenes from the Dance," *Theatre Arts Monthly,* 26:19.

——. (1943–1945). Letters to Elizabeth Sprague Coolidge, letters to Harold Spivacke, and handwritten script to Chavez.

——. (1952). "Martha Graham Speaks . . . ," excerpts transcribed by W. Sorell, ed., Student Composers' Symposium, Juilliard.

——. (1954, April 23). Letter to Louis Horst.

——. (1957). Dialogue spoken in film, *A Dancer's World,* by M. Graham. Printed in *Anthology of "Impulse," Annual of Contemporary Dance 1951–1966,* ed. M. Van Tuyl, 1969.

——. (1958, December). "Sweet Applause for a Twenty-fifth Birthday," *Dance Observer,* 25:10.

——. (1964). "About Louis Horst," *Juilliard Review Annual, 1963–1964.*

——. (1984, January 17). "I Feel So Deeply. . . ." (Letter read at Horst Celebration, Juilliard Theater.)

——. (1984, April 22). Letter quoted in "Louis Horst: A Centennial Compendium," ed. D. Sears, *Ballet Review,* Summer 1984.

——. (1985, March 31). "Martha Graham Reflects on Her Art and a Life in Dance," *New York Times,* Arts and Leisure.

——. (1987, 16 March). Personal communication.

——. (1989, January 8). "From Collaboration, a Strange Beauty Emerged," *New York Times.*

Gray, H. A. (1985, 20 September). Letter to author.

Grover, R. (1937). "At All Times . . . ," Vancouver *News-Gazette.*

Hastings, B. (1948). "The Denishawn Era," in *Chronicles of the American Dance,* ed. P. Magriel. New York: Holt.

——. (1987, September 5). Personal interview, New York City.

Hawkins, E. (1952, May). Letter to E. S. Coolidge.

Helpern, A. (1981). *The Evolution of Martha Graham's Dance Technique.* Doctoral dissertation, New York University. Ann Arbor, Mich.: University Microfilms International.

Herring, —. (1917). "Nothing Radical . . . Miss St. Denis Gives," *Musical America.* Clipping.

H. H. (1927, October 15). "Personalities: Tamiris Dances," *Musical America.*

Hill, M. (1986, January 7). Personal interviews, New York City. Audiotaped and transcribed.

Holm, H. (1984, December 4). Personal interview, New York City.

Horst, L. (1925, Summer). "The Musician Comments," *The Denishawn Magazine: A Quarterly Review Dedicated to the Art of the Dance.*

——. (1925, June 21). Letter to R. St. Denis.

——. (1929, May). "The Music Mart: Exceptional Selections from Recent Dance Events Discussed," *The Dance Magazine.*

——. (1929, September). "The Music Mart: Discussion of the Musical Selections of a Young Dancer." *The Dance Magazine,* 12:5.

——. (1929, December). "The Music Mart: Bars and Steps—The New Allies." *The Dance Magazine,* 13:2.

——. (1930, May). "The Music Mart: Music for the Modern Studio." *The Dance Magazine,* 13:7.

——. (1934, April). "Tamiris," *Dance Observer,* 1:3.

——. (1937). *Pre-Classic Dance Forms.* In *Dance Observer.* (Reprints: 1960, New York:

Kamin; 1966, New York: Dance Horizons; 1988, Princeton, N.J.: Princeton Book Co. Translation: 1955, *Danzas pre-clasicas*.)

——. (1951, August 17). "The Decade of Dance," *The New London Evening Day*.

——. (1953, July 14). "Martha Graham Gets Dance School Off to Fast Start," *The New London Evening Day*.

——. (1953, August 11). "Doris Humphrey Unfolds Theory . . . ," *The New London Evening Day*.

——. (1953, August 18). "Ted Shawn: Gentleman of Modern Dance," *The New London Evening Day*. HC NYPL-DC.

——. (1954, July 27). "Philosopher Calls Self Expression Not Work of Art . . . ," *The New London Evening Day*.

——. (1954, August 17). "Carleton Sprague Smith's Lecture Ends Dance Series," *The New London Evening Day*.

——. (1957, November). "Paul Taylor and Dance Company." *Dance Observer*. 24:9.

——. (1959–1964). Personal communication.

——, and Russell, C. (1961). *Modern Dance Forms in Relation to the Other Arts*. San Francisco: Impulse. (Reissue 1987, Princeton, N.J.: Dance Horizons/Princeton Book Co. With preface and brief biography by J. M. Soares.)

——. (1960–1961). Interviews with Jeanette Roosevelt, New York City. Audiotaped and transcribed. Personal collection, JR.

——. (1962, December). "Whither the Modern Dance?" Interview with M. Mansfield, *Perry-Mansfield Pine Bark*.

——. (1963). "Symposium. Composer/Choreographer." *Dance Perspectives 16*.

Hughes, A. (1964, January 12). "Anniversary: 'Illustrious Dean of American Dance' Celebrates His Eightieth Birthday," *New York Times*.

Hughes, R. (1990, June 25). "The Decline of the City of Mahagonny," *The New Republic,* issue 3:936.

Hoving, L. (1969, Summer). "Random Notes from a Contemporary Romantic," *Dance Perspectives 38,* ed. M. Siegel.

Humphrey, D. (1927, June 7, and 1941, Good Friday). Letters to her mother.

Ingle, T. H. (1953, August 4). "Dancers Exemplify Horst Tracings of Development of Modern Dance," *The New London Evening Day*.

Isaac, E. (1926, April 19). Article in *New York Times*. Cited in M. Armitage, 1937.

Isaacson, C. D. (1931, August). "Elegy Over a Departed Season—Dance Events Reviewed," *Dance Magazine,* 16:4.

Jackson, G. (1990, February 16). Personal interview. Audiotaped and transcribed.

Jahn, D. (1960). [Three Scores by Louis Horst]. New York: Orchesis Publications.

Johnson, Hazel. (1984, June 21). Personal interview.

Johnson, Hunter. (1978, December 27). Interview by T. Bowers.

Jowitt, D. (1981, Spring). "A Conversation with Bessie Schönberg: American Modern Dance: The Early Years," *Ballet Review, 9:1*.

——. (1984, Fall). "Interview with Sybil Shearer," *Ballet Review, 12:2*.

Kanner, J. (1955, May). "Interview with Mr. Modern Dance," High School of Performing Arts *POGO Press*. Clipping.

Kemp, F. (1927, March). "Martha Graham," *Dance Magazine, 7:5*.

Kendall, E. (1979). *Where She Danced*. New York: Alfred Knopf.

Kirstein, L. (1937, October). "Ballet: Introduction and Credo," *Dance Observer, 4:8*.

——. (1938, September 3). "Martha Graham at Bennington," *Nation,* 147:10.

——. (1970). *Movement and Metaphor: Four Centuries of Ballet.* New York: Praeger.

Kisselgoff, A. (1984, February 19). "Martha Graham," *New York Times.*

Koegler, H. (1974, Spring). "In the Shadow of the Swastika: Dance in Germany, 1927–1936." *Dance Perspectives 57.*

Kriegsman, S. A. (1981). *Modern Dance in America: The Bennington Years.* Boston: G. K. Hall.

Lamentation. (1943). Film. Title: "A Motion Picture Study of Martha Graham from Her Dance *Lamentation.*" Produced by the Harmon Foundation jointly with Simon and Herta Moselsio. NYPL-DC.

Lang, P. (1988, November 7), Personal conversation, telephone.

Lass, A. (1985, August–September). "In the Pit: An Old Pro Tells What It Was Like to Play for the Silents," *American Heritage.*

Leatherman, L. (1966). *Martha Graham: Portrait of the Lady as an Artist.* New York: Alfred Knopf.

Lepeschkin, J. (1974, June 30). Letter to NYPL-DC.

Levinson, A. (1991). *André Levinson on Dance: Writings from Paris in the Twenties.* Ed. J. Acocella and Lynn Garafola. Middletown, Conn.: Wesleyan University Press.

Lewitan, J. (1931, June). *Der Tanz.* Cited by H. Koegler, "In the Shadow of the Swastika: Dance in Germany, 1927–1936." *Dance Perspectives 57,* Spring 1974.

Limón, J. (1965). "The Modern Dance an Unpopular Art," *The Juilliard Review Annual 1964– 1965.*

Lippincott, G. (1964). "A Quiet Genius Himself — Louis Horst," *AAHPER Journal.*

Lippold, R. (1946, March). "Martha Graham and Dance Company," *Dance Observer,* 13:3.

Lisitzsky, G. (1934, May 5). "We Visit Martha," *Dynamics.*

Lloyd, M. (1936, March 3). "Relation of Music to Movement . . . ," *Christian Science Monitor.*

——. (1937). "Lloyd 1935," in *Martha Graham: The Early Years,* ed. M. Armitage. (Originally published in *Christian Science Monitor.*)

——. (1953, July). "The Personal Equation," *Christian Science Monitor.*

Lloyd, N. (1951, November). "American Composers Write for the Dance," *Dance Observer,* 18:9. (Reprinted 1957, *A Decade of Dance,* Connecticut College, New London.)

——. (1953, August 4). "Dance Encyclopedia: Horst Tracing," *The New London Evening Day.*

——. (1954, July 20). "Louis Horst Heard in Second Lecture at School of Dance," *The New London Evening Day.*

——. (1965). "About Louis Horst," *Juilliard Review Annual, 1963–1964.*

Lloyd, R. (1988, March 5). Personal interview. Audiotaped and transcribed.

Lohoefer (De Boeck), E. (1988, August 18). Personal interview, Washington, D.C. Audiotaped and transcribed.

"Louis Horst Has Been Called. . . ." (1932, December 4). *New York American.*

Love, P. (1934). "Mary Austin: Review of *The American Rhythm,*" *Dance Observer,* 1:8.

Luening, O. (1980). *The Odyssey of an American Composer.* New York: Scribners.

——. (1989, July 7). Personal interview. Audiotaped and transcribed.

Luhan, M. D. (May 1925). "A Bridge between Two Cultures," *Theatre Arts Monthly,* 9:5.

McDonagh, D. (1970). *Rise and Fall and Rise of Modern Dance.* (Reprint 1990, Pennington, N.J.: A Cappella Books.)

——. (1973, April). "A conversation with Gertrude Shurr," *Ballet Review,* 4:5.

——. (1973). *Martha Graham: A Biography.* New York: Praeger.

McGeary, G. (1984, June 20). Personal interview, Hastings, N.Y. Audiotaped and transcribed.

McGehee, H. (1985, September 29). Letter to author.

——. (1990, May 2). Personal conversation.

Mansfield, P. (1962, December). "Whither the Modern Dance?" *Perry-Mansfield Pine Bark.*

Marsh, L. (1927, October 15). "Horst Again Proved . . . ," *New York World.* Clipping.

Martin, J. (1929, March 4). "Martha Graham's Recital . . . ," *New York Times.* Clipping.

——. (1929, November 10). "The Dance: A Unique Theatre project," *New York Times.*

——. (1930, January 6). "Program of Four Stars," *New York Times.*

——. (1931, February 15). "Joint Efforts," *New York Times.*

——. (1931, March). "In the Realm of the Dance," *Drama 21,* no. 6.

——. (1932, November 14). "New York Dance Events . . . ," *New York Times.*

——. (1932, November 21). "Martha Graham in 3 . . . ," *New York Times.* Clipping.

——. (1932, December 4). "Choric Dance, Louis Horst Had Been . . . ," *New York Times.*

——. (1933, January 8). "The Dance: The First Experiment at Radio City," *New York Times.*

——. (1936). *America Dancing.* (Reprint 1978, New York: Dance Horizons.)

——. (1945). "More Kind than Wise," *New York Times.* In *Martha Graham: A Biography.* New York: Praeger, 1973.

——. (1946, August 4). "Words from Wigman," *New York Times.*

——. (1946, November 10). "The Dance: A Debut," *New York Times.*

——. (1947, March 16). "The Dance: Graham," *New York Times.*

——. (1948, February 27). "A Characteristically Excellent Score . . . ," *New York Times.*

——. (1955, March 15). Capezio Award program.

——. (1955, April). "Louis Horst Wins the 4th Capezio," *Dance Magazine.*

Meisner, S. (1984). Video. *Sanford Meisner: The Theater's Best Kept Secret,* "American Masters," PBC-TV, Jac Venza, executive director; Susan Lacy, executive producer; Kent Paul, producer; Playhouse Repertory Company.

Morgan, B. (1939, March 12). "The war makes me more. . . ." Letter to Catherine Paul-Boncour. Private collection.

——. (1941). *Martha Graham: Sixteen Dances in Photographs.* Text: G. Beiswanger and L. Horst. New York: Duell, Sloan and Pearce. (Revised edition, Dobbs Ferry, N.Y.: Morgan & Morgan, 1980.)

——. (1984, January 2). Personal interview, Scarsdale, N.Y.

Morton, F. (1935, October). Article in *The Theatre Arts Monthly,* 19:10.

Nietzsche, F. (1886). *Beyond Good and Evil.* (Trans. W. Kaufmann, New York: Vintage, 1966.)

——. (1887). *The Gay Science.* (Trans. W. Kaufmann, New York: Vintage, 1974.)

Nikolais, A. (1989, August 11). Personal interview, Stockton, N.J. Audiotaped and transcribed.

Nixon, M. (August–September 1957). "Dance Composition," *Dance Observer,* 24:7.

O'Donnell, M. (1979). Interview by E. Kendall. NYPL-DC.

——. (1979). Interview by L. Small.

Osgood, B. (1988, August 18). Personal communication. Telephone.

Page, R. (1978). *Page by Page.* New York: Dance Horizons.

Palmer, W. (1978). *Theatrical Dancing in America.* South Brunswick, N.J., and New York: A. S. Barnes and Co.

Paris, B. (1989). *Louise Brooks.* New York: Knopf.

Park, R. (1953, September 3). Letter to Louis Horst.

Parker, H. T. [H.T.P.] (1932, April 9). "Revelations to Bostonians of Martha Graham," Boston

Transcript. In *Motion Arrested: Dance Reviews of H. T. Parker,* ed. O. Holmes. Middletown, Conn.: 1982.

——. (1932, May 18). "No Dancer Has Brought . . . ," Boston *Transcript.*

——. (n.d.). "Skillful Hands . . . ," Boston *Transcript.*

Pease, E. (1953). *Louis Horst: His Theories on Modern Dance Composition.* Doctoral dissertation, University of Michigan. Ann Arbor, Mich.: University Microfilms International.

——. (1965). "Epilogue: A Conversation with Louis Horst" [from 1952 tapes], *Impulse 1965.*

Phelps, M. (1949, April). "On the Modern Forms of Louis Horst," *Dance Observer,* 16:4.

Rall, P. (1917, June 9). "I Muse Upon . . . ," Los Angeles *Record.*

Riegger, W. (1937). "Riegger 1937." In *Martha Graham: The Early Years,* ed. M. Armitage. New York: Da Capo.

Ririe, S. (1986, July 12). Personal interview, New York City. Audiotaped and transcribed.

Roberts, W. (1928, August). "Interview with Martha Graham," *Dance Magazine,* 10:4. Cited in Armitage, 1937.

Roosevelt, E. (1936). Letter to Martha Graham. Roosevelt Archives, New York.

Roosevelt, J. (1960–1961). Interviews with Louis Horst, New York City. Audiotaped and transcribed.

Rose, P. (1984). *Parallel Lives.* New York: Vintage.

Rosenblatt, E. (1941, August–September). "Bennington 1941," *Dance Observer,* 8:7.

Ross, B. (1974, Winter). "Person and Performer," in *Eddy, About Dance,* ed. J. Nuctern.

Rudhyar, D. (1925 or 1926, July 2, 14, August 27). Letters to M. D. Luhan.

Rudko, D. (1980, August 22). Personal interview, Upper Montclair, N.J. Audiotaped and transcribed.

——. (1988, April 4). Personal interview, New York City.

Sabin, R. (1948, April). "Martha Graham and Company," *Dance Observer,* 15:4.

——. (1953, January). "Louis Horst and Modern Dance in America, Part I—Beginnings: The Denishawn Years," *Dance Magazine,* 27:1.

——. (1955, May). "Louis Horst Receives 4th Annual . . . ," *Dance Observer,* 22:5.

——. (1959, February). "Moral Challenge," *Dance Observer,* 26:2.

——. (1964). *Graham Program 63–64* (article on Graham).

St. Denis, R. (1919, November 12). Diary. Unpublished manuscript.

——. (1925, July 7). Unsigned letter to Louis Horst.

——. (1930, February 16). Untitled essay on marriage, unpublished manuscript.

——. *An Unfinished Life.* London: George G. Harrap. (Reprint 1971, New York: Dance Horizons.)

Sargeant, G. Graham. (1987, March 13). Personal interview, Tucson, Ariz. Audiotaped and transcribed.

Sargeant, W. (1937). "Sargeant 1937," in *Martha Graham: The Early Years,* ed. M. Armitage. San Francisco: Armitage.

Saylor, O., ed. (1930). *Revolt in the Arts.* New York: Brentano's.

Schickel, R. (1984). *D. W. Griffith: An American Life.* New York: Simon & Schuster.

Schoenberg, A. (1967). "Editor's Preface" (1965), "Letter to D. Moore" (16 April 1938), in *Fundamentals of Musical Composition,* ed. Strang. New York: St. Martin's Press.

——. (1975). "New Music" (1923), "Heart and Brain in Music" (1946), in *Style and Idea: Selected Writings of Arnold Schoenberg,* ed. Stein. Berkeley: University of California Press.

Schumach, M. (1954, January 17). "Dance Maestro . . . ," *New York Times.*

Schuman, W. (1955, March 16). Letter to Louis Horst.

Seldes, M. (1986, October 2). Personal interview.

Severin, R. (1947, March 25). "The Season in Review," *Musical America.*

Shawn, T. (1921, November 7). Letter to R. St. Denis.

———. (1925). Diaries.

———. (1930, November). "Being Aware . . . ," *The Forward: The New York Three Arts Club,* 18:11.

———. (1960). *One Thousand and One Night Stands.* New York: Doubleday.

———. (1969, May). Interview by M. Horosko. Reminiscences from childhood to the dissolution of Denishawn. NYPL-DC.

Shelton, S. (1981). *Divine Dancer: Ruth St. Denis.* Garden City, N.Y.: Doubleday.

Sherman (Lehac), J. (1976). *Soaring: The Diary and Letters of a Denishawn Dancer in the Far East, 1925–1926.* Middletown, Conn.: Wesleyan University Press.

———. (1979). *The Drama of Denishawn Dance.* Middletown, Conn.: Wesleyan University Press.

———. (1983). *Denishawn: The Enduring Influence.* Boston: Twayne.

———. (1987, May 26). Letter to J. Soares quoting A. Douglas.

Sherman, R. (1974, April 4). Interview with Martha Graham. "The Listening Room," WQXR-FM, New York.

Shurr, G. (1987, March 14). Personal interview, Tucson, Ariz. Audiotaped and transcribed.

Smith, C. S. (1948, April). "Dance Observer Benefit," *Musical America.*

———. (1953). "It Looked . . . ," *Musical America.*

Smith, N. W. (1974, January). Letter.

Soares, J. (1958–1964). Private papers, class notes, and personal conversations.

———. (1981). "Louis Horst" in *Dictionary of American Biography,* ed. J. Garraty, Supplement 7, 1961–65. New York: Scribners.

———. (1987). "Preface" and "Biographical Note," in *Modern Dance Forms in Relation to the Other Arts,* L. Horst. Princeton, N.J.: Dance Horizons/Princeton Book Co. (Reprint of 1961 edition.)

———. (1988). "Biographical Note," in *Pre-Classic Dance Forms,* L. Horst. Princeton, N.J.: Princeton Book Co. (Reprint of 1937 edition.)

———. (1989). "Louis Horst and His Influence on Modernism in Twentieth-Century Dance," in *Proceedings: Society of Dance History Scholars Twelfth Annual Conference.* Riverside, Calif.: University of California, Riverside.

Sokolow, A. (1987, March 19). Personal interview. Audiotaped and transcribed.

"Some Vivid, Reedy Snatches. . . ." (1935, February 25). *New York Times.*

Sorell, W. (1954, January 10). "Keeping Step," *Providence Journal.*

———. (1964, March). "Louis Horst 1884–1964," *Dance Magazine,* 38:3.

———. (1969). *Hanya Holm: The Biography of an Artist.* Middletown, Conn.: Wesleyan University Press.

Stodelle, E. (1984). *Deep Song.* New York: Schirmer Books.

Tamiris, H. (1989/90, Fall/Winter). "Tamiris in Her Own Voice: Draft of an Autobiography," *Studies in Dance History,* 1:1.

Taylor, P. (1987). *Private Domain.* New York: Knopf.

Taylor, R. (1989, May 20). Personal interview. New York City. Audiotaped and transcribed.

Terry, W. (1934, December 28). "Martha Graham Dances . . . ," *New York Herald Tribune.*

———. (1936, July 21). "All Aspects of the Dance Found at Bennington Summer School," *Boston Herald.* (Reprinted 1978, *I Was There.* New York: Dekker).

——. (1939, December 28). "Martha Graham Dances in New Satirical Work," *New York Herald Tribune.* (Reprinted 1978, *I Was There,* New York: Dekker.)

——. (1942, January 25). "Y.M.H.A. Dance Center." *New York Herald Tribune.* (Reprinted 1978, *I Was There,* New York: Dekker.)

——. (1946, September 1). "The Major Function of a Dance Critic Summarized, Discussed," *New York Herald Tribune.*

——. (1947, July 3). "Ruth St. Denis, 70," *New York Herald Tribune.*

——. (1954, January). "Modern Dance in Washington," Modern Dance Council of Washington, Dance Council Bulletin, 2:1.

——. (1959). ". . . For Martha Graham," *ACA Bulletin,* 8:4.

——. (1975). "Revolt, A New Frontier," *Frontiers of Dance: The Life of Martha Graham.* New York: Thomas Y. Crowell.

Thompson, B. L. (1940, Summer). Film. *Compositions in Modern Forms by the Martha Graham Dance Group.* NYPL-DC.

Tobias, T. (Spring 1981). "A Conversation with May O'Donnell: American Modern Dance: The Early Years," *Ballet Review,* 9:1.

Turbyfill, M. (1930?). Biographical Notes. *Page Kreutzberg* (unpaged).

Umanya. (1990, May 2). Personal conversation, Lynchburg, Va.

Van Tuyl, M. (1954). Notes. Typescript.

——. (1954, March). "Louis Horst Considers the Question," *Impulse 1954.*

——, ed. (1969). *Anthology of "Impulse": Annual of Contemporary Dance 1951–1966.* New York: Dance Horizons.

——. (1986, March 12). Personal communication. Telephone.

Wagner, C. (1927, October 10). "Tamiris at the Little Theatre," *Morning Telegraph.*

Wallach, E. (1955, March 15). Capezio Award Program.

Watkins, M. (1930, April). "Dance Events Reviewed," *The Dance Magazine.*

Wigman, M. (n.d.). "Composition: The Law. The Idea. The Theme," trans. L. Horst. Typescript.

Woodward, J. (1984, April 22). "Neighborhood Playhouse: The Actors Remember." Tribute to Louis Horst, Theater of Riverside Church, New York City.

Yuriko. (1988, February 18). Personal communication. Telephone.

Brief Chronology

1884 Born 12 January 1884, Kansas City, Missouri.

1890 Family — Conrad, Carolina, and sister May — moves to Bethlehem, Pennsylvania.

1892 Family moves to San Francisco. Conrad joins San Francisco Orchestra. Louis begins violin studies.

1898 Louis graduates from Cosmopolitan Public School. Studies in keyboard harmony and counterpoint.

1902 Passes exam for San Francisco musician's union. Freelance jobs for next three years: Elk Saloon, Reno; Cafe Zinfand and Techaw Tavern, San Francisco. Violin studies with John Marquandt, piano with Sam Fleischman, and oboe.

1905 Camping and hiking trips.

1906 Earthquake destroys San Francisco. Becomes a pit musician; Eureka, California, Margarita Theatre; Oakland, California, MacDonaugh Theatre.

1907 Plays at Novelty Theatre and Van Ness Theatre, San Francisco. Aquarium Grill and Cafe San Francisco. Offers private lessons. Cruise to Mazatlan, Mexico. Van Ness Theatre; The Casino, Santa Cruz.

1909 Elected member of board of directors, musician's union. Golden Pheasant Cafe, Monroe Hotel. Marries Bessie (Betty) Cunningham, November 29.

1910 Pit musician, Columbia Theatre, Columbia Boys Band. Accompanist, Ruth St. Denis in her program *Oriental Dances*.

1911 New York City. Various freelance jobs. Six-month contract at Princess Hotel, Hamilton, Bermuda.

1912 Return to New York City. Maplewood Hotel, New Hampshire; mountain climbing and cross-country travels with Betty. Return to San Francisco.

1913 Columbia Theatre, Solari's Grill. Ensemble trio. Accompanist for singers. Returns to Maplewood Hotel.

1915 Alcazar and Cort Theatres. Studies organ with Wallace Sabin. Father dies June 24. Joins the Denishawn Dance Company to begin ten-year association.

1916–[1925] "Conductor and Musical Director" for the Denishawn Company. Denishawn's Los Angeles summer school music head. Extensive company touring through 1925 on vaudeville and concert tours arranged by Orpheum and Pantages circuits, followed by three Mayer cross-continental tours.

1918 Composes *Dance of the Royal Ballet of Siam.*

1919 *Japanese Spear Dance.* Begins liaison with Martha Graham.

1923 Composes *A Sahara Romance.* Arranges *Cuadro Flamenco, Ishtar of the Seven Gates* for Denishawn.

1924 *Pompeiian Murals, Introduction to Byzantine Dance* for Denishawn. *Danse Impertinente, Ylang-Ylang* for Betty Horst.

1925 Resigns from Denishawn; last performance March 25. Travels to Vienna to study with Richard Stöhr at the Conservatory of Music. Writes songs *Scène Javanaise* and *A Viennese Nocturne.* Returns to New York City. Begins to rehearse with Graham.

1926 Accompanist, dance classes at Denishawn and Anderson-Milton schools. Pianist and conductor for Bolm, Montero, Niles, Page, under contract with Mayer. Accompanist, Graham's first New York City concert on 18 April 1926 (*Masques*), and second on 28 November 1926 (*Alt-Wein, Three Poems of the East* [called "first original score for dance"]) and Page (*Two Balinese Rhapsodies*). Composition studies with Max Persin. Accompanist for Denishawn and Leo Staats summer schools.

1927 Accompanist for concerts with Johansson, Graham, Ito, Niles, Tamiris, Page, and others. Musical director for various John Murray Anderson shows for next two years.

1928 Begins to teach: Neighborhood Playhouse, New York City (until 1964), and Perry-Mansfield Dance Camp, Steamboat Springs, Colorado (for next five years, and 1946). Writes first article for *The Dance Magazine.* Accompanist, concerts for de Mille, Humphrey-Weidman, Kreutzberg, and Graham (*Fragments*). Bolm tour. Score for Weidman (*Japanese Actor*).

1929 Collaboration and touring with Graham (*Heretic*) and de Mille (*Spring Song, Civil War Songs*). Mother dies March 10. Teaches Music Applied to Movement at Neighborhood Playhouse.

1930 Pianist for first Dance Repertory Theatre season. De Mille (*Julia Dances*), Strawbridge (*Heroic Hymn*). Visit to Indian pueblos in New Mexico with Graham (returning annually for the next four years). Teaches Music Appreciation at Perry-Mansfield.

1931 Music director for second Dance Repertory Theatre season. Graham (*Primitive Mysteries*). Production of *Electra.* Summer travels with Graham (on Guggenheim grant) to Mexico. Publishes exercises written to accompany dance studies for Portia Mansfield.

1932 De Mille (*Orchesography*). Production of *Decameron.* Graham (*Chorus of Youth—Companions, Choric Dance*). Radio City Music Hall opening. Teaches at Sarah Lawrence College through 1940.

1933 Graham (*Tragic Patterns, Six Miracle Plays*). Humphrey (*The Pleasures of Counterpoint*). Teaches Survey and Use of Music in Relation to the Dance.

1934 First issue of *Dance Observer,* continuing as editor and contributor until his death. First faculty of Bennington School of Dance. Graham (*Celebration, American Provincials*). Teaches An Analysis of Dance Composition from the Standpoint of the Musical Forms of Many Periods. At Sarah Lawrence, Composition in Dance Forms. New School lecture on Pre-Classic Dance Forms.

1935 Teachers College Conference. At Bennington teaches courses Pre-Classic Dance Forms and Modern Dance Forms. Graham (*Frontier*). Music for Theatre productions: *Noah; Panic*. De Mille (*Mountain White*).

1936   March–April: transcontinental tour with Graham. Graham (*Horizons*). Director of program in music composition for the dance at Bennington.

1937   February 26: performance at White House. Bryan film clip of Graham and Horst in studio. March–April: Graham with twelve dancers (Washington, California). Graham affair with Carlus Dyer. Chairman of Dance Teachers Advisory Committee. *Dance Observer* publishes *Pre-Classic Dance Forms*.

1938   Spring tour. Horst, Graham, and Hawkins. Teachers College course. Fonaroff assistant.

1939   Lives at 1 West 67th Street (Hotel des Artistes). Hawkins moves into 29 West 12th Street with Graham (for twelve years). Graham (*Columbiad*). January 30: World's Fair opening. Bennington at Mills College.

1940   Bennington. Graham (*El Penitente*).

1941   Teaches at Graham Studio. Bennington.

1942   Erdman (*Medusa*). Fonaroff (*Little Theodolina, Yankee Doodle*). Adelphi, 1942–1943. Teaches at Graham Studio. Bennington.

1943   Moves to 55 West 11th Street. July: Graham in residence at Bennington. Horst teaches course at Barnard College. Teaches at Graham Studio. Scores for two Bryan films.

1944   Head of YM-YWHA Modern Dance School with Martha Graham. Dudley (*The Ninth Psalm*).

1945   March 27: Receives National Section on Dance of the National Education Association Ruth Bloomer Award for creation and development of modern dance in America. Teaches Group Composition. Fellowship Award from Rita Morgenthau.

1946   Gray (*The Prophet Said Three*), Fonaroff (*Born to Weep*). Returns to Perry-Mansfield Camp.

1947   Yuriko (*Tale of Seizure*).

1948   McGehee (*Man with a Load of Mischief*). Summer: Connecticut College School of the Dance. Begins reviewing for *The New London Evening Day* until his death. Severs professional association as conductor with the Martha Graham Dance Company.

1949   Lippincott (*La Danse des Mortes*). Yuriko (*Servant of the Pillars*). Scores for film (*Pacific Island*).

1950   Lippincott (*If Love were Love*). Teaches at Barnard College, 1950–1951.

1951   Teaching for the Juilliard Dance Division begins. Teaching Pre-Classic Dance Forms, Modern Dance Forms, and Group Forms every semester until his death. Sixteen articles: Award from Board of Editors of the Encyclopedia Britannica. Score for Bryan film (*Rural Women*).

1952   Mild heart attack; advised to limit performances at the keyboard. Lippincott (*Goddess of the Moon*).

1953   Score for film *Flower Arrangements of Colonial Williamsburg*.

1955   Capezio Award.

1959   Kanda (*Island Memory, Young Moon*).

1961   *Impulse* publication of *Modern Dance Forms in Relation to the Other Arts*.

1962   Moves to East 62nd Street and York Avenue.

1963   December 15: Honorary doctorate, Wayne State University. Creative Award, American Academy of Physical Education.

1964   January 4: Enters Doctor's Hospital. Dies January 23. Fonaroff and Graham at bedside.

Scores by Louis Horst

C: date and place composition signed
Ch: choreographer
D: director
P: premiere (date and place)
I: instrumentation, if other than piano
SD: set design
MD: music director
MS: manuscript note
Pub: date published
R: date and place recorded
Dis: distributor
FC: film collection
N: incidental note
PN: program note

1908
1. *Passion Danza*
Arrangement of music by M. Magallanes
P: 14 February, San Francisco (Thompson's Grill)
I: Violin, piano

1918
2. *Dance of the Royal Ballet of Siam, or Ballet of Siam*
Ch: Ruth St. Denis
P: 19 November, Denver (Orpheum Theatre)
I: Small orchestra

1919
3. *Japanese Spear Dance,* or *Danse Japonesque,* or *Spear Dance Japonesque*
Ch: Ted Shawn
P: 3 November, Los Angeles (Pantages Theatre)
I: Small orchestra
N: Performed as part of *Julnar of the Sea,* 1919–1921.
Retitled *Danse Japonesque,* 13 July 1923

1923
4. *A Sahara Romance*
C: August, Peterborough, New Hampshire
MS: [Ded.] to Betty

5. *Cuadro Flamenco*
Arrangement of Spanish dance and folk music
Ch: Ted Shawn
P: 15 October, Atlantic City, New Jersey (Apollo Theatre)
I: Small orchestra

6. *Ishtar of the Seven Gates*
Arrangement of music by Charles Tomlinson Griffes
Ch: Ruth St. Denis
P: 15 October, Atlantic City, New Jersey (Apollo Theatre)
I: Small orchestra

1924

7. *Pompeiian Murals*
Suite for Piano: Prelude to Dawn; Dancer with
Tambourine; Flora; Bacchante
Ch: Ruth St. Denis
P: 1 January, Quincy, Illinois (Empire Theatre)
MS: [Ded.] to Martha Graham
N: *Dancer with Tambourine* score became
Byzantine Dance, 1925, choreography by
Ruth St. Denis.

8. *Danse Impertinente*
Ch: Ruth Austin and Betty Horst
P: 13 June, School of the Theatre of Golden
Bough, Carmel, California

9. *Ylang-Ylang*
Song: words by Bryant Coleman
C: 19 July, Carmel, California (Theatre of the
Golden Bough)
I: Voice, piano
N: Song recital by singer Lawrence Strauss.

10. *Introduction to Byzantine Dance*
Introduction to No. 2 of *Pompeiian Murals*
Ch: Ruth St. Denis
C: September, New York
P: 6 October, Newburgh, New York (Academy of Music)
MS: "This Introduction to Byzantine Dance is
the property of Ruth St. Denis."

1925

11. *Thin Ivory Petals*
Song: poem by C. Wentworth
C: Spring, on U.S. tour
I: Voice, piano

12. *Tango*
Ch: Ted Shawn
P: 6 March, South Bend, Indiana (Oliver Theatre)

13. *Autumnal*
Song: poem by Henry Faust
C: April 1925, on U.S. tour
P: 18 April, New York (Guild Theatre)
I: Voice, piano

14. *Scène Javanaise*
C: 22 June 1925, Vienna, Austria
Ch: Martha Graham

P: 23 May, Rochester, New York (Kilbourn
Hall, Eastman School)
MS: "Parts of this composition were incorporated in the Balinese Rhapsodies of Ruth Page,
and are her property."

15. *Toys*
Song: poem by Arthur Symons
C: 25 June, Vienna, Austria
I: Voice, piano

16. *Harvest Dirge*
Song: poem by Alfred Kreymborg
C: 2 August, Vienna, Austria
I: Voice, piano

17. *Mule Pack*
Song: poem by William Haskell Simpson
C: 11 August, Vienna, Austria
I: Voice, piano

18. *A Viennese Nocturne*
Ballet-Pantomime in 1 act
C: November, New York
MS: Includes typescript of scenario with two
magazine illustrations

19. *Change*
Song: poem by Witter Bynner
C: 4 December, New York
I: Voice, piano

1926

20. *Blind Weavers*
Song: poem by Lucille Rice
C: 2 March, New York
MS: [Ded.] to Mabel Zoeckler
I: Voice, piano

21. *Two Balinese Rhapsodies*
Religious Dance; Pleasure Dance
Ch: Ruth Page
P: 20 March, Ithaca, New York (Bailey Hall)
N: Performed as Balinese Rhapsody, January
1932, Newark, New Jersey.

22. *Four Songs*
Harvest Dirge; Toys; Change; Blind Weavers
C: See entries 15, 16, 19, 20
P: 14 April, Utica, New York (New Century
Auditorium)
I: Voice, piano

23. *Masques*
Ch: Martha Graham
P: 18 April, New York (48th Street Theatre)
MS: Title, Masques for Piano.

24. *Alt-Wien*
Arrangement of music by Leopold Godowsky
C: 25 November 1926
Ch: Martha Graham
P: 28 November, New York (Klaw Theatre)

25. *Three Poems of the East*
"On listening to a flute by moonlight"; "She like a dancer puts her 'broidered garments on"; "In measure while the gnats of music whirr the little amber-coloured dance moves"
Ch: Martha Graham
P: 28 November, New York (Klaw Theatre)
N: "She like a dancer puts her 'broidered garments on" retitled *East Indian Dance,* 27 January 1927, New York (Guild Theatre). "On listening to a flute by moonlight" retitled *Chinese Poem,* 12 February 1928, New York (Civic Repertory Theatre).

1927
26. *Dancing Shoes*
Popular Song: words by Hugh Anderson
C: June, New York
P: 4 July, Boston (Statler Hotel, New England Shoe and Leather Exposition.)
D: John Murray Anderson
MD: Louis Horst for show *Dancing Shoes*
I: Voice, piano

1928
27. *Fragments: Tragedy — Comedy*
Ch: Martha Graham
P: 22 April, New York (Little Theatre)
I: Flute, gong

28. *Japanese Actor: XVIIth Century*
Ch: Charles Weidman
C: 2 July, Steamboat Springs, Colorado
P: 28 October, New York (Civic Repertory Theatre)

29. *Rhythmic Design*
Five Studies in Rhythm in Relation to Design
C: 25 July, Steamboat Springs, Colorado
Ch: Portia Mansfield and Charlotte Perry

N: These studies are included in the *Musical Settings* collection published in 1939.

30. *Gypsy Song for a Romantic Play*
C: August, Steamboat Springs, Colorado
I: Voice, piano

1929
31. *Spring Song*
Arrangement of thirteenth-century work by John of Fornsete
Ch: Agnes de Mille
P: 17 February, New York (Martin Beck Theatre)
I: Voice, bugle, trumpet, piano

32. *Civil War Songs*
Arrangement of traditional songs
Ch: Agnes de Mille
P: 17 February, New York (Martin Beck Theatre)
I: Voice, piano

33. *Heretic*
Arrangement of old Breton song
Ch: Martha Graham
P: 14 April, New York (Booth Theatre)

34. *Two Songs for a Play by Villon — The Lord of Royal France* and *The Motley Road*
C: September

1930
35. *Julia Dances*
Arrangement of music by Thomas Weelkes
Ch: Agnes de Mille
P: 26 January, New York (MacDowell Club House)

36. *Heroic Hymn*
"The Sun of God Goes Forth to War"
Ch: Edwin Strawbridge
P: 28 March, New York (Booth Theatre)
I: Vocal chorus

1931
37. *Primitive Mysteries — Hymn to the Virgin, Crucifixus, Hosanna*
Ch: Martha Graham
P: 2 February, New York (Craig Theatre)
I: Piano, flute, oboe

38. *Prelude, Entrance and Lamentation for Electra*
Incidental music for dances in the play of *Electra* by Sophocles
D: (of chorus) Martha Graham
P: 18 May, Boston (Jordan Hall)
I: Gongs, cymbals, big tom-tom, tympanies, flute, chords on piano
MS: "Much of the material in this composition was incorporated in "Dance for Furies," Tragic Pattern, No. 3." (Horst note appears in "Lamentation" section of manuscript.)

39. *Ouija Dance*
Ch: Portia Mansfield
P: 22 August, Steamboat Springs, Colorado (Perry-Mansfield Theatre)

40. *Musical Settings: Correctives in Dance Form*
Book I: 30 Exercises for Dance Movements (1st Series); 40 Exercises for Dance Movements (2nd Series). Book II: Crescendo: 11 Exercises.
Pub: Fischer and Company, September 1931

41. *Tension and Release*
Ch: Portia Mansfield
P: 13 October, Pelham Manor, New York (The Manor House)

1932
42. *Orchesography*
Arrangement of music by Arbeau
Ch: Agnes de Mille
P: 8 January, New York (MacDowell Club)

43. *Etruscan Dance*
Ch: Portia Mansfield
P: 26 August, Steamboat Springs, Colorado (Perry-Mansfield Theatre)

44. *Rhythmica*
Ch: Portia Mansfield
P: 26 August, Steamboat Springs, Colorado (Perry-Mansfield Theatre)

45. *Tales from the Decameron* (Boccaccio)
Arrangement of twelfth-century by Carlos Salzedo
troubadour airs

D: Sydney Thompson
P: 13 November, New York (Town Hall)
I: Piano, voice
N: For a later program (17 February 1935), Horst arranged interludes of early Italian music for Sydney Thompson's program of scenes from the *Decameron* for flute, clarinet, bass clarinet, trumpet, percussion, soprano, and baritone.

46. *Chorus of Youth — Companions*
Ch: Martha Graham
P: 20 November, New York (Guild Theatre)
I: Flute, oboe, cello, clarinet, baritone, piano

47. *Choric Dance for an Antique Greek Tragedy — A Chorus of Furies*
C: September, New York
Ch: Martha Graham
P: 27 December, New York (Radio City Music Hall, Opening Inaugural Program)

1933
48. *Six Miracle Plays* (of the eleventh century)
Le Nativity, The Miraculous Birth and the Midwives, Les Trois Rois, Les Trois Maries, Lamentation of Virgin Mary, The Magdalen.
Ch: Martha Graham
P: 5 February, New York (for Stage Alliance at Guild Theatre)

49. *Throwing*
Dramatic Stylization No. 1
C: March, New York
Ch: Portia Mansfield

50. *The Pleasures of Counterpoint*
C: March
Ch: Doris Humphrey
P: 15 April, New York (Guild Theatre)
N: First performance with No. 2 (composer Harvey Pollins) and No. 3. (original score marked *The Pleasures of Counterpoint No. 2*, by Horst. HC NYPL-MD).

51. *Tragic Patterns*
Three Choric Dances for an Antique Greek Tragedy (later, *Three Tragic Patterns*)
Chorus of Supplicants
C: May, New York
Chorus for Maenads

C: April, New York
Chorus for Furies (see 47)
C: December 1932, New York
Ch: Martha Graham
P: 4 May, New York (Guild Theatre)
I: Flute, oboe, clarinet, bass, baritone, piano

52. *Pulling*
C: July, Steamboat Springs, Colorado (Perry-Mansfield Camp)
Ch: Portia Mansfield

53. *Stride and Strike*
C: July, Steamboat Springs, Colorado (Perry-Mansfield Camp)
Ch: Charlotte Perry

54. *Gymnastics — Nos. 1 and 2*
C: July, Steamboat Springs, Colorado
Ch: Portia Mansfield
N: Nos. 50, 52, 53, 54 (Throwing, Pulling, Stride and Strike, Gymnastics) published by J. Fischer and Brothers, 1933.

1934
55. *Celebration*
Ch: Martha Graham
P: 18 February, New York (Guild Theatre)
I: Piano, trumpet, clarinet, drum
N: Sometimes subtitled *Dance of Rejoicing*.

56. *American Provincials — Act of Piety; Act of Judgment*
Ch: Martha Graham
P: 11 November, New York (Guild Theatre)
I: Seven instruments, soprano, and baritone

1935
57. *Mountain White* (Theme and Variations)
Arrangement of traditional song "She'll Be Comin' Round the Mountain"
Ch: Agnes de Mille
P: 3 February, New York (Guild Theatre)
N: Sometimes subtitled *Improvisations on a Square Dance Theme*.

58. *Noah*
Incidental music for the play by André Obey
Choreographer: Anna Sokolow
D: Pierre Fresnay
P: 13 February, New York (Longacre Theatre)

I: Oboe, Hammond electric organ or piano.
Pub: Samuel French, 1935
N: Horst's personal chronology: "Wrote and directed dances for Pierre Fresnay's production of Obey's *Noah*, conducted 1st week at Theatre. Feb."

59. *Panic*
Incidental music for the play by Archibald MacLeish
Ch: Martha Graham
P: 9 March, New York (St. Nicholas Arena)
N: In Horst's personal chronology, "Played for MG part."

60. *Frontier — American Perspective of the Plains*
Ch: Martha Graham
P: 28 April, New York (Guild Theatre)
SD: Isami Noguchi
N: Also titled: *Perspective — No. 1 and No. 2* and *Perspective No. 1 — Frontier; Perspective No. 2 — Marching Song* (score by Lehman Engel).

1936
61. *Horizons*
Migration (New Trails); Dominion (Sanctified Power); Building Motif (Homesteading); Dance of Rejoicing.
Ch: Martha Graham
P: 23 February, New York (Guild Theatre)
SD: Alexander Calder
N: Interlude for Mobiles followed Dance of Rejoicing for 23 February performance. Review states, "Before each of 3 parts she presented a different group of mobiles by Alexander Calder, mechanically operated." Also, Dance of Rejoicing from *Horizons* performed 26 February 1937 at the White House, Washington, D.C. and 2 March 1937 in New York (Guild Theatre). Program note: "Music for Dance of Rejoicing is based on a Southern hill shout."

1937
62. *Study in Americana*
Variations on a Middle West Theme: Theme and Six Variations

Ch: Ruth Ann Heisey
P: 14 August, Bennington, Vermont (Bennington College Student Demonstration)
N: As *American Greetings,* choreography by Alwin Nikolais, September, New London, Connecticut. Later called *Seven American Variations for Americana Study. Variations on an American Theme: Theme and Six Variations* for student demonstration, 11 August 1939, Oakland, California (Bennington School of the Dance at Mills College). Score for *Ki Yippee Yay. Square Dance,* choreography by Gertrude Lippincott, 22 March 1947, Lafayette, Indiana (Perdue University, Ezra Fowler Hall).

1938
63. *Militant Hymn*
Solo from *American Document*
Ch: Martha Graham
P: 1 May, Flushing Meadows, New York (New York World's Fair Preview Pageant)
N: First performance of *American Document,* 1938, with score by Ray Green does not include this solo music.

1939
64. *Tribute to Peace*
Ch: Martha Graham
P: 30 April, Flushing Meadows, New York (New York World's Fair)

65. *American Stride*
Words by Mary Phelps
D: Martha Graham and Laura Elliott
P: 16 May, New York (Heckscher Theatre)
MS: "An original project written especially for the students of the Neighborhood Playhouse and developed by them."

66. *Street Scene* from *California Suite*
Ch: Composition demonstration
P: August, Oakland, California (Mills College, Lisser Hall)

67. *Musical Settings*
Rhythmic Design; Correctives in Dance Form; Correctives in Rhythmic Design; Rhythmic Design; 60 Exercises in Rhythmic Movement.
Pub: J. Fischer and Brothers, 1939.

68. *Columbiad*
C: December, New York
Ch: Martha Graham
P: 27 December, New York (St. James Theatre)

1940
69. *El Penitente* (The Penitent)
Entrance of Performers; Flagellation of Penitent; Vision of Penitent — The Virgin Pleads, The Christ Blesses; Death Cart — The Death Cart is the Symbol for Sin; Seduction — The Magdalen Seduces the Penitent; The Fall of Man; The Christ Condemns; The Penitent Bears the Cross on his Back; The Crucifixion — The Penitent Atones and Wins Absolution; The Festival Dance.
C: June–July 1940
Ch: Martha Graham
P: 11 August, Bennington, Vermont (College Theatre)
I: Flute (piccolo), oboe, clarinet, bassoon, violin, cello, drum.
N: The drum is a special Indian type with a high, dry tone. Guitar interludes were originally intended, to be played by a guitarist on stage.
SD: Arch Lauterer (for the 1947 revival, Isami Noguchi added a mask and redesigned the decor).
Pub: New York: Liberal Press, 1945; New York: The Orchesis Publications, 1960.

1941
70. *Yankee Doodle Greets Columbus, 1492*
Ch: Nina Fonaroff
P: 25 May (in progress), New York (Humphrey-Weidman Studio Theatre)
N: Retitled *Yankee Doodle, American Prodigy; An American Fantasy.* Also performed 15 August 1941, Bennington, Vermont (College Theatre).

1942
71. *The Transformations of Medusa*
Maid of the Secret Isle; Lady of the Wild Things; Queen of the Gorgons.
Ch: Jean Erdman

P: 1 August, Bennington, Vermont (College Theatre)

N: *Maid of the Secret Isle* later retitled *Temple Virgin.*

72. *Little Theodolina, Queen of the Amazons*
Fantasy of a little creature
Theodolina, the huntress; Theodolina dances for joy; Theodolina has a thought; Theodolina flies through space.
Ch: Nina Fonaroff
P: 1 August, Bennington, Vermont (College Theatre)
N: Score included four exercises in different Greek modes that Horst had composed previously. According to Fonaroff, "I used them ready-made except . . . he wrote something for the last part."

1943
72. *Graduation Day — The Hills are Ready for Climbing*
Ch: Pearl Lang
P: 24 March, New York (Humphrey-Weidman Studio Theatre)

73. *Housing in Chile*
Score for a film by Julien Bryan
C: August, New York
I: Violin, bass, piano
R: 17 August 1943, New York (RCA Studios)
FC: International Film Foundation, Museum of Modern Art, New York

74. *Atacama Desert* (North Chile)
Score for a film by Julien Bryan
I: Piano, small ensemble
R: 23 December, New York (RCA Studios)
FC: Indiana University Film Collection; International Film Foundation, New York

1944
75. *The Ninth Psalm*
In Memory of Irene Lewisohn
D: Mary Barrett
C: Jane Dudley
P: 24 May, New York (Kaufmann Auditorium YM-YWHA.)

76. *Hot Sunday*
C: With Norman Lloyd
Ch: (used by) Gertrude Lippincott
P: 15 August, San Francisco (San Francisco Dance League)
N: Choreography by Lippincott reworked as a group piece, 14 January 1948, St. Paul, Minnesota (Hamline University). Originally composed as a jazz study.

1945
77. *The Lonely*
Incidental music for a text by Horton Foote
Ch: Martha Graham
P: New York (Neighborhood Playhouse)

1946
78. *Three South American Dances for Piano*
Ch: (used by) Gertrude Lippincott, *Invitacion*
P: 22 January, South Hadley, Massachusetts (Mount Holyoke College)
Pub: New York: Motif Publications, Choreomusic, Orchesis Publications, 1960
N: Orchestrated by Henry Denecke, 29 October 1947 for "A Percussion Concert," The Walker Art Center, Woman's Club Assembly, Minneapolis, Minnesota.
PN: "Three short sections using melodies and rhythms of various Latin American countries."

79. *The Prophet Said Three — Prologue; Dialogue of Rocks*
Dance-drama with text by John Malcolm Brinnen
Ch: Harriette Ann Gray
D: Charlotte Perry
P: 23 August, Steamboat Springs, Colorado (Perry-Mansfield Dance Theatre)
N: Negative photostats of each section except "Square Dance." HC NYPL-MD. Parts of this score were used for *Taken with Tongues,* choreography by Harriette Ann Gray, 1948.

80. *In Memoriam*
Ch: Harriette Ann Gray
N: A solo in memory of her brother.

81. *Humiliation*
Ch: Edith Wiener
P: 18 September, New York

82. *Born to Weep*
Ch: Nina Fonaroff
P: 27 October, New York (Kaufmann Auditorium YM-YWHA)

1947
83. *Relent to Tears*
Ch: Edith Wiener
P: 10 May, San Francisco Dance League (Marines' Memorial Theatre)
N: On a program shared with Ann Halprin and Welland Lathrop.

84. *Archaic Movement Study based on the Agamemnon Tragedy*
P: 15 May, New York
(The Children's Center Theatre)
N: A final demonstration at the Neighborhood Playhouse School of the Theatre, with Richard Boone as Agamemnon and Marian Seldes as Clytemnestra.

85. *Tale of Seizure*
Ch: Yuriko
P: 29 November, New York (School of Needle Trades)
N: Reworked with full score for small orchestra and set by Isamu Noguchi, 19 February 1948, New York (Maxine Elliott Theatre). Score dated 24 November 1947. HC NYPL-MD. PN: "This dance is a tale of seizure by the inner world of ancestral pattern, the struggle to become free, and the final victory."

1948
86. *Man with a Load of Mischief*
Ch: Helen McGehee
P: 7 March, New York (Kaufmann Auditorium, YM-YWHA)

87. *Ki Yipee Yay*
Ch: Gertrude Lippincott
P: 21 April, Charleston, Illinois, (Eastern Illinois State College)
PN: "Composed in the manner reminiscent of a Western square dance."

88. *Ominous Horizon*
Ch: Tao Strong
P: 2 August, New London, Connecticut (Palmer Auditorium)
N: Also performed at Griswold Estate, Old Lyme, Connecticut, 13 August. New York premiere 20 February 1949, New York (Kaufmann Auditorium, YM-YWHA).

89. *Death Croon*
Ch: Beth Osgood
P: 9 December, Lisser Hall, Oakland, California (Mills College)
SD: Joan Larkey
PN: "And is it not a sad thing to be drowned twice, once by the waves and once by the tears of your folks?" In Hebridean stories the exasperated spirits of the drowned ones appear to frighten the men out of their tears and sorrow. Based on John Synge's *Riders to the Sea*. "This music has been composed especially for the dance."

1949
90. *La Danse des Mortes*, or *Dance of the Dead*
Dance and the Abbess; Death and the Lady; Death and the Maiden
Ch: Gertrude Lippincott
P: 1 May, New York (Kaufmann Auditorium YM-YWHA)
N: Commissioned by Gertrude Lippincott. Orchestrated by Thomas Nee, 2 November, St. Paul, Minnesota (Hamline University). Reworked version *Figures on an Altar Panel*—The Abbess, The Lady, The Maiden, 26 February 1959, Fredricksburg, Virginia (Mary Washington College, University of Virginia). Reworked as a duet *La Danse des Mortes*, 30 April 1960, San Marcos, Texas (Southwest Texas State College).

91. *Pacific Island*
Score for a film by Julien Bryan.
R: 20 June, New York (RCA Studio)
I: Flute and prepared piano
FC & Dis: International Film Foundation, New York

N: Manuscript includes diagram for preparing piano.

92. *Santo*
Also called *Santo Labanada*
C: New York City
Ch: Jane McLean
N: "The score is solemn, dramatic, and minor key dominates the sound. We met in my studio at 70 West 3rd Street very often to rehearse. He thought my conception of the Santo deep and fine—a very high complement from Louis."

93. *Servant of the Pillars*
Ch: Yuriko
P: 23 October, New York (YM-YWHA)

94. *Caged*
Ch: Lin Pei-Fan
P: 1 November, Minneapolis, Minnesota (YMCA)

1950
95. *If Love Were Love*
Originally called *My Own True Love*
Ch: Gertrude Lippincott
P: 25 February, Granville, Ohio (Denison University)
N: Reworked as a trio *The Love-Quickened Heart,* 22 January 1954, Fargo (North Dakota State Agricultural College). Later called *Ghosts of the Heart.*

96. *Sorceress*
Ch: Charlotte Griswold
P: 5 May

1951
97. *Rural Women*
A film by Julian Bryan
R: 24 April, New York (Reeves Studio)

FC: International Film Foundation, New York

1952
98. *Goddess of the Moon*
Waxing; Full; Waning.
Ch: Gertrude Lippincott
P: 15 February, Baltimore (Baltimore Museum of Art)
N: Commissioned by Gertrude Lippincott for the work. Working title for Horst *Moon Phases.*

1953
99. *Flower Arrangements of Colonial Williamsburg*
Film by Art Smith
R: 16 October, New York (RCA Studio)
FC: International Film Foundation, New York
N: "Official" film for Colonial Williamsburg, Virginia.

1959
100. *Island Memory*
Ch: Akiko Kanda
P: 4 March, New York (Contemporary Dance Productions, YM-YWHA)
N: Based on Haiku poem by Buson.
PN: "The halo of the moon, Is it not the scent of plum-blossom, Rising up to Heaven?"

101. *Young Moon*
Ch: Akiko Kanda
P: 4 March, New York (Contemporary Dance Productions, YM-YWHA)
N: Based on Haiku Poem by Buson.
PN: "Agitatedly, The Swallow flies out of the chamber of Gold."

Index

About the Author   Janet Mansfield Soares first met Louis
Horst as a young dancer at Juilliard. She became his
assistant while pursuing a career as a performer and
choreographer under his tutelage. Since 1964 she has
taught dance composition courses based on his work at
Juilliard and Barnard College, where she is currently Chair
of the Dance Department.

Library of Congress Cataloging-in-Publication Data
Soares, Janet Mansfield.
Louis Horst, musician in a dancer's world / Janet
Mansfield Soares.
Includes bibliographical references and index.
ISBN 0-8223-1226-3 (acid-free paper)
1. Horst, Louis.   2. Composers — United States —
Biography.   3. Modern dance — United States —
History.   I. Title.
ML410.H86S5   1992
784.18'82'092 — dc20
[B]   91-32933 CIP   MN